Why Don't We Just...?

Why Don't We Just...?

An Oklahoma Childhood

Patty Mac Sloan Hewitt

Published by Piscataqua Press
32 Daniel St., Portsmouth, NH 03801
Ppressbooks.com

ISBN: 978-1-950381-78-4

Printed in the United States of America

To my mother and father,
Patricia Smith Sloan and William Henderson Sloan
who brought me into this world,

and to
Janet Ruth,
who led me through my childhood,

and to
my husband, Michael Case Hewitt
who has been by my side ever since.

Through the Rear-View Mirror

*W*hy Don't We Just...? is a look backward to a decade that began sixty years ago. It is a story of girlhood friend-ships, especially between Janet Ruth and me. We were born at the end of World War II. We tip-toed through the Korean War, came of age during the Eisenhower years, participated in the beginnings of integration, sowed seeds of a lifetime friendship through girlhood antics and were both married with a child by the end of that decade. In those ten years, we leapt from breaking a window to get into the high school to jump on a trampoline, to declaring adulthood. As unmarried women, we missed Title IX, birth control pills, the Sexual Revolution, the Civil Rights Movement, the Women's Move-ment, legalized abortion, and drugs (well, we did try diet pills). We adopted our parents' generation faster than what was to follow us.

Janet Ruth and I often remarked later that we grew up in a bubble, and we had – a wealthy oil community in Oklahoma, site of the state's first commercial oil well and birthplace of Phillips Petroleum. Before our arrival, the town had gone through as many evolutions as the ones we were to miss. From a rowdy, oil-derricked, erector-set outpost in Indian Territory, it evolved into a sophisticated oil company town in the state of Oklahoma, and we arrived at the height of the paternalistic generosity showered on Bartlesville by Phillips.

I first saw Janet Ruth on a softball field in the sixth grade during a grudge match between our two grade schools. We did not actually meet that day, but her athletic skills made her the one everyone spoke of. It would be our first and last school-sponsored *girl's* athletic event, but it provided the be-ginnings of our childhood friendship.

1

Neither of us hailed from Oklahoma. I was born in Washington, D.C, christened Patricia McBride Sloan, but called Patty Mac the day I was born. Janet Ruth was born in Lafayette, Louisiana, though her parents Hank and Ruth Pickering came from Boston. Both our dads came to Bartlesville as oil-company engineers, hers to work for Phillips and mine to work for Cities Service.

We were opposites. I, the oldest of three, was bossy – a judgmental stickler for rules. She never bossed; she led. And everyone followed. As for obeying rules, she didn't. She read signs that read, "Keep out" or "Do not..." as invitations. And, as for judgment, she was only ever on the receiving end. She knew she was caught when she heard, "Janet Ruth!" or "Janet Ruth Pickering!" Her full name was proof she'd been busted, and she would have to work harder to cover her tracks the next time. Her dad would often cave to her antics, but Mama Ruth was tougher.

Also, she was funny. Not the joke telling, stand-up-comedy-routine kind of funny, but the quiet-quips-or-suggestions-or-observations kind of funny. It was never what anyone expected. And it often happened in places like churches, classrooms, or the movies so that when I wanted to laugh, I had to try to stifle it, which only made me laugh more until the coke spewed out my nose, or I wet my pants. As soon as I saw the glint in her eye, and her why-not eyebrows pleading, "Why don't we just...?" I was helpless to refuse her lead. At times I tried to play the role of conscience, but, mostly, I was all-in.

We weren't girly-girls, though I was probably more girly than Janet Ruth. We both had tom-boy streaks and excessive energy. We might have been satisfied if we could have played soccer, lacrosse, field hockey, or run track, but this was before Title IX. Our schools only offered girls physical education through junior high and then no P.E. or girls' sports in high school. Reluctantly, we accepted our fate. But with ideas, energy, and freedom to wander, we created the adventures and misadventures of these stories. Over the years, as I told the tales to my children and grandchildren, the name, Janet Ruth, became synonymous with a little bit of mischief or a lot of trouble."

In writing these stories, I've drawn on my own memory, memories of family and friends, and from books written about larger events at the time. With the exception of myself, my family and a few others, I have modified names of most of the characters. When referring to Blacks and Native Americans in the early stories, I have chosen words used at the time, whereas, when speaking from the perspective of today, I have tried to use what is now preferred. I have included anecdotal history of the town and state to help the reader more fully understand the implications of living in an oil company town in the state of Oklahoma. When appropriate, I've tried to provide windows into some of the other worlds around us, but I only really know my story. I know now that being white brought privilege, and I was lucky, not so much with the wealth of means, but with the wealth of belonging, of friendships with many, and one in particular—Janet Ruth. As she once wrote me, "We were our childhoods. I cannot remember mine without recalling yours."

A Country Mile

It was springtime recess on the playground in 1956 at McKinley Grade School in Bartlesville, Oklahoma. The brick school, at 16th and Keeler, was in a modest neighborhood of asbestos-sided ranches, brick Tudors, and stucco, porch-fronted bungalows. The street was flat, but the land sloped down behind the school, creating upper and lower playing grounds. The ball field filled the lower level and fronted Johnstone, a thoroughfare of sorts at the time: there was a stoplight at one intersection on the way to town. Surrounded by a chain-link fence, the ball field was normally a hard-packed, sere, dirt stage – barely distinguishable from the sandbag bases. That day it was a fertile meadow thanks to the spring rains we'd welcomed. It was the best season for recess.

The boys crowded the upper playground behind the school. They were dressed in the preteen uniform of the day: short-sleeved white tee-shirts designed appropriately for underwear, but nonetheless, worn for outerwear, Levi jeans, and Converse high-top sneakers prominently displayed with the All-Star circle. Fierce tether-ball matches thump-pause-thumped at the two stations to enthusiastic cheers. Those awaiting their turn either rough-housed with their buddies or jumped off the four-foot cement wall dividing the upper ground from the baseball field below. That wall was responsible for one or two good injuries a season, but if there were no mishaps, the boys raced back up the steps and leaped again until their tether ball turn came up. It was Monday, so girls had the lower playing field. They wore blouses with their Levis and canvas Keds on their feet.

"Listen up! Listen up, people," Mr. Ryder said. He was my homeroom teacher, and that's how he addressed our class. But he was speaking to the girls' softball team, so why were we "people"? He did like to be in charge, and I guess he figured he'd get our attention. But he already had it. For most of us, he was our first male teacher, and I think many of us had a teeny-weeny crush on this tall, handsome man. We really liked him, so we listened-up.

He went on, "The annual sixth grade girls' softball match between McKinley and Garfield School is Friday morning, and since they have shellacked us the last two years, we gotta break their winning streak." Often teachers tip-toed around girls, but he was used to dealing with boys, where you just ordered them to do things. But we got it. No trophy, just glory. All spring during recess, we'd been playing softball. But that was about the only time I played. I'm sure it was the same for most of the other girls, but now there was an event on the horizon.

Since Garfield was our big rival, some kids were already chanting, "Garbage-field vs. Mc-Cleanly! Garbage-field vs. Mc-Cleanly," in that operatic voice kids make. Of course, not me (goodie two-shoes), but I was trying to get into this competition thing. I was now in sixth grade, and this would be our only chance to beat Garfield before we all moved on to junior high.

I was ready, sort of. I always wished I could do things that boys did, like play sports, have a paper route, or swim naked at the Y, but this formal competition was a little scary. I had never been in a real one. As I anxiously mulled this over, my eyes caught sight of the Canter's house next door – three brothers, known to be fierce Yankee fans and super baseball players. They must be good because they were boys, I concluded. I was a decent hitter, a middling catcher, but a pathetic thrower, with neither my oomph nor direction ever measuring up. No wonder, I figured. I was just a girl. But maybe I could pull this off.

Soon everyone was talking about a player on the Garfield team called Janet Ruth Pickering who "could play like a boy!" *Well, that would be something.* I was used to girls playing like girls which pretty much meant that they weren't very good. Of course, no one seemed to want to teach us, or practice with us, or give us an opportunity to play. That some girl was really good was surprising – and a little intimidating. *How did that happen?* I wondered. But there was no time to chicken out now, and there was no reason to practice either, as I recall.

Friday came quickly, and soon after reporting to school, our team boarded a bus and headed the few blocks over to Garfield. We were the visiting team, and they were already warming up when we arrived. We scanned the field. The rains had worked wonders on their diamond too, creating a lush arena for this event – building the tension and increasing my anxiety never in short supply. Our team poured out of the bus, and as soon as we assembled by the field, we all looked for signs of the girl we'd heard about.

"Who is she?" I asked Virginia, one of my teammates.

"I think it's the girl with the big thick braids." We both saw, at that moment, her hurling a ball dead-eye to one of her teammates. She looked strong and athletic in her Levi jeans and white tee shirt, her braided hair flying behind her when she ran and threw. We were mesmerized; her fielding was just as impressive.

Wow, she is good! Here we go. Fortunately, we didn't have too long to worry; Mr. Ryder called us for a huddle. There were no pre-game routines for this event. Coach Ryder just called out player positions, and when he got to me, yelled, "Center field!"

Oh no. And to the softball god: *Please...send the balls to left or right field!*

Our team took our positions, and I guess we held our own

for a while. But then, the bases were loaded with Garfield players, and the girl with the braids was up. As she picked up her bat and strode confidently to the plate, took her stance, cocked her head, focused her eyes on the pitcher, I saw an inkling of what was to come. I realized that even if I caught the ball, I would be expected to throw it somewhere useful. That seemed unlikely. I sidled closer to the infield. As the pitch was launched, Virginia, seeing me move, yelled, "Wrong way! Go way out! She can hit the ball a country mile!"

"What's a country-mile?" I yelled, continuing to run in the wrong direction as the bat cracked, and the ball sailed over my head, into home run territory – a grand slam and win for the Garfield team.

"Oh nooo, Patty Mac!" my teammates shouted. My legs froze and my arms hung limply by my side. I stood stunned and stupefied, but in awe of this incredible girl with the beautiful braids, who "played like a boy." She must be Janet Ruth Pickering.

Well, she wasn't. After I'd remembered this event for 68 years and after she'd read the first version of the story, Janet Ruth told me that she *might* have cut her braids in the third grade, and the girl I saw *might* have been Vicki Norris, another ace for their team who did have a great set of braids. Janet Ruth had been the pitcher that day.

So, the truth is, I stunk, they won, and Janet Ruth Pickering was there, just not the player I thought. I finally got to know her in the eighth grade, and as she would say to me in future years, "the Pickerings never let the truth get in the way of a good story," so I haven't. But know that from here on, I will tell the truth and nothing but, or at least something close to it.

I won this for dancing at the pet and hobby Show May. 6, 1954

Kids at McKinley thought they went to the best school in town. The highlight of the year was the Pet and Hobby Show held every spring. There you could bring your dog, your stamp collection, do a dance or race one of your classmates, and you'd get a ribbon.

Bartles, Johnstone and Keeler

I grew up in the northeast Oklahoma town of Bartlesville, an area of craggy hills and rolling plains now called Green Country. The town is bisected by the Caney River, an uninviting brown waterway filled with ugly catfish and water moccasins. Dirty or not, water is water and copses of elms, cottonwoods, and scrub oak line the Caney's banks and stretch beyond. Where the river meanders through the center of the town, a patch of land called Johnstone Park runs alongside. In the springtime, it was a favorite spot that drew my family to the Caney, but not too near.

When I was a child, Easter time was usually beautiful, and if the timing was right, purple violets blanketed the banks and borders of the river. And, along with Christ dying on the cross and getting resurrected, the Easter bunny came. It wasn't difficult to figure out which was more exciting to a kid. We awoke to an egg hunt and sometimes a box that held live, dyed, pastel-colored chicks, ducks, or rabbits. Of course, we thought the Easter bunny brought them, but truth was, his agent got them at the feed or dime store. The animals varied year to year, but if they were chicks, we'd hear them chirping before we got to the living room. We couldn't wait until after church to take them to Johnstone Park and let them run loose in the flowers. Chicks grow so quickly those first few days that it was our only chance to play with them, unpenned and outside.

We were excited to have our new pets, though they always came with the caveat that they were temporary, ours to raise until they grew up. We gave them names anyway – like Henrietta and Delilah, and those of that plucky Biblical trio,

Shadrach, Meshach, and Abednego who survived King Nebu-chadnezzar's fiery hell. Maybe we hoped the names would bless our barnyard critters with survival genes.

After a few days' play, our new friends moved to a cage in the backyard to reach adulthood by summer's end. When fall arrived, we tearfully said good-bye after finding them a new home, usually with a local farmer who always "swore on a stack of Bibles," he would not eat them... *Right.*

The Caney River was a focal feature for early settlers. This region of the country was part of The Louisiana Purchase, and the area surrounding the river later became the northeastern part of Oklahoma. But in 1830, under Andrew Jackson's Indian Removal Act, this territory was set aside to be parceled out to various Native American tribes as exchange for their lands east of the Mississippi. It was hardly a fair swap. Many of the Native American settlers had successful businesses and farms they were forced to leave behind. Some tribes went willingly, others didn't.

The most famous migration was that of the people of the "Five Civilized Tribes," which included the Cherokee, Choctaw, Chickasaw, Creek, and Seminole Tribes who were forced from their homelands in Georgia, Florida, Alabama, North and South Carolina, and Mississippi. As many of them were landowners, they owned slaves as workforce for their land. When they were forced to move, the slaves they owned were forced to move as well. All trekked across the country on a path that became known as the Trail of Tears, an avenue of illness and death. Ten thousand were thought to have died on the journey. When they finally arrived, each tribes' survivors were assigned a specific area in "Indian Territory" as it was now called.

The slaves who survived the journey remained in servitude until Reconstruction. Then, as Freedmen, many joined the tribal rolls of their owners, as treaties demanded and if their owners cooperated. My schoolmate Ada Lee Bean whose

11

great-grandmother made the journey as a slave, told me that one of her cousins was deeded acreage and then found murdered some time later. Often these types of murders were to transfer head rights to someone else.

Soon white men came to work in the area, but they couldn't acquire land unless they married into an American Indian tribe. And, so, they began to do exactly that. In 1873, years before statehood, a man named Jake Bartles moved near the Caney River. From an old photo he appeared to be a Grizzly Adams kind of guy, older looking than his years, but enterprising: he married Nannie Mae Journeycake, the widowed daughter of a Delaware chief, Charles Journeycake. This entitled him to settle in the Territory, where he bought land and a grist mill from the first white man to move there, Nelson Carr, who had already married into the Cherokee tribe.

Bartles' mill and store, located on the north side of the Caney, became successful with the help of employees William Johnstone and George Keeler. In time, those young fellows married into American Indian tribes, enabling them to acquire property as well.

Naturally, when certain outsiders began to see the successes of their fellow white men in this area, more wanted to move to the Territory. Most of the land was now owned by various tribes, but there was one empty area, cleverly designated "Unassigned Lands." In the late 1800s, this region became known, and people began to badger the government to open it up. Their persistent clamoring eventually gave them the nickname, "Boomers." Finally, Congress and President Benjamin Harrison relented and announced that a land run would take place precisely at noon on April 22, 1889. Like antsy sprinters awaiting the gun at a track meet, these zealous land-claimers jumped the gun, some by sneaking in days early and hiding in the hills, and others by heading off by the thousands before noon on April 22, overwhelming officials. They staked their claims for 160 acres each and were labeled

"Sooners" – because they came in early.

Later, those nicknames made their way into the University of Oklahoma fight song:

"Boomer Sooner, Boomer Sooner, Boomer Sooner, Boomer Sooner, Boomer Sooner, Boomer Sooner, Boomer Sooner, OKU. I'm a Sooner born and Sooner bred, and when I die, I'll be sooner dead. Rah Oklahoma, Rah Oklahoma, Rah Oklahoma – O K U!!

That's it. It's a spirited song – just a little light on lyric variety.

Back at the Caney River, William Johnstone and George Keeler, aspiring entrepreneurs, decided that they could do as well as Jake Bartles. They quit working for him, brought some neighbors along, moved to the south side of the river and opened their own mill and store. When the railway depot and post office arrived on their side, their community leaped ahead of Bartles. I'll bet old Jake wasn't too happy about that.

One day in 1897 while George Keeler was riding along a creek on his side of the river, his horse refused to drink the water. That and the colorful sheen on the water's surface signaled to Keeler there could be oil nearby. Nearly forty years earlier, oil had been discovered in Titusville, Pennsylvania and since that time, prospectors everywhere had searched for signs of it. There had been drillings in the Territory for a number of years, with disappointing results. But on this hunch, Keeler partnered with Johnstone and another man, Frank Overlees, to drill, and on April 15, 1897, they struck oil.

Their gusher created the first commercial oil well in the Territory and was christened Nellie Johnstone No. 1. Today that derrick stands at the entrance to Johnstone Park, not far from the picnic areas and near the violet fields where our chickens, ducks and rabbits had played at Easter time.

At the time of the 1897 find, the Johnstone/Keeler settlement had reached the number of people required to incorporate, and, ironically, they named the town Bartlesville, after their competitor and former boss. Despite the honor, Jake Bartles refused to hang around and play second fiddle. Instead, he log-rolled his house and store four miles north and founded the town of Dewey, Oklahoma, named for the famous Admiral. It later became well-known as the home of Tom Mix, the popular silent movie cowboy.

During our childhood, we went to school and became friends with the great-grandchildren of William Johnstone and William Keeler. Their fathers, both grandsons of those early settlers, eventually became executives of Phillips Petroleum Company. And William Keeler was once elected chief of the Cherokee Nation.

Bartlesville Boomtown

When Janet Ruth and I grew up, Johnstone Park had the only wooden oil derrick for miles around, but in the early days of oil exploration, those four-sided angled towers erupted everywhere; they represented a lot of looking, but not always a lot of finding.

Before Keeler and Johnstone brought in that first well, there were other fortune-hunters exploring for oil. Whale oil was the source of fuel for lighting, so, when it became scarce, kerosene oil became the valuable commodity to replace it. And that came from oil in the ground. The hunt was on, and it was all over the northeast part of Indian Territory.

Citgo can trace some of its early roots to Bartlesville and to Henry and Edwin Foster, banking brothers from Rhode Island, who were some of those early explorers. Since they didn't own the land, they had to acquire leases from the American Indians who did own it. These leases varied in the length of time that allowed for exploring. But the Foster brothers were lucky. They were able to connect with an Osage Indian advocate who obtained a lengthy lease from the tribe for drilling rights. If they were successful, everyone would profit.

Years went by with minimal luck and then Henry died, leaving the drilling project in the hands of a reluctant heir, a man called H.V. Foster. H.V. had no interest in settling in Indian Territory, but it happened that the Nellie Johnstone no. 1 discovery was just the mule kick he needed. When he learned of that find, he decided to continue drilling, and within months discovered the first of many wells, enriching himself as well as the Osage tribal landholders.

After the find, Foster joined together a number of small oil

15

companies, and created Indian Territory Illuminating Oil Company, I.T.I.O., named for the kerosene oil product used for home-lighting. This was the company where my mother first worked after graduating from Bartlesville Business College. Mr. Foster became a wealthy man and community leader who built a beautiful Spanish-colonial style mansion in Bartlesville. His house sat on a small hill surrounded by several acres of land including a pond.

Once, in high school, Janet Ruth, Virginia and I snuck onto the property to go skinny-dipping in that pond. By this time, the property was vacant, and as it had been one of my childhood wishes to "swim naked at the Y," which never happened, this was my chance (for the naked part). Three of us tromped through the underbrush towards the murky pond. We got as far as taking off our shoes and socks when Virginia wondered if there might not be water moccasins lurking in the reeds of the muddy water. It was amazing how quickly we reshod our feet and abandoned that idea. Chills ran down our spines, and we never went back.

Today the property is home to Bartlesville Wesleyan College, and Foster's home is an administrative building. Years later, I.T.I.O. joined the food chain of oil companies and merged with a series of other companies to become Cities Service, and ultimately, Citgo.

As the wealth of the Osage tribe grew from the oil on their land, so did the greed and avarice of the white man. The Osage's good fortune was quickly manhandled. Local government officials enacted guardianship laws requiring white overseers to manage tribal member's money as they felt the Natives were not fit to do so. That pipeline of money from the oil company became a soaker hose with its many exits, to enrich anyone who could get their hands on any part of it as it slogged its way to the tribal owners. Eloquently revealed in *Killers of the Flower Moon* by David Grann, beginning in

1916, and extending into the 1930s, the Osage began suffering mysterious deaths and obvious murders. After years of extensive investigation, some 600 of those deaths were classified as murders – all a plot to acquire Osage headrights to their oil. The murder cases and the plots' investigative conclusion, were led by a Texas Ranger and newly turned FBI investigator John White.

The Bartlesville boomtown was only 25 miles away from the rocks and rolling hills of the Osage, but little of this was noticed. A city was being planted; brick and mortar were replacing oil derricks and a shanty town. Company housing sprang up as well as mansions. Fortunes were made, and lost, but even if one wasn't becoming a millionaire, there were plenty of good paying jobs to make a life and raise a family. People saw that the Osage were growing wealthy, but Phillips Petroleum Company and Cities Service were as well.

Phillips' history began in the early 1900s when the Department of the Interior opened up more land-leasing through open auctions. That got the attention of three Iowa brothers, Frank, L.E., and Waite Phillips. They had been entrepreneurs dabbling in barbering, coal mining, and banking in Iowa. I'm not sure how those dabblings related to oil, but the brothers were drawn to Bartlesville to try to strike it rich. Smart, driven and determined, but with limited resources for repetitive drillings, luck and hunches had to blossom quickly before the money ran out. Waite, being an independent guy, decided to strike out on his own, but the other two persevered in Bartlesville. With three dry holes and money for only one more try, they struck oil on September 6, 1905, naming the gusher Anna Anderson no. 1 after the little Delaware girl whose land allotment they leased in Juan, Oklahoma. More wells followed, and by 1917 the Phillips Petroleum Company was established with Frank and L.E. at the helm. Meanwhile, Waite settled fifty miles away in Tulsa, eventually making his own fortune in oil.

The automobile arrived, airplanes were coming, and all drove demand for gasoline as fuel. The Phillips' brothers' timing was perfect. Business begets business, and Frank quickly saw the need to create some new ways of doing banking with these oil prospectors. Old fashioned bankers were afraid to take the risks and leverages that oil exploration required, so Frank and L.E. quickly jumped on board, buying failing banks and starting new ones. It turned out that they were quite flexible in their banking style. When the noted bank robber Henry Starr, son of Belle Starr, wanted to take out a legitimate loan from one of Frank's banks, Frank felt he was earnest and would re-pay. He did, and went on to deposit his money there. Word got out that Frank was a fair man, and other such notables quietly did their banking with Frank. With all the bank robberies happening in Oklahoma in those days, it seemed the Phillips' banks were never robbed!

Janet Ruth's and my family came to Bartlesville in the late 1940s and early 1950s to ride the prosperity of the oil boom. By the late 1950s and early 1960s, Bartlesville was a town of 25,000 people, anchored by the strong presence of Cities Service and Phillips Petroleum. Employees arrived from all over the country – and world, giving the town a flavor and color unsuspected by those who would visit, and probably unappreciated by those who lived there. I was certainly clueless. With all those oil companies and related businesses though, it was easy to understand how one's first question to any new acquaintance wasn't to ask if their parent worked in the oil business, but for which company? My world had a unique slant to it, and living in a company town would touch all aspects of my daily life.

Early days of downtown Bartlesville.
Printed with the courtesy of The Bartlesville Area
History Museum, Bartleville, Oklahoma

Growing Up

Sixth grade ended and summer began – every day hot and humid, with highs in the 90s or 100s. Dad fitted our first air conditioner into a living room window, and we loved it. But since it only cooled that room, we still roasted while trying to sleep. Nightly, when we couldn't switch cheeks on our sweat-drenched pillows one more time, we dragged our bed palettes into that air-conditioned room. There you could forget how hot it was until you opened the front door in the morning to get the newspaper and a blast of hot air greeted you, so hot it made you gasp.

Naturally, most kids wanted to spend the day swimming. There were ponds and lakes nearby, pools at private clubs if your parents were lucky enough to belong, or the indoor pool at Phillips' gymnasium if you were connected to "The Company" (as people referred to Phillips). I went swimming at Sani-Pool, the overly chlorinated public pool that signaled to anyone who entered that no polio virus was growing there. Just to make sure we were thoroughly disinfected, we had to wade through a chlorine footbath on the way in and out of the locker room.

The Salk and Sabin vaccines were just coming into use, but there were still cases of polio; places like swimming pools and movie theaters were suspected of spreading illness. We all watched telethons from the March of Dimes and saw kids in braces – or worse, in iron lungs – that condemned them to life in a metal cage that performed their breathing. It was every mother's dread that her child might contract the disease, and, of course, the very places we all wanted to go to in the summer were the movies and swimming pools.

Anyone for kick the can?

I only knew one girl who got polio, and I have no idea where she got it. She used crutches, and I thought it looked fun – like swinging on a jungle gym.

At night, despite the hot winds, the absence of sun provided just enough respite to entice neighborhood kids outside for catching lightning bugs, games of kick-the-can, or just sitting around talking, if we could stand the chiggers living in the grass. The bites of those little mites could make you itch for hours and be sorry you ever sat down. But we loved being outside. Some nights it looked like someone pulled a blanket of black sky and stars to the ground and turned those sparkles into catchable fireflies. We chased the flashes with partially cupped hands until we captured one, felt the flutter inside, and then ran to put it in a mason jar, hoping to keep our little headlight until we got the top back on. We'd already punched air-holes through the lids so that we could catch enough to create our own natural flashlight. Lit by them and serenaded by the vibrating engines of summer cicadas, we sat on the corner of 18th Street and Cherokee Place, full of excitement and apprehension at what 7th grade had in store.

One night, my friends Susie Reinfeld and Lynn Hobart who lived up the block came over to play. We sat down to rest after a game of kick-the-can, and talk quickly turned to what junior high might be like. Susie jumped right in to hold court. She was curious about everything and with an older sister to question, she had answers, and loved being the one to give them out. Lynn and I were spellbound recipients, and other kids stopped to listen.

"So...everyone gets their own locker – for coats, books or anything else you want to store. Then a bell rings. That means homeroom. It's the longest class, and you stay there for two hours. After that, when the bell rings, you go to another room for another subject with another teacher."

I liked the idea of moving around and having different

teachers for various subjects. My kindergarten report card described me as lacking self-control, but what five- year old had it? I guess I finally got some, but I still got restless. This schedule sounded good for a squirmer like me.

Throughout grade school, we went home for lunch. We had an hour, and providing I didn't play "I was blind" on the way home (which I often did), it was plenty of time to eat and return to school. I have no idea why I tried pretending I was blind. I guess I always noticed things, and when people were different, I wondered how it felt to be like them. Anyway, even with my weird game, I usually made it back. Now, according to Susie, we'd be staying and eating at the cafeteria in half that time.

"And the food's awful, like hospital food," she said, and we all agreed, as if we'd had a lot of experience in that area. But then she got to the good part – the description of the lunch ladies.

"They have to wear hair nets that end up dropping down just over their eyebrows. It's hilarious. Their hair is tucked inside so tight you can't hardly tell if they're a man or a lady. But really...you know who the ladies are. They wear coral nylon dresses with sweaters over their shoulders. And then they add these fancy chains which clamp to each side of the sweater to keep it from falling off. And they wear a lot of jewelry, and a lot of make-up. Maybe they think it gives you something to look at besides their hairnets and ugly dresses."

Lynn wanted to know what was on their feet.

"Oh, yeah!" Susie said, "I almost forgot that part. They roll their hose just below their knees, and they wear those Etta Jetticks...you know...old lady shoes." By this time, we had forgotten about the chiggers and were rolling in the grass, laughing. It sounded like Halloween.

But Susie wasn't finished.

"My sister says the really cool thing to do for lunch is to go to Ferndell's." Ferndell's was located just west of the school on 9th Street, and a man named Otis Beck ran the store. They were famous for selling Frito chili pies and peach cobbler both served in paper boats with a wooden spoon. We thought it sounded great, but then Susie said, "I'm not sure if we're supposed to go there, 'cause there might be some rule about not leaving school at lunch time. But lotsa kids do."

"Yeah, I heard about that place," I said.

"Me, too," said Lynn, "and I hear they have 'cat fights' there."

"What's a cat fight?" I asked. Susie jumped right in.

"Well they're fights between girls where they rip off each other's blouses and scratch each other's faces."

Lynn and I recoiled.

"Really," she continued, "it happened ... or maybe it happened once."

"Are they goin' after girls like us?".

"Nah...these are fights between friends – over some boy, usually,"

Some friend, I thought.

About this time, Eddie, another neighborhood kid, showed up. He was two years older than we were, cocky, and seemed to know his way around – or thought he did. Actually, any older kid commanded respect from us, and with his attitude, we were appropriatcly cowed.

"You know they can stuff you in your locker and slam the door on you if they feel like it," he said. "Or sometimes they just empty out a trash barrel, throw you in, and roll you down the hill." Both Lynn and I were terrified, but Susie interrupted.

"Aw, Eddie, you don't know what you're talking about. My sister says that's just a bunch of baloney, and everyone tells those stories to scare the little kids." Susie was a fast talker: the hardly-takes-a-break-when-they-talk-and-you-can't-get-a-word-in kind. Eddie wasn't. He met his match, and backed off.

24

Susie's interest in everyone and everything made her a font of knowledge. She liked knowing what was going on, and we liked having a source. We could always ask Susie.

Fall finally arrived, when all the 6th graders in town melded into the 7th grade at a formidable three-story, red brick school called Central Junior High. (St. John's Catholic School went through the eighth grade, so we didn't meet the Catholic kids until 9th grade.)

Our new school was well named (many of us could walk). At Central Junior High, we joined kids from schools called Horace Mann, Washington, Jefferson, Garfield, Jane Phillips, or Limestone, each named for a President, an educator, a well-known local figure, or a native rock. The kids from Douglass, the "Negro school," did not arrive until the following year. We were still segregated.

At Central, you climbed a flight of stairs to reach the front door, and once inside, there were endless hallways of lockers and linoleum, with stairwells to the rafters. We kept a lookout for trash barrels, but nothing Eddie predicted came to pass. Finding our classrooms and arriving on time seemed the biggest challenges.

For many of us, school was over a mile away. Most families had only one car, and fathers took it to work or their wives drove them. A mile walk was not drive-worthy anyway, so we were expected to walk to school and pretty much anywhere else we went. Since we wanted to walk together, we walk-pooled: the girl who lived farthest away walked to the next closest friend's house and so on, until everyone was collected, allowing all of us to arrive at school together. Strength in numbers, ready for the likes of Eddie.

During that first week we were eager to try on make-up, but our parents had nixed that, so we left for school with scrubbed faces. However, my friend Jan Everett had acquired some lipsticks. She waited until we had collected the last girl, then surprised us as she pulled lipsticks from her pockets and began passing them around like communion. We applied the colors with no mirrors and no stopping. Tangee was the most natural, but I liked Revlon's "Persian Melon." My guess is we missed our targets a few times, but we were thrilled with our initiation into the world of make-up and deceit.

Boys still wore blue jeans, the Levi's brand almost exclusively, with varying types of T-shirts or wing-collared, short-sleeved shirts. The Converse high-top sneaker was still popular, but this was Oklahoma, so there was a hard-core group of boys who wore cowboy boots. Those boots worked for horseback riding, walking down the hallways at school, or going to the prom.

Girls wore Levi's, too, when they wore jeans, but that was mostly for play or weekends. At school we wore full, printed cotton skirts with blouses or sweater sets when it got cold. On our feet, we had black and white saddle-shoes and Weejun penny-loafers, a sturdy version of today's loafer. Cordovan-colored, they featured coin slots which we filled with a shiny penny. Some girls wore Pappagallo ballet-flats, colorful and cute, but they were never in my family's budget. For play, we wore a canvas, lace-tie shoe called Keds, an early version of today's sneaker. They were sensible: they could get wet, dry-out and be ready to wear again.

Those full skirts we wore were gathered at the waist and held aloft by a myriad of petticoats. These were made of a netting material sewn onto an elastic waistband. We starched them weekly and stiffly with liquid starch and then air-dried the whole mess on a clothesline. One petticoat was never enough – the more crinolines the better. When you got dressed you just stepped through the waistband of that underskirt and pulled them up, one after another, like layering on hula hoops. Then you slipped your skirt over the whole buoyant umbrella and were on your way. At school, there was often a competition to see who was wearing the most petticoats. One day Susie and I joined a group of balloon-skirted girls huddled in a corner, and she immediately began organizing.

"O.K., I've got on three today. Can anyone beat that?"

"No," I said. "I've got on three, too."

Virginia spoke up, "Well, actually, I have on four." We required proof before declaring a winner, so she pulled up her skirt, and separated the layers of crinolines, counting each as she pulled the hems towards her.

"All right. Can anyone top that?" Susie said, just as Jan came running up, out of breath and clearly buoyant with skirt and petticoats.

"Mama got me a new one, and I have *five* on," she said. We were amazed, but like Virginia, she had to lift her skirt and prove the count before we elected her winner.

Our weekly washing did a job on those petticoat waistbands. They overstretched, and often needed safety-pin fixes to keep them tight. I was always in a hurry, and once while running down the hallway to a class, I felt a snap and sudden loosening, and realized that one of those crinolines had given way and was headed to my ankles. With a step-dance move, I released myself from this ankle-tackling petticoat as it dropped to the ground, kept right on running, and never looked back. I was mortified. Later, when I came out of class, I saw that someone had taken it away, relieving me of having to re-claim it. Still mortified, I'm pretty sure that I wouldn't have owned up to it.

By December we had settled into our new routines. Hallways seemed shorter, stairs less steep, and the way from room to room not so confusing. My homeroom teacher, Miss Ora Lee Cupp, was a long-time local schoolmarm who peppered her lectures with, "Doncha see?" We watched as she endlessly diagramed sentences into webs of words, and then concluded with, "Doncha see?"

Sometimes we did, and sometimes we didn't. And sometimes, when it got really boring, we counted the "Doncha sees?"

Every day in homeroom, we began with forgettable morning announcements read by the principal over the loudspeaker. Forgettable until the morning of December 13, 1956. That day there was no cheerful greeting; that alone caught our attention. Kids were often talking before announcements, but the tone of the Principal's solemn voice stopped the chattering sooner. Everyone listened. And then as if he were reading a headline from the newspaper, he began to recount the morning's event at Bartlesville Airport. A Phillip's Petroleum plane had crashed. En route to Salt Lake City, Utah it had gone down on take-off.

Suddenly the silence that accompanies an impending tornado spread over the room. No one moved or spoke as the Principal announced the names of all those on board, names we all knew.

Phillips employed pilots and maintained several DC-3's at a private airfield in Bartlesville. That day six passengers, the pilot, and co-pilot were killed. Several were fathers of kids in our school and the high school, and the pilot was a favorite coach for the Frank Phillips Mens' Club Little League Baseball Team. It was hard to find anyone who did not have a connection to someone who had died.

The effect of the news brought the school, the town, and the company a sense of shock I later came to know and associate with the Kennedy assassinations, the Challenger explosion, the Oklahoma City bombing, school shootings, and, of course, 9/11. Suddenly that day, we all had to grow up. Worrying about being stuffed in lockers, or late for class, about getting lost or whether to eat at Ferndell's, deciding whether to try make-up or how many petticoats to wear, all seemed – suddenly – very unimportant.

Girlfriends

With the loss of hometown friends in the plane crash, there was a pervasive gloom at most any gathering, and I saw the sadness in some of the kids at school whose fathers had died. I didn't know most of the children well, but I felt sad when I imagined how they must be feeling.

Two of my earliest friends were Virginia Smith and Jan Everett. Jan and I met in first grade. We were both living in the Jane Phillips Addition – originally, the low-cost rental housing development created by Phillips Petroleum for their employees. When their workers began to buy their own homes, Phillips opened up the rentals to outsiders. My parents signed on because the housing was inexpensive.

Our neighborhood school was named for Jane Phillips, Frank Phillips's wife. There, I met Jan, a sweet, wheat-haired, green-eyed classmate I was drawn to like a Madam Alexander doll. We shared a very kind teacher, Miss Peggy Parker.

Jan and I share a first-grade memory of our Christmas Pageant where Frank Phillips was the guest of honor. I will never forget him. When the pageant concluded, he came onto the stage, and made a little speech whose words left my mind the instant he mentioned he was giving each of us a silver dollar. He had been doing this yearly at every school in town, including the "Negro school" called Douglass, but this was my first time to receive that silver dollar. Ada Lee Bean, who was at Douglass, recalls that the silver dollars given the six children in her family enabled her parents to buy toys at Christmastime. I, too, realized that a dollar was a lot of money, but for me it only generated greed. I mentally imagined my future

29

haul from Uncle Frank's annual generosity, only to have him up and die a few months later. I can still feel my disappointment at the news.

My friendship with Jan was disrupted when my dad's reserve unit was called up during the Korean War. Once again, his expertise in ordnance did not lead him to the front, but to an armory in Philadelphia where he served for nearly two years. I had only completed first grade when we left, so there were no histrionics on my part about the move to Beverlea Farms, on Philadelphia's outskirts where apple orchards grew all around.

Our home was the lower-level of a two-family farmhouse, where an Italian family lived upstairs. I remember that there was a lot of conversation about what a good cook their mother was, and though my mother loved her food, she must not have taken any lessons. Years later, Mom still made marinara sauce from Campbell's Tomato Soup.

My most vivid memories of our stay in Philadelphia are of seeing American history. We visited the house where Betsey Ross sewed the first American flag, and we touched the crack in the Liberty Bell. It was a lot more fun to read about those things when you had some proof they really existed.

But the highlight of the year was *almost* being on the *Howdy Doody Show*. My sister and I were booked to be in the audience, but the day before it was to air, we were cancelled. I cried all day. My sister was two years younger, and didn't really understand, but since I was crying, so did she. All day. (She was always sympathetic.) My parents must have done some back-flips writing letters because we got a reprieve later: to join the audience on *Candy Carnival*, a definite second-cousin to our lost gig. We were somewhat mollified, but the only thing I remember is being instructed by a director, sitting in front of us, yet out of camera range, to stuff our mouths with M&Ms as full and fast as we could shovel them in. It didn't top Howdy Doody.

When we returned to Oklahoma, we moved into yet another rental in Bartlesville where I entered my fourth school in four years, this one called Southview. I entered in January which was somewhat unusual, and Jan recalls the day I arrived, the teacher asked if anyone had known me when I lived in Bartlesville earlier. Shy as she was, Jan piped up that she knew me from the first grade, and that made me feel very welcome. We finished the school year together, and as the school went only to the third grade, we both transferred to McKinley in the fourth grade. We were friends again, and I went to the same school for the next three years.

One of my favorite things about Jan's family were their names. Although Jan called her mother, Mama, her real name was Jean, her dad was Jack, her younger sister was Jennifer, the cat was named Mr. Jackson-Jackson-Jackson and her bird, Dr. Jekyll. (When Jan was out of school, she got a parrot and named him José.)

Virginia Smith and I met in the fifth grade when she arrived from the local Horace Mann School in town. We lived three blocks apart, so it was easy to be friends. She was kind, trustworthy, comfortable and safe, an "old soul," as our parents might say, but also fun and quick to laugh. Hers was infectious, beginning with a deep chuckle rolling upwards from her belly, triggering the laughter of anyone around her, even if they'd missed the joke. Everyone was drawn to her. She was loyal, often the voice of reason, but rarely of judgement. When we played our memorable game against Garfield, she was the one who tried to alert me to the hit, but she never held the country- mile loss against me.

Virginia lived in the same brick Tudor house on Dewey all the years I knew her. Despite my family's many moves, I never lived too far away, so I spent a lot of time there. One of my favorite things was a little house in the backyard, numbered 1721 ½. Though, it looked like a playhouse, it was really

31

a shed, and I had an idea one summer to turn it into a club-house. Virginia liked the idea, but she realized it was her dad's tool shed and wasn't sure how he'd feel about the idea. Just then we heard his truck coming into the drive, so the time seemed right to approach him about our scheme.

"Hey, Dad! Patty Mac and I have something to ask you!" It was always good to ask your parents for something in front of a guest, and Virginia grabbed my arm for emphasis.

"Soo...we were thinking it would be fun to paint the inside of the shed and make it into a clubhouse for us. Whaddiya think?" asked Virginia.

"Well...I don't know...you know I keep my yard tools in there. Where am I goin' to put them?" Mr. Smith said.

"Oh...how about the garage? Oh, Dad, it would be so much fun. Patty Mac really wants to do this." Her dad did like me so maybe I had a little pull.

"Oh, all right. I guess I could store stuff in the garage some-where. Might have to clean some things outta there, too," he mumbled, and we had a deal.

I never seemed to be able to wheedle things out of my dad if he wasn't on board. If I kept asking, he'd just blow up, but Mr. Smith was so different. I'd seen Virginia at work already. When I slept over, and we could hear her dad snoring in the next room, she just rolled up a newspaper, walked into his room and whacked him on the head. He never woke. He just quit snoring. He really was an old softie, and Virginia and I both knew it. I wondered how he got that way.

The following Saturday I showed up to help. We all made multiple trips to the garage to transfer the stuff from the shed before we could finally sweep it out, have the dust settle, and begin painting. During the week Virginia and I had gotten the paint and brushes at Maltby's Hardware so we were ready to go (when the shed was).

If I close my eyes today, I can feel the stifling summer heat and the forehead sweat burning into my eyes as we layered white paint onto the inside walls to transform the shed. We worked side by side in that enclosed tomb with the only air coming through the door. As we worked, hundreds of dive-bombing gnats assaulted us. We swatted them away, only to glue them to the sticky walls, creating polka dots against the white. It was useless to try to remove them.

And so our first club began. We made the rules, which Virginia unearthed many years later. She still had the envelope with the original sheet of paper, its text in pencil, with numerous cursive "typos."

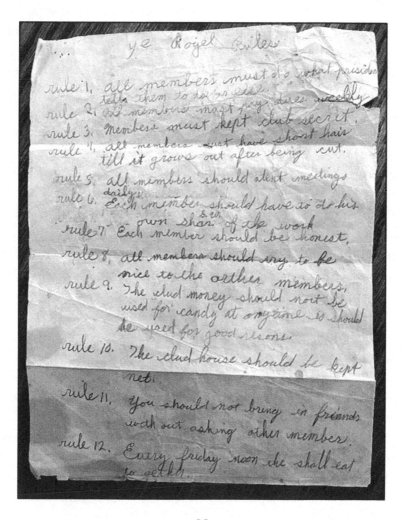

Only when all of this was set in place did we realize we couldn't solve overheating. If it's hot outside, then it's an inferno in an enclosed box, "hotter than the hinges of Hell," an Okie might say. That had not crossed our minds, all through the thinking, planning and hard work. And then there were those onerous rules.

We lost interest, and Mr. Smith got his toolshed back; he probably knew he would all along.

Through the years, Virginia, Jan and I grew our friendship worrying about make-up, crinolines and boys. And then, early in the fall of the eighth grade, the reality of life stopped us again. Like many of our fathers, Jan's dad loved to play golf. On a beautiful fall day while playing with friends, Mr. Everett suffered a heart attack. He was taken to the hospital where he lived for several days, but he was unable to recover; he was only in his 40s.

Where we lived, families kept their personal problems to themselves. I was totally unaware of Mr. Everett's heart attack until I learned he had died. Neither Virginia nor I knew Mr. Everett that well. Like most fathers, he was at work in the afternoons when we were at Jan's house. But he was her dad. We saw how sad the kids were who lost their fathers in the Phillips' plane crash, so we had some idea the sorrow Jan must be feeling. And in the corners of our minds, I think we both wondered if this could happen to us.

"So, what should we do?" I asked Virginia.

"Well, Mom says we should go visit Jan to 'express our condolences,'" she said.

I told her that's what my mom said too, and then continued, "But I don't know what to say when we get there. I don't want to make her feel sadder."

"Me, neither, but we'll think of something when the time comes. Don't worry, we'll go together."

Wakes weren't customary where we lived. Friends called on mourners at home, usually in the afternoon, and bereaved families expected unannounced guests.

That afternoon we dressed in our Sunday church clothes, walked to her house, and anxiously rang the front door. Jan answered it herself, invited us in, and led us to her bedroom. We never spoke to her Mama, but we saw her huddled with grieving friends in the living room as we passed by.

When we finally had the courage to speak, perhaps we began with how sorry we were, but I remember that we quickly began talking about anything else *but* Jan's dad, naively thinking we would take her mind off his death. We didn't stay long. She told me recently we sent flowers to her family. I'm glad, but as teenagers, we didn't understand the magnitude of his early death.

Jan's Mama became the breadwinner as a teacher and raised her two daughters alone. We went back to our lives, and Jan, too, returned to eighth grade. We were adults before we ever spoke to her of her father again.

A Slip of the Wrist

The plane crash and Jan's father's death were big events in our lives, but being kids, we were quick to find routine to avoid the discomfort and mysteries they presented.

I focused on school, and new friends. Many were in those rotating classrooms of mine, but Janet Ruth was not among them. I saw her in the hallways and, as some of my old friends got to know her, we became nodding acquaintances; we knew *of* each other. But was she interested in meeting me? Decades later she told me she heard I was "snobby," but she also heard I was "nice." It made her curious, she said.

Then one morning amid the cacophony of closing lockers, the kid telegraph reported that Janet Ruth had been knocked off a horse and broken her wrist. Once I got over the fear of being thrown into one, lockers became the gathering place for before and after-school socializing. Rumors flew fast, though there was no cyberspace to feed them. Injuries and blood made almost as good stories as who liked whom, and broken limbs were definitely big news. Since no one died this time, I wanted in on the drama – and the chance to know Janet Ruth.

Wow! She rides horses, I thought. *This girl can do anything...well...maybe not, since she ended up with a broken wrist.* But she got a cast, and the best thing about a cast was that everyone could sign it. Even me. It was like wearing a yearbook on your arm or leg.

We all waited near her locker to see if she'd be coming to school. She arrived, looking proud and healthy. By this time, she had given up her braids and had cut her hair short, a "mod Pixie," she called it. We watched as she stowed her coat in her locker and walked down the hall, proudly supporting her mummified arm with the working one. She was athletic, with broad shoulders, but wore the junior high girls' uniform – a white blouse with a circle pin and a cotton skirt shirred at the waist, belted with a cinch belt. Cinch belts were about three-inches wide and made of elastic material in varying colors. They buckled with a figure-eight clasp that interlocked, and they were always slightly smaller than your waist, thereby, *cinching* you in.

Within minutes Janet Ruth was swarmed by kids and questions. I held back because I still didn't really know her.

"What happened?" asked Jan and Virginia, my friends who did.

"Well ..." she began slowly, scanning her audience. And then she launched into a long story about how she had gone horseback riding with Judy and Linda Merrifield at Shawnee Park. Apparently Janet Ruth didn't ride very often, but when her friends invited her she thought it sounded fun, and they promised her she could ride the gentler horse called Ribbon.

When it was Janet Ruth's turn to ride, she had no problem mounting Ribbon while Judy and Linda tied Sugarfoot to a football goalpost. Ribbon had barely started to trot, when he suddenly took charge, and bolted straight for Sugarfoot, who was still tied up. Ribbon galloped right between the goalpost and the tied-up horse.

"Then, ol' Sugarfoot's reins caught me and flipped me backwards over Ribbon's butt onto a pile of horseshit!" Janet Ruth said.

"No...ick!" said Jan.

Virginia cringed.

Ouch, I thought.

Her audience, at full attention, Janet Ruth continued, "Well, at first I was really interested in getting all that horseshit off me, but suddenly I saw these funny little bones poking out in different directions from my wrist, and it was beginning to hurt bad. So they took me home, and Mom took me to

Doc Bronson. He set the bones and cast my arm. Wanna sign?"

They did, me included. I almost wished I had a cast.

A month went by, and it was nearing Christmas. Everyone was stuffing their lockers with coats and unloading books for classes, when Susie saw Janet Ruth approaching with something unusual on her arm.

"Hey, Patty Mac, take a look at Janet Ruth's arm. I think maybe she's got a new cast," she said and led us toward a better look.

Janet Ruth.

"Yep, and you're not goin' to believe this – it's red and green striped. The old dirty one's gone."

Quickly, kids gathered to admire the candy-striped plaster and to re-sign, but Janet Ruth pulled away. Then, slowly and with the theatrics of a night-club stripper, she took hold of the cast near her elbow, and began to slide it down her arm. No one spoke or moved as – inch by inch – she worked it down her forearm. As the last part neared her wrist, she held the arm still and straight as she slipped the remainder of the cast over her wrist and hand, wincing only slightly as she pulled it completely off. We were awed.

"There." she said, holding the pale arm out for all to see. Some yellow bruising was still visible around her wrist, while dead flaking skin, resembling old-crazed china, covered her forearm. Wild, black, whisker-like hairs sprouted up and down her arm like a newly planted field. It was gross.

"Yuk!" was the general consensus, but we couldn't could take our eyes away. Apparently the swelling in the arm had gone down dramatically since they'd put on the new cast, and as it only covered her wrist, she discovered it was removable. Never missing an opportunity to be the center of attention, she knew this trick would be a hit.

I was amazed. I couldn't imagine anyone trying to remove their cast for a look. I wondered what her mother was going to say when she found out about this exhibition, but I was beginning to get Janet Ruth's M.O. She'd probably just slip that petrified bandage back on, the way it came off – with no parent the wiser. She was just so funny – hilarious, actually. I had dreams of being out of the ordinary, but this girl was already there.

Janet Ruth's broken wrist ushered in our friendship. We would be old ladies before I learned that the terrific player in the McKinley/Garfield softball game was not the Janet Ruth I still admired, so this new stunt was one more thing that drew me to her.

Our era placed limitations on girls, but Janet Ruth seemed not to notice. She just went ahead as her ideas and spirit moved her. I seemed to be too bound in by rules and trying to obey them. Though, I wanted to break away, I never knew how without getting into big trouble. Especially with my dad. He was just never amused by misbehavior. Given the things Janet Ruth did, I had to wonder what her dad was like.

School days...Junior High Poker.

Goin' Explorin'

Since Janet Ruth was everything I wished to be, daring and full of nerve to do and try things we shouldn't, or which weren't expected, I loved being around her. She made me laugh until my ears ached, and talked me into things I never would have tried alone. But I wondered what she liked in me.

She said there was that "snobby but nice" thing she'd heard about, and it made her want to know me. And as she got to know more about me, she said that she liked that my mom sewed my clothes which were kind of matchy-matchy, and that she fixed up my bedroom to be "happy." But I think what she really liked was that I loved her adventures and was ready to go along with them.

O.K. I get it. It sounds about right for the depth of a junior high friendship.

Janet Ruth's closest friend from Garfield was Marie Charette, so that broken-arm entrée came with a second new friend for me. Marie was wiry and fit (probably another ace for the Garfield softball team who beat McKinley so handily). She had short, curly brown hair, and with a slight little smirk, a cocked head, and skinny arms akimbo (a position she assumed often), she resembled an elf – another perfect accomplice for implementing Janet Ruth's ideas. With my friends Susie Reinfeld, Jan Everett, and Virginia Smith, we six began to run around together, and our adventures began.

Exploring, for early Indian Territory settlers, meant searching for land and oil. But for us, it could cover any activity on foot we could dream up. "Goin' explorin'" sounded harmless when we told our parents, so it was the excuse we used to go off for a number of hours with no explanation. The unspoken rule was, "Be back by dinner." When we could drive, we graduated to, "We're goin' out for a coke." Everyone knew if you asked someone if they wanted a coke, you might get, "Sure, I'll have a Dr. Pepper" as a response. "Coke" was generic for any pop or soda. And then it became generic for going with our friends to hang out.

Explorin' in the rain never took us too far, but like werewolves who come out when the moon is full, Janet Ruth and I were like a couple of water ghouls who couldn't get out the door or window fast enough when the skies opened up – especially in a warm summer rain. Early on we discovered that neither of us ran the other direction in a rainstorm; we headed towards it. And when it did rain, as Okies say, the water came down "like a cow pissin' on a flat rock." In minutes, streets and curbs channeled little rivers, and Janet Ruth and I and every kid in the neighborhood waded or rode their bike through the ankle-deep streams. I even saw a couple of teenage boys haul out a raft to ride the little rapids down the street. After a day of mucking around in those waters, our mothers figured we needed a typhoid shot. Good thing it didn't happen too often.

South and west of town was Circle Mountain, a thickly forested arc of a hill known for warding off tornadoes. Accessible by a two or three mile walk or bike ride, it was a draw many times we went exploring. There were farms along the way, as well as a creek, and numerous shacks were tucked here and there throughout the wooded hills. Dirt roads veined their way around and up and down Circle Mountain to reach these cabins. Some were abandoned, others were not. Sometimes they were a little scary looking, but like an amusement ride, there was a thrill in that. The fear didn't stop us, and no one in our families seemed to worry; so, we just said good-bye, and that we'd be back when we got back.

We did hear that girls could get raped, though. Janet Ruth and I were one of the last of our friends to get our periods, and quite proud of that. We thought the whole thing was disgusting, and secretly felt we might somehow have escaped that nuisance – which gives you an idea of how naïve we were. She and I often led the way to Circle Mountain, bravely announcing since we hadn't *started*, we could enter the scary places first so that if we got raped, it wouldn't matter so much because we couldn't get pregnant. We automatically assumed if you got raped, you'd get pregnant. I'm not sure we processed all of the girls' Disney health film in the fifth grade. It was our only experience with sex education and, at the time, we felt they were referring to another species.

I usually went on these Circle Mountain adventures, but one Saturday when I couldn't go, Janet Ruth, Marie, Virginia, and Jan headed off on foot to explore the mountain, Gap Road and Sand Creek, another of those muddy waters which fed the Caney River. Like many small streams, its length was often more impressive than its depth, depending on the season and the rain. Their experience that day was divulged to me the following morning, complete with dialogue and retold so many times among the five of us, it became legendary.

When the girls reached the base of the mountain, they headed to an old shanty that had been a one-room schoolhouse, our usual first stop. It was a popular destination for vandals, and they quickly discovered someone had recently broken the windows and removed the sash cords and weights which were now strewn all over the ground – a clear invitation to investigate. They found broken toilets which they guessed to have been broken up by the sash weights. Nevertheless, the girls picked the weights up and began twirling them by the cord, drawing figure-eights in the air as if they were sparklers. Just about this time Officer Cronin and his cruiser rolled up, and he lowered his window.

"Hey, what's going on here? And what are you doin' with those sash cords?" Apparently, police routinely patrolled the area, on the lookout for vandals. Terrified, the four dropped the contraband and froze. But before anyone else could act, Jan stepped forward, walked to his car, looked in through the window, and said, "Who are you?" (Virginia, Marie and Janet Ruth had no doubt who he was.)

"I'm a police officer," he said.

"Well, lemme see your badge," Jan said. The rest of the group shuddered when they heard this. They couldn't imagine what she was thinking.

"Perhaps you girls need to take a little ride with me down to the station!" Now the others were really worried. She needed to shut up! But she stood her ground, this blonde, green-eyed mini-me of Marilyn Monroe with the baby-doll voice no one seemed able to resist. Every boy in school was secretly or openly in love with Jan Ellen Everett. She went on to whine, "But Officer, my mama doesn't allow me to get in a car with strangers!"

I guess her charms subdued Officer Cronin too, because he finally gave up. He must have realized they were innocent curiosity seekers, but still he was officious enough to order them to get out of there. Relieved, they took off and headed towards Sand Creek. Just as relieved, I bet, the officer left too.

Since they were free to explore more, they headed on down the road where they came to an area being cleared for construction with a front-loader sitting, unattended, in the middle of the field. Janet Ruth led the way, and when she saw it, commented it "looked interesting." Marie, too, felt an adventure brewing, as she'd been friends with Janet Ruth for a while and knew that goin' explorin' with her had to end with something fun. But Virginia and Jan were nervous. They were still shaken from the threat of a ride to the police station and didn't want to get into trouble.

"What are you guys dreaming up now?" Virginia said. (We always said "you guys," male or female.)

"Aw... nothing, really. Just lookin'," Janet Ruth said. But as she spoke, she and Marie climbed aboard for a closer look.

Virginia, always sensible, reminded them that they might not want to mess around with the knobs and levers. I guess they ignored her, because the next thing anyone knew the machine began to grind and rumble and lurched forward. Janet Ruth later *swore* that they were just pretending with the knobs and such, but somehow they engaged one, and once the thing started, they had no idea how to make it stop. At first it moved slowly, but it quickly gained momentum, while digging the dirt in front, and in a few seconds was on its way. Startled, but enjoying this surprise ride, Janet Ruth and Marie looked ahead, but suddenly sobered up when they realized the only way this machine was going to stop was when it hit something, and that something was going to be Sand Creek!

Mesmerized by this tableau, Jan and Virginia saw it too, and yelled, "Jump! Jump!!"

Janet Ruth and Marie saw their future if they didn't leap, and both dove onto the dirt just before the loader careened over the bank and into the water. Jan and Virginia raced to their friends and found them shaken by their near-miss, but unharmed.

The four re-assembled by the bank to gaze at the upended corpse. All they could see was the diesel engine flapper above the water. Relief and terror washed over them as reality sunk in: they were O.K., but that front-loader wasn't.

Officer Cronin was long gone, and no one saw any witnesses. Though they were sorry for what they'd done, no one had money for reparations or any desire to go to jail, which seemed a real possibility. Burdened with guilt, they made their way home and, (except to me), pledged secrecy. The following week there was a notice in the newspaper:

REWARD FOR ANY INFORMATION REGARDING THE
VANDALISM OF A FRONT-LOADER DRIVEN INTO
SAND CREEK

This cemented it. The pledge had been made, invoking Omerta — the vow of silence that would be kept for years — which I have just broken.

Epilogue:

Pam Head is a friend who we came to know a couple of years later. Sixty years after this event when I began to write these stories, I interviewed many of my old friends for their memories. When I asked Pam if she had any knowledge of this one, she paused slowly, and then said there had been a lot of talk about it at her house. I was surprised because we girls never spoke of it. The talk came from her cousin who *owned* the machine that went into the creek! She knew one half of the story, and I knew the other. We were both speechless, and then began to laugh. Who could ever believe that this event could have intertwined all of us and yet never come out in all those years? Her cousin tried to discover who did it, suspecting teenage boys with a car, but couldn't find any tire tracks. He never suspected four eighth grade girls, on foot, with an inflated case of curiosity.

The Sloan Family

My family are the Sloans. My dad, William, was called Bill, and my mom was, Patricia (Patty) Sloan, neé Smith. Both were the youngest in their large families – Dad the last of six, and my mother the youngest of seven. According to my many aunts and uncles, they were babied, pampered and until the 1930s, reasonably spoiled. The Great Depression dramatically changed the lives of both families. Before it, they had been able to afford college for their older children, but choices were limited for the youngest children.

Dad was of average height, handsome and trim with an engaging smile, glacier-blue eyes, and wavy dark hair. As heredity took over, his hair receded, but there were no combovers for him. He had the remainder burred to a buzz-cut, and that's how I remember him.

Dad was always ambitious, and often spoke of his disappointment at not being able to accept his admission to Rice University because of the Depression's effect on his family's income. He and his brother Jack enrolled in Army R.O.T.C. at Texas A & M instead and received military commissions along with their degrees. That scholarship still wasn't enough, so to pay the rest of his way, Dad worked multiple jobs, tutoring fellow students in engineering courses and playing bridge for money. He was an excellent player and found games where someone wanted to win badly enough that they paid him to play with them. There was never any money left for transportation costs so he hitchhiked the 370 miles from home to school, which amazed me. Dad played bridge for the rest of his life, but I did not know until after his death what a good player he was.

His civil engineering degree led him to his first job in Bartlesville to work with a fledgling oil company that would later become Cities Service. Around that time he met my mother. Then, in 1940, when the war in Europe had begun, he was called to military duty at the Office of the Chief of Ordnance at The Pentagon in Washington, D.C. In testimony to the urgent need for this office, it opened in the one completed wing, while the other four sides of The Pentagon were still under construction.

In March of 1941 President Roosevelt signed the Lend-Lease Act where the United States promised to send military aid in the form of food, weapons and equipment to Allied Forces – effectively ending the United States' neutral status. Mom and Dad married on August 7, 1941, with Dad scheduled to muster out the following December. But the Japanese attack on Pearl Harbor on December 7 brought a declaration of war, and all discharges were cancelled. Mom and Dad remained in Washington for the remainder of the war, where he continued his work with the Lend-Lease program.

My sister and I were born during this time. When the war ended, we returned to Oklahoma for several years, and Dad resumed work at Cities Service. He was called up again when the Korean War began, for his expertise in ordnance, this time to serve at an Armory in Pennsylvania. He was one of the most patriotic men I ever knew, though he never advertised his service. I believe he always felt a certain guilt for not being sent overseas. To him, war veterans were those who served in battle.

Between wars, Dad spent his entire career in the oil and gas business, always hoping to start his own company, but he never achieved that independence. While two wars interrupted his career, I have to wonder if his emotionally volatile personality didn't contribute to his disappointments.

So many memories of my dad involve anger. He was hot-tempered and often impatient, and I realize that nearly any emotion (he felt) could evoke anger – worry, fear, anxiety or uncertainty. He was never physically abusive, but his anger was hurtful. Or he was Mr. Happy-Go-Lucky and quite loving.

Alcohol, too, could bring on his temper. Though no one (but me) called him an alcoholic, I saw his testiness arise when he'd had a drink or two. As kids, we were never sure whether we'd meet the lion or the lamb when he entered the room.

Despite his unpredictability, I remained outspoken and committed to reason, and so I would challenge his crazy behavior only to incur his fury and a "Goddamnit Patty Mac!" My sister claims she heard that so often she thought it was one word.

Our arguments could be brought on by the simplest things. He had a fit when I wanted to "frost" (add highlights to) my hair. You'd think I was becoming a prostitute. And another time when I wanted to go camping with friends in college, he forbade it, with no explanation. He confessed that he worried about rapists in the camp, and after a lot of tears and my mother's intervention, he finally relented. But with every new thing I wanted to do, we had war before peace. It definitely took the joy out of trying new things.

My sister was a quick study and took a different approach. Quietly, she followed my inroads, letting me bushwhack her path to adulthood. When my brother came along, he became the family clown, and ignored Dad's rages. Or so it seemed.

Dad's outbursts were embarrassing, and since I couldn't predict when they would happen, I never enjoyed having friends at my house. I spent most of my free time at their houses instead. And now when I look back, I remember that my closest friends had the most openly loving and patient fathers, fathers I was fond of all my life.

At the end of my junior year of high school, a headhunter approached my dad to be general manager of an oil and gas company in Calgary, Alberta, Canada. Though this would not be his own business, it was a huge opportunity which he accepted and where he stayed for six years. But things began to unravel. His contract was not renewed, and our family returned to Bartlesville with few explanations and no next-job for dad in sight.

Three years went by with no job, and the results were weighing heavily. A relative in Arkansas who owned a convenience store wanted to take a vacation so my Dad and then eighteen-year-old brother Chip volunteered to work there while the family was gone. Chip and Dad had barely taken over when the stress of responsibility took its toll. Dad's drinking increased, and one night my brother was awakened by the noise of Dad throwing ice cubes against a wall. Normally my brother would have seen this scene as hilarious, but he immediately knew it wasn't. Dad was disoriented, babbling nonsensically, and clearly breaking down. Without calling our mother to add hours to her worry, Chip put Dad in the car and began the seven-hour drive back to Oklahoma.

Dad had never been comfortable with Chip's driving, or anyone else's really, and in Dad's defense, Chip had wrecked two cars in his first month with a license, which was then revoked for a year. Now a year had gone by with no problems, but in the passenger seat and sick as he was, Dad was going to be the driver whether he was behind the wheel or not. Chip couldn't concentrate with the ragtime talk and Dad's imaginary bracing and braking. Eventually, he pulled over and quietly drew Dad out of the car and into the backseat. Dad finally calmed down with him – a first.

When they returned, Dad was immediately hospitalized, first locally and then in a Veteran's Hospital in Colorado. His "nervous breakdown" was diagnosed, and a name was given to his erratic behavior – manic-depression, today called bipolar disorder. Several weeks later, he was discharged with heavy medication but no other treatment.

Modern psychopharmacologic drugs and psychotherapy

might have altered my dad's future had they been available, but his working career was over. At age 52, my mom took over as breadwinner, and went to work for Phillips. She built a career in the international department, while my dad was mostly homebound. He told her he had made every major decision in their life incorrectly, and now it was her turn to make decisions. And as my mom said later, he meant it.

In my usual try-to-fix-it way, I attempted to get him help, but by then, I lived in Boston. He and Mom were in Oklahoma so options were limited. Mom worked full-time and was just trying to financially survive, and the shame that surrounded mental illness made things worse. People seemed to think it was something you could just toughen through and get over. And if you couldn't, it was seen as weakness.

As we were able, my husband and I helped financially. I knew I married the right man when my husband took out a loan to pay off my parent's mortgage as foreclosure threatened. It would be awhile before we owned a home, but that loan saved my family.

Dad did love us, and he began to show it more as he aged, but there remained a sadness in him the rest of his life. Partly, it was the medication, but beyond that it was his disappointment that he never achieved the heights in business he hoped for.

At the age of eighty-seven, he succumbed to cancer. I was with him daily for the last three weeks of his life, lying by his side, watching *I Love Lucy* re-runs, forever grateful for that gift of time with him. Over the years since he first became ill, we had made our peace, and at the end, I felt pride in his life for the first time. I realized that sometimes life's greatest accomplishments are those one makes dealing with the limitations one has to face. I finally saw that. I just hope he did.

My mother was everyone's darling from the moment she arrived. Twenty years younger than her oldest sister, she charmed everyone. Well, maybe not her cats. Mom loved those curly-headed kittens, but her preferred method of carrying them around was to encircle her chubby little hands around their necks, leaving their bodies to hang loose, taffy-pulled by gravity.

As she got older, she wore a live garter snake around her neck, enjoying neighbors' responses when they discovered it was real. Twelve year old pictures show her playing the ukulele, doing headstands and swinging a golf club. You knew she didn't want to miss a thing. Apparently she was the female version of her beloved father.

Mom grew up in Emporia, Kansas, and years later when I read the play *Our Town*, I always imagined my mother's home on Neosho Street to be like the one in Grover's Corners. Their quiet neighborhood of elm-tunneled streets included William Allen White, the nationally famous editor of *The Emporia Gazette*, and the Clogston family, whose father was a Nabisco salesman.

This salesman had a ready market-research group for his products. Living next door to Mom's family with their seven children and various come-and-go relatives, he'd arrive there with his black leather accordion-expandable suitcase and begin to unfold the compartments to reveal the latest Nabisco treats. Oreos were Mom's favorites.

When she was eleven this world ended with her father's untimely death from peritonitis. Her mother tried to run her husband's optometry business, but inexperience and the Depression led to its demise. My mother, a perpetual optimist, continued to be a happy child. Besides being beautiful, she was smart, but she was more interested in friends and fun than school. The sixth daughter born to a forty-two-year-old mother, my grandmother must have had little reserve left for this vivacious chickadee. When my grandmother learned some of Mom's friends smoked and had multiple boyfriends (probably Mom did, too), my grandmother sent her to spend her senior year with her older sister Meredith, and her family in Red Wing, Minnesota. Things didn't change much. Mom began where she left off, making lifelong friends, having multiple boyfriends and being a social success.

She could have attended Emporia State Teacher's College to study teaching or nursing, but Mom had no interest in either career. A second older sister, Marjorie, called "Didge," (pronounced Di-jee) stepped up to take the hand-off from Meredith, and my mom moved in with her and her family.

Didge and her husband lived in Bartlesville, where Didge's husband Homer was a geologist for Phillips. Mom enrolled in Bartlesville Business College, graduated and took a job with I.T.I.O. (Indian Territory Illuminating Oil Company), later to become Cities Service. It was there that she met my dad.

Mom was the voice of reason in the family. No matter how erratic Dad could be, she was our lodestone. And she could calm Dad. During the time of the hair frosting episode, she convinced him I wasn't headed to the red-light district. When I wanted to go camping with friends in college, she made him realize that every male in camp wouldn't be a rapist.

It's hard to remember a cross word with my mother.

Until she outlived her reunions, Mom returned to both high schools to reunite with old friends. My dad died when she was 83, and then at 89 she met 89-year-old Charles Peters at the retirement community where she lived. They were a couple until he died at age 97. At one point she told me they might have gotten married had they been younger, but at this stage it would just mess up their Social Security and Veterans' benefits. They enjoyed socializing, music, bridge and each other. The eight years they shared were a gift to both.

Charles' death, and that of Mom's seventeen-year-old Shih-tzu Daisy a year later were a blow, but she continued to play piano and the occasional bridge game. At age 98, she performed with her grandson Adam's wife Stephanie on a YouTube video called *Recipe Archaeology*. They made cranberry ice, a recipe from Mom's mother. The video concludes with Mom at the piano.

Throughout her life, she stayed connected to family and friends through letters, phone calls, visits, and later, email. And then, at 99 ½ years, a heart episode, pneumonia, and two falls sent her on a downhill progression.

She told me she'd "make it to 100 and that's it!" And she did. At one hundred years, one month and 28 days, she died on Valentine's Day of 2019.

My sister Pam, two years younger than me, was adorable. When she was young, she had a precious little speech impediment affecting her r's, most noticeable when she said "Wudolph the Wed Nosed Weindeer, Woy Wogers or Twigger." It charmed everyone, but Mom felt it might not be so cute later on, and enrolled her in Mrs. Verian Chaney's "Expression Class" (elocution class, really), with hopes of correcting her speech and shyness.

By our early teens Pam had her "r's" down pat, was beautiful, popular, and a good student. She reached my height and passed me a little. Soon we found ourselves sharing clothes — and a double bed. A big mistake, on both counts.

"Where is my white blouse?" I'd yell.

"Uh...I wore it...yesterday," she'd confess.

"What!! You never asked me! Mom! Pam took my blouse without asking..."

We didn't have a closet full of clothes so it might have made economic sense to share, but the rules were spelled out only in arguments. And we had a lot.

Our sleeping arrangements were the second battleground. We shared a double bed with a charming white iron headboard scrolled into a heart, with a medallion in the middle. That little circle marked the surveying post for the center line that separated her side from mine. Not a finger or a toe was allowed to cross that line; I learned to sleep like a corpse.

Other than those difficulties, we got along great. I loved her friends, and I loved to boss her around, which happened a lot because my parents were always putting me in charge. I took to the job like a warden at the pen (the penitentiary,that is). My sister didn't like my attitude, but she saw life was smoother if she appeared to go along. My brother didn't care. He simply ignored me. And so did Pam, really. She'd smile sweetly and then do exactly what she wanted.

My family lived in Calgary, Alberta from 1961 to 1968 where both my siblings attended school. But as Pam approached her senior year of high school, she decided she would like to go back to Bartlesville to finish and graduate high school with her childhood friends. Her closest friend, Carol Candy and her family invited her to live with them, so with Mom and Dad's approval, she made the move.

In the spring of that year, Carol wanted to compete in the Miss Bartlesville contest, and her whole family thought Pam should participate too. Though our mother had been Miss Bartlesville of 1941, my shy sister would never have wanted to participate in such an event. But Carol and her mom insisted. With a lot of enthusiasm and some in-house pressure they convinced Pam to sign on.

Beauty contests included swimsuit and evening gown parades, and Pam was pretty, tall, and slender so she qualified there. The biggest hurdle was the talent contest. Carol was a talented dancer. Pam didn't dance, sing, play an instrument or throw a baton around. What she did do was to call Mrs. Verian Chaney (from the Expression classes) and ask for help in performing a dramatic reading.

The evening of the performance arrived, and so did I, from college. The rest of my family flew in from Canada to attend, along with Pam's high school graduation later in the week. We met at the Civic Center Auditorium, an impressive theater, where we found our seats, settled in and began the wait as the energy from candidates' family and friends filled the room. I was just plain nervous, praying for no disasters.

Finally, the production began. Parades of contestants, first in bathing suits and then in evening gowns strolled across the stage. Pam looked great. As long as she didn't trip, we weren't worried about that part. But then came the talent portion. We heard concertos, arias, and Carol danced beautifully. Then it was Pam's turn. As she walked to center stage, I scrunched down in my seat, squinting my eyes to filter out any catastrophe that might unfold. And then she began a soliloquy as Emily from the play, *Our Town*. Her sweet voice washed over the auditorium, and it wasn't awful. I sat a little taller. She continued, and drew me and the audience into the moving scene where, after dying in childbirth, Emily is allowed to return to Grover's Corners to revisit a day of her choice, her twelfth birthday. As Pam delivered Emily's emotional response to the beauties that people do not see, I relaxed, sat tall and was enthralled by her performance. By the ending, I was fully erect and moved to tears.

As the audience applauded, I elbowed my seatmate to the left, "That's my sister!" It was the first moment in my life that I remember feeling happier for someone else than I had ever felt for myself.

Pam didn't win and neither did Carol, but that might depend on how you define winning. They were second and first runners-up, respectively, and Pam was Miss Congeniality (no surprise there). She went on to college and graduate school to become a speech pathologist and audiologist, first treating patients, and then teaching in the speech pathology program at The University of Oklahoma. I guess Mom and Mrs. Verian Chaney were onto something.

Our brother Chip was born when Pam and I were five and seven. We were playing in a yellow rubber dinghy in the backyard of Aunt Didge and Uncle Homers' house when my aunt called us over to deliver the news. We were ecstatic. Within two weeks, I began selling tickets to neighborhood kids to come and see him. My sales were going quite well, when my horrified mother found out about my enterprise and made me return the money. I was shattered.

While Pam saw my brother as a sibling, I viewed him as a project. I taught him baby tricks like "so big" with his little arms over his head, and how to hold up one finger when asked how old he was. He never seemed to be able to walk outdoors without holding a leaf in each hand, but he's the one who made up that trick. I showed him off at any opportunity (no fees involved).

As time went by, Pam and Chip squabbled like most siblings, but about the only time he really made me mad was at my thirteenth birthday, a slumber party. He and his friend J.B. decided to annoy us, and J.B, as Chip later claimed, came up with the idea of running naked through the room. Chip was all-in. My friends and I were in the living room laughing and talking when, after stripping elsewhere, my brother streaked through. He was only slightly horrified to discover that his buddy had chickened out at the last minute.

Chip was creative. His room was a fun-house of airplane and car models, perched, stashed and hanging everywhere. Some were from kits and others were from scratch; he would have loved Legos. Soon after the Sputnik launch in 1957, he decided to enter a Valentine contest promoted on the radio. He cut out a wooden heart, affixed legs to the bottom and covered the surface with a cushiony material to resemble a launch pad. He placed a toy rocket on the pad, decorated the edges with more hearts and wrote, "You're out of this World!" It may sound trite now, but it was pretty clever in 1957. He won the contest at six years of age.

Chip loved music. His favorite TV show was a country and western one called *The Leon McAuliffe Show*. When the music played, he grabbed the living room floor lamp, dipped it, and mimed, twanging away on the lamp post. He learned to play a little piano, a lot of drums, and later he excelled on the banjo and guitar.

In college, Chip became an architect. Money was always

an issue for our family so once he opted to hitchhike home from the University of Kansas to Calgary. It was a long way and would involve a lot of riding segments so he created a giant wooden hand, with fingers clenched and thumb extended, hitching-style. Then he screwed a cup-hook onto the front to hold the signs for his next destination. A stick was attached to the back and extended below so he could hold the sign high. It worked perfectly. One ride ended and another showed up. Until he got to Montana. Recently there had been a heinous crime: a hitchhiker had killed and *eaten* part of the truck driver who had given him a lift. This did not bode well for rides in that state. However, it was only a small hiccup for my hilarious brother. He just added an additional sentence after his current destination. "I'M A VEGETARIAN." He had more offers than he could accept.

He grew up, still plays music, and continues as an architect. His sense of humor drives a lot of his creations beyond the buildings and homes he designs. Over the years, he painted a topographic map of the world on a 1932 Kelvinator refrigerator, and created postcards from airline barf bags. He'd close them flat, draw some hysterical scene like a bird's eye view of the interior airplane seating with his family dispersed throughout the plane, and entitle it, "Convenient Family Airline Seating." Then he'd stamp and address the front and mail it.

One Christmas he created a life-size cardboard nativity scene depicted with "Simpson" characters. And after he married, he began an ongoing Valentine for his wife Susan. It is drawn with pen and ink against a red background and builds upon the first scene he created, adding events of the past year, chronicling their life with their children, Alex and Charlotte. He has drawn one for every year of their marriage, and could fill a gallery with those Valentines.

And it's probable that my birthday party wasn't the only

place he ever streaked. I knew he was special from the moment he arrived.

The Sloan family preparing to leave for Philadelphia. It was a bad hair day for Mom. Credit: © USA Today Network

Top Ten Good Things
about being routed through
New York and St. Louis to Tulsa

10. Meet entire TWA
    Flight Attendant Corps

9. Finally master locatton of
   emergency exits and flotation devices.

8. Three bags of honey roasted
   peanuts makes a handful.

7. Thorough baggage handlers at
   JFK sift out unwanted jewelry.

6. Three out of four family
   members get turn at window seat.

5. Able to pretend we are
   going to Vegas for 2/3 trip.

4. Three chances to cash in on
   lucrative flight insurance.

3. Enough barf bags for 3 years
   of correspondance.

2. Get over infatuation with the
   glamour of airline travel.

1. Two words: THE MILES.

A Barf-bag Letter from my Brother.

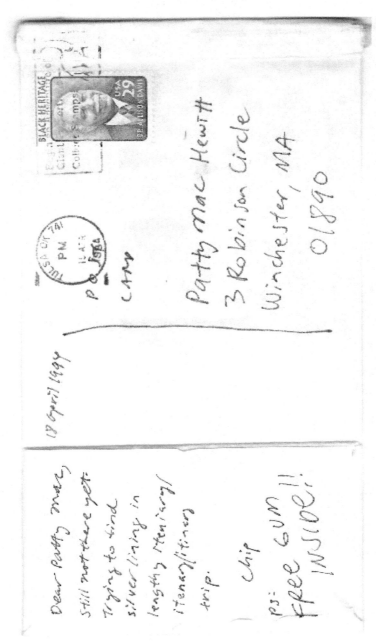

18 April 1994

Patty Mac Hewitt
3 Robinson Circle
Winchester, MA
01890

Dear Patty Mac,

Still not there yet.
Trying to find
silver lining in
lengthy itinerary/
itemization/itinerance
trip.

Chip

P.S.
FREE GUM!!
INSIDE!

Mom and Dad on their wedding day, August 7, 1941.

Goin' to Town

I See Bartlesville

Patty Sloan

I see Bart - les - ville, I see Bart - les - ville,

I see Bart - les - ville, Tra la la la la la!

The first person to catch a glimpse of the Bartlesville skyline sang out this chant whenever we returned home
from an outing. Mom liked to sing so she made up this song
and game to keep the kids entertained for the last twenty
minutes of a trip. Thanks to Phillips Petroleum Company,
Cities Service, H.C. Price Company and the Union and First
National Banks, we had a mini-city skyline on the Oklahoma
plains. The view was particularly dramatic coming into town
from the southwest on the old Barnsdall Road (Route 123)
past Frank Phillips' Woolaroc Lodge, Ranch, and Museum. As
the car crested the last hill and descended the back side of
Circle Mountain, the skyline appeared like a theatrical cur-
tain parting on opening night. We loved it, and once someone
spotted the first building and then broke into song, we all
joined in as we headed home.

But on Saturday mornings, when Janet Ruth and I chose

walking to town to go explorin', those office towers became the brick and mortar buildings where our dads worked – not quite as interesting as Eng's Café (the Chinese restaurant owned by a schoolmate's family), movie theaters, clothing stores, hamburger joints, or the shoeshine shop.

Downtown streets were laid out in a grid like most midwestern towns (and we did consider ourselves midwestern). If you're doubtful, check out an atlas with a two-page map of the lower 48 states, and it's pretty obvious that Oklahoma is about as midway to the west as one can get. I bet there is even a crease down the middle of the state.

North/south streets in town had names like Osage, Delaware, Cherokee, Choctaw, and Chickasaw – all, Oklahoma tribes. Then there were Johnstone and Keeler, named for the fellows who poached Jake Bartles' settlers and drew the town across the river. Those early settlers even included a street called Dewey, the town Bartles founded when he got incensed and moved north. East/west streets were mostly numbered except for Third, which became Frank Phillips Boulevard, a thoroughfare from the west side of town to the east where the town ultimately grew. This was precisely the area that Jake Bartles tried to settle; another poor guy busted ahead of his time.

Cherokee was my favorite street to walk along, where the elms that lined it stretched their branches out until they kissed those on the opposite side, creating an arbor.

There were some fine homes to admire, too, including the in-town mansion of Frank Phillips, but in the spring, we liked to cut over to Dewey to walk by Mr. Bryce's house, a single-story white stucco home with attached portico. Once there'd been a clay tennis court surrounded by chain-link fencing lying just beyond that portico, but by our time, the court had been repurposed as a spectacular garden. Despite the leftover tennis fencing, the garden flowers invited on-lookers like us to smell and enjoy the seasonal blossoms.

"I see Bartlesville!"
Photo Credit: Kathy Spears Hughes

The irises were my favorite. Hundreds bloomed in shades
of yellow, purple, and white, their unique scent, not sweet,
but alerting to their presence, tickling our noses as we
pressed our faces against the mesh fencing. I never smell an
iris that doesn't resurrect memories of that garden.

Continuing down Dewey, we reached the Price Tower, the
talk of the town during 1957 and 1958. This skyscraper was
first designed by Frank Lloyd Wright in the 1920s as an
apartment complex in New York City, but it was never built
because of the Depression. When H.C. Price, owner of a successful pipeline construction corporation decided he needed a
building, he contracted with Wright, who resurrected the design to recreate the nineteen-story tower in prairie
Bartlesville. The project began in 1952 and was completed in

1956. Wright called it his "Lone Pine...the tree that escaped the crowded forest."

We loved that building. With its colorful copper and glass cantilevered windows, and modernistic style, it was distinct from anything else around. For a brief time, when my dad was attempting to start a business, he had an office in that building. It is Frank Lloyd Wright's only skyscraper.

The Price Tower, designed by Frank Lloyd Wright.
Photo courtesy: Bartlesville Area History Museum

In 2003, after housing offices and apartments for many years, the lower level of the building was remodeled into an Arts Center, and the remainder converted into a boutique hotel with a restaurant, a drawing card for many of Wright's architecture pilgrims.

To reach the shopping area, we walked a block over to Johnstone, first passing by the Y.M.C.A., and then the newer Y.W.C.A., both across the street from the post office, with its stone facade and granite stairs. Finally, we reached the area of retail shops. With all the businessmen in Phillips and Cities Service, there was a flourishing market for suits, dress shirts, ties and hats and – with the same loyalty that led you to buy gas from the company that employed you – the townspeople shopped locally. There were May Brothers, Dan's Men and Boys' Shops, Zofness Brothers for shoes, The London Shop, Young's and Martin's Department Store – just to name a few. A lot of men walked around town looking like F.B.I. agents.

There were even more shops for women. Bartlesville was a social town, and just about anything was an excuse to get together and dress up. Many white women who had children and whose husbands worked for the oil companies didn't work, so many filled their days participating in clubs – bridge, poker, church, sorority, or Masonic clubs – or they volunteered for philanthropic efforts.

Mrs. Patterson, a friend of everybody it seemed, used just about any excuse she could find to throw a party. I'm not sure you actually needed to know her all that well, but she'd make you feel you did with the twinkliest eyes and warmest smile you ever met. If your mother's sister came from Houston for a visit, Mrs. Patterson would have a coffee to gather your friends to greet her. And if things were a little slow in the news department, the event might even make the society page of *The Examiner-Enterprise*.

Montaldo's was the dressiest ladies' shop in town. In 1940,

when my mother was working for Indian Territory Illuminating Oil Company, they sponsored her for the Miss Bartlesville contest. As she occasionally modeled for them, Montaldo's donated a gown to her for the competition. When she won, her title took her to Kansas City to compete in the American Horse Show Beauty Pageant, where she came in 4th out of 63 contestants. Many years later when she recounted this event for a newspaper article, she told of the Hollywood judges who had been brought to Kansas City to select the winners.

"Once the votes were taken and delivered," Mom said, "the celebrities made a hasty exit, probably to escape the angry mothers."

Janet Ruth and I usually walked by the shops, including Koppel's and Edwards, popular stores for teenage girls. With no money to spend, neither of us was a shopper. My family didn't have enough, and Janet Ruth's family was intent on keeping what they had. But at Koppel's every fall, we usually got suckered into the "Miss Therma-Jac" contest. Therma-Jac was a clothing line, and I guess this was a big sales promotion.

"Whaddiya think, Patty Mac? Wanna go try on clothes for the contest and get our pictures taken?" Janet Ruth asked.

"Oh...sure...we never win, but what-the-heck, let's go try," I said, and off we went to paw through the racks of the new fall line, find something we liked and try it on. Then in the photography corner, we'd pose, and have our picture taken and posted to provide another entry for the contest. The winner got some of the clothing and their picture in the paper as "Miss Therma-Jac!" We never won, but we tried every year. We were always up for something free.

On most Saturdays when we went to town, Janet Ruth and I headed for the cobbler's shop, the Dewey Avenue Shoe Shop, run by Mr. Tony K. Yeahontis, the Greek proprietor who repaired and polished shoes and boots and sold replacement shoelaces. I'm not sure how we first got there, but we loved giving him business, and he treated us like we were his best customers.

His shop was small with a couple of chairs for shoe shining, a check-out counter and a workroom in the back. A quick peek through the window determined whether we had a wait, and if it looked quiet, we bounded through the door.

"Hi, Mr. Yeahontis!" we'd call.

"Whoa...well, where you two been? I no see you too often," he said. I, of course, explained that we had to save up our babysitting money before we could come.

"Ah, sure, I know," he smiled. "You ready for the shine to-day?" and pointed to the high wooden seats with brass stirrups.

"Yep, just let us get these pennies out of our loafers," said Janet Ruth. Then we hopped up, slid our shod feet into the stirrups and fingered the coins out of the slots of our loafers. We wanted to make sure that the shoes got the full shine with nothing in the way.

I'm not sure which we liked better – the shine – or the storytelling. Mr. Yeahontis grew up in Greece, so his stories all came from his childhood. Sadly, those stories are lost from my memory, but his accent, enthusiasm, and drama are not. And neither is the art of the shine.

And so, the story and shine began. First Mr. Yeahontis washed away the Oklahoma red clay and dust from each shoe with a damp cloth. Sometimes he had to rinse the cloth more than once to do the job well, but by the time the second shoe was cleaned, the first had dried well enough to begin applying the polish. He then took a soft, clean cloth, dipped it into the matching paste color of our cordovan shoes. With a bowl of water nearby, he dabbed one drop of water onto the pasted cloth before carefully painting the shoe. He repeated this step with every fresh dab of paste he applied to the cloth. He covered the top, sides, and exposed heels and sole edges in this manner until all was covered. The polish brought out the scent of new leather, and the excitement of new shoes. Since we didn't get new shoes often, this was the next best thing. By the time the second shoe had been painted, the first was dry enough to begin the brush brandishing on all sides. The flourish matched the emotion of the story, soon to end, as was the shine. At the tale's finale, he set the brush aside, picked up his polishing cloth, and whipped it up, down, and sideways along the shoe to finish, snapping occasionally for further drama. When we could practically see our faces reflected in our shoes, the shine and story ended.

It was a great adventure worth much more than he was paid, but we settled our bill, thanked him, waved off, and headed next door for a Coney Island hot dog.

I've lost my taste for that specialty, but not for a shoeshine. If I'm wearing eligible footwear, I never pass up a stand without getting a polish. And if I've got a good talker, I'm taken back to days with Janet Ruth and Mr. Yeahontis.

We never won, but we were always hopeful.
We were always looking for something free.

Mom and Pop Pickering

The door never shut at the Pickerings. Someone was always following the last one through, and everybody seemed welcome. I was no exception. In no time Pop Pickering was teasing me, making me feel I'd been around forever. Maybe he thought I might be a good influence on Janet Ruth. Oh, he loved his mischievous daughter, but I think he figured it couldn't hurt to sand down a few rough edges.

Mr. and Mrs. Pickering both grew up in Medford, Massachusetts, and were childhood sweethearts. Hank was bright and spent his final year of high school at Phillips Exeter Academy to graduate and then went off to M.I.T. to complete a degree in Mining Engineering. He married Ruth Goldman after graduation and moved to New Jersey, where, of all places, his new mining job at Franklin Mines required him to go underground. He'd spent no time in a mine and found he didn't like it one bit. It didn't take him long to realize that oil was also underground, and you didn't have to go there in person, so he moved to a career in oil exploration and production. That's how he always told the story, but I bet he also saw the sea change coming in energy sources.

Janet Ruth's parents lived in several states before coming to Bartlesville, Oklahoma in 1951 for Mr. Pickering's job at Phillips Petroleum Company. By then, they had two children, Janet Ruth and Cort, ages seven and ten. Their first home was temporary, at the Phillips Apartment Hotel where they lived while looking for a house. Janet Ruth and her brother Cort loved exploring that multi-storied building with its elevators, back hallways, and in-house restaurant. But those adventures were kiddie rides compared to what they found on

the roof, site of the building's cooling system and other me-
chanics.The chat-covered surface had plenty of loose stones
for hurling, first at each other, and then over the roof's edge
to the grass below. But nothing was more fun than tossing
those rocks into the central air conditioning fan to be blown
back. I'm not sure how long that lasted before the kids were
discovered, but the hotel staff and the Pickerings were soon
grateful when they found their home.

Phillips Apartment Hotel.
Photo courtesy: Bartlesville Area History Museum

After rejecting the one-story ranches and bungalows common to the area, they moved into a two-story white colonial
more typical of Boston than Bartlesville. Mom Pickering always liked to say, "nice people go upstairs to bed." So, they

did, and a year later Sherry arrived, the youngest of the three by eight years.

At the time of our friendship, Mr. Pickering worked in the older of the two Phillips buildings – a darker brick, nineteen-story structure with an adjacent tower. The newer Adams Building was a block away and was named for the current chairman and chief executive of Phillips, "Boots" Adams, successor to Frank Phillips himself.

Luckily for Janet Ruth and me, with all the floors in those buildings, Mr. Pickering's office was located at ground level with a window that looked out onto the sidewalk. What's more, the window opened, and Mr. Pickering liked seeing us and opening that window whenever we were roaming in the neighborhood. If we reached really high on our tiptoes, we could knock on the lower half of the window to get his attention, and most often it worked. He never seemed too busy to see us, and though the window could only open part-way, it was enough for him to appear in the space and, with his head cocked sideways, greet the two of us with a gentle "Hi, Babe" (his pet name for Janet Ruth).I was always amazed by his welcome. My dad was so serious about "business;" he never wanted an interruption from home, not even a phone call. I would never have thought of knocking on his window, even if I could have reached it.

One day we got more than a greeting. Phillips expected employees to participate in community service so when we surprised Mr. Pickering with a visit, he surprised us with, "Hey, I've got a great idea for you two. I'm working on a fund-raiser for The Crippled Children of Washington County selling little white lilies. I think you'd be dandy sales-girls downtown!" (He really liked the word "dandy.")

*The Phillips Building and the First NationalBank Building.
If we reached up on our tip-toes, we could knock on Pop
Pickering's street-level window to say hi.*
Photo: Bartlesville Area History Museum

I said it sounded fun to me, but from the look on Janet Ruth's face I guessed she suspected there was more to the story. But her dad didn't give her a chance to back out. He mentioned there were some costumes involved, but we wouldn't have to worry about coming up with them; they had just the right *rabbit suits* for us to wear. A wry grin crossed his face as Janet Ruth started to protest, but I overrode her arguments. I really liked her dad and wanted to help him out.

So, on the next Saturday, Janet Ruth and I hawked lilies in our bunny rabbit suits on the streets of downtown Bartlesville. We felt ridiculous, but we got our picture in the newspaper, so we agreed it was definitely worth it; we loved publicity.

As a result of that photo, I got a job from a neighbor who owned a florist shop to help deliver flowers at Eastertime. The wrinkle was that I had to wear that same rabbit suit, but I liked making money. It turned out to be a lot of fun, riding with the driver, an old African-American man named Henry who told stories as we delivered flowers house to house. I caused quite a commotion when kids opened the door to find a rabbit delivering the bouquets. Looking back, it seems I never turned down an opportunity to make money or to listen to a good storyteller.

Janet Ruth's dad was really special – big, with a gentle manner, and always with a warm smile. And he was funny, like Janet Ruth or maybe she was funny, like him. When we got older, but still didn't drink, he advised us that if we were ever having a martini, one should be our limit. If you had two, "you had to be careful, else you'd be telling folks you were having "tee martoonis!"

There's a famous Pickering story that once when he'd *had* "tee martoonis" over at a neighborhood barbeque, he and his friend Don needed to use the bathroom. Meanwhile, Janet Ruth and the neighborhood kids, playing outdoors and curious about what the grown-ups were doing, had climbed a nearby tree to spy on the goings-on. About the time they were situated on their branches, the two men got up for a bathroom break. Perhaps because they were busy cooking or maybe they were just lazy, they decided to forego the steps to the house bathroom and just go whizz under the tree where the kids were perched like crows on branches. It took a lot of will-power for those "crows" not to explode with laughter before the two of them were through and out of earshot. Hank and Don never knew.

Mama Ruth was a lot more serious than Hank. She was short, had a full head of dark hair, and spoke with a thick Boston accent, which set her well apart from most folks in town. She was not big, but sturdy, in body and demeanor. And while Hank was actually heavy, Mama Ruth had to *be* the heavy; she made the rules and enforced them. I'm not sure she liked that role, but someone had to do it, and it was clear Hank never would. In fact, he would often intervene when she tried to enforce something. His favorite crisis breaker was to recite the poem, "Ruthless Ruth."

> *Ruthless Ruth, the girl uncouth,*
> *that brought the smirch on the Baptist church,*
> *in Keokuk, I-O-Way.*

I tried to find that poem in full, and came up with "The Ballad of Yukon Jake" by Edward E. Paramore, Jr. He definitely writes about a "Ruthless Ruth," but not with the same words Mr. Pickering recited. Clearly, Mr. Pickering created his own version.

Sometimes this poetic intervention drove Mama Ruth crazy, but by its end, she had usually given up on whatever was making her mad, and was quietly laughing with the rest of us.

Mama Ruth never lost that Boston accent, and I loved to hear her talk. She'd offer you a little "vaniller ice cream", and she had a lot of good "idears." If *you* didn't, she'd reply with a "hmmph..." I had never heard anyone speak like that, so I thought it was pretty funny.

She was thrifty, too. Some might say cheap, always looking to save a penny. Once, Janet Ruth wanted a prom dress from somewhere other than C.R. Anthony (a moderately-priced emporium), but Mama Ruth's comeback was to offer to make a dress out of the dining room draperies.

Janet Ruth declined.

I laughed. I knew Mama Ruth was serious.

In her elder years when Mrs. Pickering was complaining of the difficulty of getting a pizza in Odessa, Texas, her son-in-law Tom told her she could order over the phone and have it delivered for free.

"It's not free," she said. "Ya gotta tip 'em a dollah!"

All through our growing-up years, the Pickering house was a draw for kids. Mr. Pickering loved to spend time in the kitchen, declaring he was "cookin' up something tasty." On Saturday, it was Boston baked beans. On Sunday, it was breakfast. Sometimes when he was making one of those Sunday breakfasts, a strange kid wandered into the kitchen after spending Saturday night in the den as an uninvited guest, usually one of Cort's friends. The kid might have had "tee martoonis" himself, but he'd be greeted, asked a few questions and then offered breakfast. Who wouldn't love a family like that?

"Here comes Peter Cottontail."
Patty Mac and Janet Ruth.
Photo ©USA Today Network

Beaver's Bend

Although much of Oklahoma fits the image of sweeping plains, Beaver's Bend is actually a lake and mountain recreation area in southeastern Oklahoma within the Kiamichi Mountain range and the Ouachita (pronounced Wash-i-tah) National Forest. It's a popular summer recreation area, and numerous church camps claimed locations there. Janet Ruth, Marie, and I went to Episcopal Church camp there for two summers. Most kids went to their own church's camp, but I found my way to Beaver's Bend because of Janet Ruth.

Churches were everywhere in our town. If you didn't require a temple or a mosque, you could probably find a church home in Bartlesville. Most of my friends were mainstream Protestants, but I met my first Catholic friend, Pam Oulde, in the ninth grade after she finished at St. John's Catholic School. My first Jewish friend, John Ross, was my boyfriend Mike's close friend. His dad was our family's veterinarian, having come west from Brooklyn to go to vet school at Kansas State. He made his way to Bartlesville when a vet practice became available. His family found a religious home fifty miles away in Tulsa, but that was not too handy for John's dating and meeting nice Jewish girls. There were several Jewish families in town, but none had daughters John's age, so the three of us often hung out together, shooting baskets or going to movies.

Both my parents grew up Presbyterians and attended First Presbyterian Church in Bartlesville. Kids didn't usually church shop; you just went where your parents went. Our church was a formidable brick, Gothic-styled building with an

ivy-covered tower housing a sanctuary, windowed with magnificent stained-glass stories from the Bible. It appeared as
serious as its theology, but it was healthy, as they say, with
just enough wealthy oil executives supporting it, and enough
ordinary folk attending. And though the congregation was
welcoming, the doctrine of predestination (which I heard as
meaning God had already ordained everything) made the
church services – and life in general – seem humorless and
out of my control. As I was a regular, attending Sunday
school, church, and choir since I was very young, you might
imagine with my *exploring* tendencies, I sometimes got bored.
I often resorted to sitting in the balcony during sermons,
counting the congregants' bald heads to keep myself entertained.

I did like our church organist and choir director a lot. Her
name was Francis Yates, or Mrs. G.V.N. Yates as she was formally called. She seemed old (to me, anyway), but she was a
bit of a local celebrity. As a young woman, she composed "The
Twelfth Street Rag," a popular jazz song of the 1920's celebrating Twelfth Street in Kansas City. Fortunately, or unfortunately, she sold the rights for $50 (or so the story went) and
Wikipedia gives the author credit to Euday Bowman. She was
happy with $50 at the time, but I think when the song became
famous it made her sad not to be given a writing credit. But
we credited her. Nearly every week at the end of junior choir
rehearsal, the kids begged her to play it. She beamed, took
her place on the organ bench, and despite her matronly appearance, the sound that poured out of that organ convinced
anyone listening she *owned* that song. The place rocked!

I became a lapsed Presbyterian one Palm Sunday. Janet
Ruth's family were Episcopalians at St. Luke's. Their church,
a beautiful grey-stone building with walled gardens behind,
and a signature red front door, was only a few blocks away
from the Presbyterians. On Palm Sunday she invited me to
come to church with her family, and I did. It was my first visit

to a different church, and as was customary, we all dressed in our best clothes and shoes.

When we entered the church, the greeter presented each of us with a palm frond, and as we took them in hand, we followed instructions and proceeded single file around the room, waving our branches as the musical prelude filled the sanctuary. Mr. Pickering was in the lead with Mama Ruth next, and the rest of us followed. Never missing an opportunity to tease "Ruthless Ruth," Mr. Pickering perched his branch over his shoulder and began bouncing slightly up and down causing the palm to bend and flex, so that with every step it would reach behind him and tickle Mama Ruth across her nose.

Quickly, we saw how he did it, and in no time, we mimicked him. Around and around the church we went with those palms flippin' the face or nose of the one behind us. No one could say a word. It was hilarious.

I guess I decided that day they just had more fun over at St. Luke's. As Virginia Cary Hudson wrote in *O Ye Jigs and Juleps*, the Baptists (and perhaps the Presbyterians) would sing about "plunging sinners in a bloody fountain drawn from Emmanuel's veins" while "we (the Episcopalians) sing about "Crown Him Lord of All." So, I joined the Episcopal Youth Group with Marie and Janet Ruth and went to Evening Prayer and learned to say The Lord's Prayer "forever and ever." And in the summer the three of us went to summer camp at Beaver's Bend.

I loved camp. Kids came from all over the state, and we quickly found the exploring types. There were plenty of organized activities, but we decided to create some adventures of our own (the main one having to do with obtaining communion wine). Episcopalians (and Catholics) drink real wine when they take communion, not grape juice like most of the Protestants.

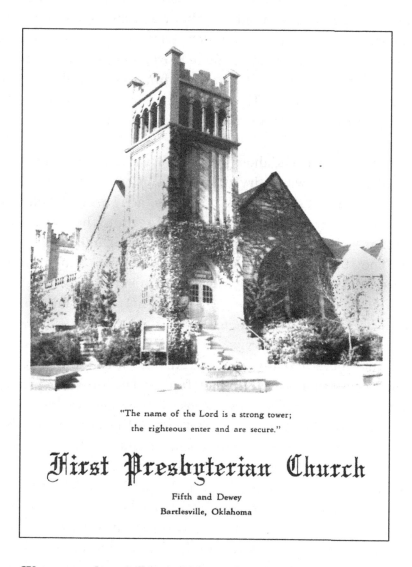

"The name of the Lord is a strong tower;
the righteous enter and are secure."

First Presbyterian Church

Fifth and Dewey
Bartlesville, Oklahoma

We got modern in the 1960s and replaced the building.
Bulletin photo courtesy of First Presbyterian Church,
Bartlesville, Oklahoma.

At camp, communion wine was served to *all* the campers, no matter your denomination. This was new to me, so when Marie, Janet Ruth, and our new friend, Chuck, suggested breaking into the sacristy to taste more, it seemed like a good idea. Word was that little sacristy cabin was not well secured so it was worth a try. The whole idea was one of those, "Do not..." situations that drew Janet Ruth – and the rest of us – to try it.

In those days, Oklahomans had a lot of conflicted feelings about liquor. It was a dry state, prohibition not ending until 1959, finally dispelling Will Roger's adage, "Oklahomans would vote dry as long as they could stagger to the polls." But as that saying inferred, there was plenty of imbibing going on. The 1959 vote only allowed the sale of liquor in package stores; the sale of liquor by the drink (in bars or restaurants) would not pass for another 25 years. In 1984, Oklahoma finally became the last state to do so.

Now, during those dry years, it was anybody's guess to figure out where it really *was* dry. Anyone who wanted to get liquor could find it easily. In my family, Dad drove to Caney, Kansas, twenty miles away across the border, where there were no prohibition laws. My sister and I loved to make the ride with him; it was an outing that might involve getting a hamburger. But if he couldn't make the drive, he'd just call and place his order with "Trigger Bealler," a local bootlegger who'd come to our door and bring the liquor wrapped discreetly in a brown paper bag. I always felt it was like Christmas receiving that package. And I knew who was knocking by the doors they used: the milkman came to your front door, and your bootlegger delivered to your back door.

Our schoolmate Ada Lee Bean recalled that in the "Negro" part of town there were a few illegal taverns called "Do Drop Inns," which sold whiskey and beer. The whiskey was either branded whiskey or moonshine, and the beer was home brew or "chock." There would be a raid from time to time, but, according to her sources, there was always advance knowledge and not much came of the raids.

We didn't talk openly about our bootlegger so I'm not sure if the Pickerings used his services. There were other ways to get around the law. People belonged to private clubs, such as Hillcrest Country Club where you could store a personal bottle if you were a member. Clubs such as the VFW, Elks, Lions, and Knights of Columbus were popular, some offering lifetime memberships in windowless bars and an opportunity to store a bottle of your choice, with your name on it. And the law said "no sharing was allowed..." *Right...*

If you didn't belong to one of these clubs, you could always go to Rosalie's Steak House, a western speakeasy where they kept a cache of booze stashed under a trap door in the center of the dance floor. Though they had problems with episodic sheriff raids and seasonal Caney River floodings, the place always reopened. It seemed to only take a little creativity to get around the law.

With all that drinking, I'm really not sure why it took so long to change the law. Perhaps it had to do with appearances; people cared a lot about appearances. I think it was the looking over the shoulder part that really kept the law under wraps.

So...back at camp, Janet Ruth, Marie, and I were really not much different from Adam and Eve and the forbidden fruit, and the rest of the folks in the state. It seemed important to break into that sacristy and taste the wine.

We launched our mission in the dark, and with our new buddy Chuck willing to help us, four culprits headed to this refuge of banned beverages. I don't recall being nervous. The most difficult part of the stunt was to stifle the laughs. It just seemed that when you're a kid, the more off limits the scheme was, the funnier it was, and the more you needed to keep quiet to pull it off. I guess there was a lot of laughing in those other cabins that night because no one stopped us. We found the unoccupied cabin quickly, and with a flashlight and some of Janet Ruth's adept jiggling, we were through the door. *Now what?*

There were a number of bottles on the shelves, but one had already been opened and re-stoppered, which was good, because we hadn't thought to bring along a wine opener. We didn't have glasses so we began passing the bottle around, each taking a taste, communion-style, leaving plenty so no one would be the wiser.

Actually, the wine wasn't very good; it reminded me of vinegar. I think it might have *turned* in all that heat. Truth was, the plan and execution were actually a lot more fun than the drink. And we were pretty smug we never got caught.

After that, it was back to organized activities, the most popular one being swimming. One day, as we were "fixing to get our suits on," Janet Ruth took me aside and told me that she had just gotten her period! That hadn't happened to either of us yet, so we were unprepared. And it had been three years since that sex education class in the 5th grade, so we didn't remember much. But what we did know was that we needed supplies. Fortunately, there were lots of girls at camp, so after some discreet requests, we came up with Kotex pads and cardboard plungers called tampons to deal with this situation.

The pad was easy enough to install, but Janet Ruth still wanted to go swimming. Our friends told us she should use a tampon, so with a box of them in hand, the two of us headed to the girls' bathroom. Janet Ruth took a stall near the back, went inside, then closed the door while I held the supplies outside.

The mood was tense, and we were both quiet. You'd think we were surgeons headed for the O.R. But instead of a scalpel, she asked for a plunger. I began doling them out to her from underneath the door. At first there was no response, but then

the mutterings, grunts, and ouches began, as one after another rejected tampon came rolling out from under the door,
slightly destroyed by the bloody cramming as they failed to
navigate this foreign territory.

"Where on earth is this hole?" she finally yelled.

I began to laugh so hard that I could barely keep re-fueling
her. Eventually, in a final try, the plunger scored, and the
deed was done. The two of us, now doubled over in laughter,
chucked the leftovers in the trash and exited the toilets victo-
rious in Janet Ruth's entry into womanhood. We were off to
swim. Amazing what you can learn at church camp.

Camp and Campers
Circled, L-R, Marie, Patty Mac, and standing behind,
Janet Ruth. We were 14 years old.

The March

The Supreme Court's 1954 ruling in *Brown v. Board of Education* that racial segregation in the public schools was unconstitutional, was not quickly implemented in our town. School segregation was the reality in Bartlesville until 1956 when Jane Morrison became the first African American when she entered the high school. Others followed, but it was not until 1958, the year Janet Ruth and I entered 8th grade, that Black students joined us there.

I was completely unaware of the historic significance of what was going on. There were no lively political discussions around our dinner table, though my dad railed against the Democrats from time to time. I recall no conversations about integration among my family or friends. Clearly, I lived in my own world.

Bartlesville was predominantly white, though many in the community could claim full-blood American Indian heritage, or some partial Native heritage. All that early intermarrying had produced a significant multi-ethnic population throughout the state.

Since so many people claimed Native heritage, it was not surprising that my family had close friends, Leann and Will Nelson, with such roots. Their daughter Janette was a little younger than I, and their son Ruse was a friend of my brother's. Mr. Nelson sold insurance for a living, but his passions were golf and photography. He won the Oklahoma Amateur Open in golf in 1938 and 1940, and he took every good photograph in our family albums.

Leann was warm and wiry and had the most hilarious laugh. It turned into gasps halfway through, as if she were straining for air, building steam to finish. I think she was so overcome with laughter that she started a second laugh before she finished the first. It sure got my attention, and you couldn't help but laugh with her. Mrs. Nelson loved golf, too, but what I remember most was she was always helping someone. I was fascinated with her jewelry: silver and turquoise bangles and rings never missing from her hands and wrists, which seemed to always be carrying a casserole to some needy friend – assembled between golf rounds, I guessed.

Both the Nelsons often spoke of their Delaware roots and attended periodic weekend pow-wows to connect with other tribal members. We kids were fascinated with those stories. The Nelsons were like many multi-ethnic Oklahomans we knew. It seemed to me that some Native heritage was a badge of honor. When I learned that if we were a "quarter Indian" we might qualify for a tribal roll and collect some oil money or land, I pestered my mother to research our genealogy. We located one female Choctaw forebear, but, disappointingly, we did not qualify for any windfall. Being a little different always seemed appealing to me.

At the time of integration, the Bartlesville African-American population was small, around 800 people out of 20,000. Through Ada Lee Bean, a former classmate who was one of the first to integrate our junior high, I learned that many in her community could trace their forebears to the slaves owned by Native Americans forced to settle in Indian Territory. Ada Lee and I never really knew each other as children, except as classroom acquaintances, but from the little interaction we did have, I never forgot her. I located her three years ago, and we have shared many stories. As she has told me, I have tried to relate some of her stories as they paralleled mine.

Ada Lee's study of her own family genealogy revealed that her great-grandmother, at the age of 12 walked the Trail of Tears as a Cherokee slave. She found similar histories for some of her family's friends and neighbors in Bartlesville. Following the Civil War, Reconstruction-era treaties with Native American tribes required that slaves be treated as family and entered onto tribal rolls to receive head rights. Not all of these former slave owners were eager to share, and some made entitlement difficult. Nevertheless, today qualified descendants of those African Americans are now entitled to be full members of the tribes who once enslaved their ancestors.

Once freed, many African Americans continued to work for their former owners or, if they were given any land, set out to farm on their own. Others worked as teachers, hairdressers, barbers, shopkeepers, or in health fields, but only within their community. Employment outside was severely restricted, limited mainly to working as a domestic, in hotels or for the railroad.

My contact with "colored people," which was how most of us referred to African Americans then, was limited to observation. We had no "maid," though I had friends who had "colored help." I was aware that they lived on the "West Side," but I had no idea that boundaries determined where they could live since the early 1900s. According to Josie Marie Oulds in her article entitled "Bartlesville's West Side Story" in Bartlesville's *1997 Centennial* publication, published by the town's *Examiner-Enterprise* newspaper, "Negroes were not to live east of Santa Fe, or south of Seventh Street except for one block on Maple and one block on 9th St. There were "three main areas (where they lived) – the Y where the two sets of railroad tracks meet near 5th and Santa Fe, The Brickyard – from Virginia to Bucy (also known as Shackle Rods from the sound of pumping oil wells), and The Bottom – from Second Street north on Johnstone."

Ada Lee told me that many families did not have indoor plumbing. Many of the homes were outside designated city limits, so the town was not obliged to provide sewerage or water lines. She remembers a generous neighbor, with a very long hose who supplied them with water. Meanwhile white families who lived blocks away had all those facilities.

At home, I don't recall my mother making any racial remarks, or uttering slurs about anyone for that matter. She saw the best in whomever she met, was always forgiving, and spent her life making new friends. My dad, on the other hand, could have been first cousin to Archie Bunker of *All in the Family*. Though he grew up in the Rio Grande Valley of Texas with many Mexican friends and acquaintances, he could paint an entire ethnic group for the crime of one who had offended his moral code.

In contrast, I saw him treat *individuals* of different backgrounds with courtesy, respect, and compassion. Once Dad was stranded in a snowstorm in Pennsylvania where a Black family took him in for the night so he could dig out his car in the morning. Weeks later at Christmas, he made the drive, again at night, bringing gifts for the family, which he left anonymously on their porch. The dichotomy of his actions and speech confused me, but I guess his deeds impressed me more than his words.

When the "colored kids" arrived in the eighth grade, it was just one more new thing to me. There were no barricades or placards anywhere. The new kids just came to school.

In English class, Ada Lee Bean sat across the aisle, one desk ahead of me. She was tall and looked older than some of my friends. Now I'd say she looked "mature," though more because of her demeanor than her appearance. And I would say I was immature then. She appeared to know no one at first, but soon enough our little neighborhood was chatting. It didn't take long to discover that she was smart, even though she wasn't one of those kids who waved their arm like a flag in a gale if they knew the answer to a question.

We were required to do numerous report writings in that class, and often a lot of effort went into creating covers for the themes. I cannot recall the assignment that led to one of my more elaborate covers, but we were given several weeks to produce it. My magnum opus was about the book, *Toussaint, The Slave Who Freed Haiti,* the story of a former slave who led Haiti to independence from France. For the cover, I wood-burned the title onto a lightweight piece of wood, used a second piece for the back and then lacquered all four sides to finish. Lastly, after drilling two holes near the spine on each side, I put the report between the front and back pieces and tied it all together with two shoelaces. Clearly, I spent more time on that cover than the essay itself, in which I might have plagiarized some. I cannot honestly say, but, amazingly, I do still have the report.

On the day we were to turn in our masterpieces, I looked across the aisle at Ada Lee's theme. Her cover was a piece of tan construction paper with the title simply printed, "The Bean Sprouts." Beneath that she had glued eight various dark beans, of different sizes and shapes, stair-stepping from left to right to represent her parents and the six children in her family. Ada Lee remembers that their bodies were colorful stick figures made with either crayons or yarn. A sudden clap of thunder couldn't have surprised me more. I was stunned by the cleverness of her art which was simple, yet powerfully expressed her feelings about her family and her place in the world. At once, I saw her as a peer who had, in her creative simplicity, outdone my effort. We were just two teenage girls, both good students, colored differently. It was a significant moment for me.

I met other Black students in my classes, all of them smart and well prepared. Ada Lee told me they all felt they'd been intentionally separated when they entered, so that no class had more than one or two Black students. Music class was the exception.

They were all together on the first day when the teacher asked them to sing "Old Man River," but not the version Paul Robeson made famous. It was the one with the racist lyrics he refused to sing, the version that repeatedly used the "N" word. They were all horrified. But one girl, who was incredibly funny according to Ada Lee, immediately began playing dumb, questioning the teacher about the lyrics and repeatedly using the "N" word until the teacher was completely flustered. Over the next couple of weeks, the teacher continued to challenge their music skills (singing parts, sight-singing, etc.), all of which they'd mastered at Douglass from their music teacher there. At the end of two weeks, the teacher resigned.

Clearly, the Douglass teachers had prepared them well, but when integration came, we didn't benefit from their teachers; none came to our schools. And during those years we were separated, Douglass was dealt cast-offs for their material needs. Books were second-hand, and their band uniforms were old College High outfits whose colors were black and gold, while Douglass' were purple and white.

I knew nothing of this at the time. My connections with the Black students were superficial and never extended beyond school – except for once. And I have never forgotten that.

One day before class, Janet Ruth and I began talking about Y-Teens when Ada Lee joined us. Y-Teens was an after-school club for teenage girls, held at the YWCA in town, led by volunteer mothers. Most of their activities were indoor, crafty projects which didn't interest us much, but the socializing and food were a draw. With no sports available to us, there weren't a lot of other options. During one of our discussions about Y-Teens, Ada Lee asked when we met.

"Every Thursday at the Y after school. We meet outside on the front steps to walk over together. Why doncha come?" Janet Ruth said. Ada Lee said she'd think about it.

On the following Thursday, as I and my friends were assembling to leave, Ada Lee and a couple of her friends showed up to go with us. She and I immediately paired up to talk and walk, leading the way over the few blocks to the Y.

We were too busy chatting to notice any jaws agape when we got to the building, but when we entered the meeting room, we were met with an appalled silence. We stopped talking and everyone behind us went mute as we all saw the look of horror on Mrs. Milburn's face. When she found her voice, her shock turned to anger and a blur of rage.

Though I didn't hear her words, I knew that the meeting was cancelled and that we'd all been ordered to leave. But we didn't know what we had done wrong. We were speechless and confused, but we all quietly filed out of the building, separated, and made our way home. It was difficult to explain to our parents what had happened. In our minds, it was an inexplicable consequence to a simple act. All I recall is that my mother quietly listened, and that she wasn't angry with me.

Because Ada Lee and I walked through the door first, I took the blame that day. (Janet Ruth had a remarkable knack for being involved in things, and a Houdini-like gift for escaping blame.) The following day I was called to the vice-principal's office at school. This was never good since he was the school disciplinarian. Today, I might joke that his job and title said it all. He was second in command, and in charge of junior high – vice. But I saw no humor that day. As I waited outside his office, I was terrified. I had never been in trouble at school before. And I still couldn't understand what we had done wrong. Then the door opened, and the vice-principal appeared,

"Patty Mac Sloan?"

"Yes, Sir," I said.

"Please come in and take a seat," he said while ushering me in. I had barely sat when he proceeded to lecture me, telling me that "under no circumstances was I ever to lead a march on anything again." Paralyzed, I nodded in submission. Only now do I understand how an innocent person could be pressured into acknowledging guilt; I would have said anything to get my aggressor off my back.

I had no idea we were "leading a march." In hindsight, I wish I could say it *was* a premeditated act. But it was nothing so courageous. We were just a bunch of girls walking together to something that should have welcomed all of us.

I never went back to Y-teens. I don't even know if it ever started up again. At the same time, I just accepted the outcome. It was out of my control, like the limitations on girls.

I do not recall any of the Black students participating in after-school activities until high school, when slowly, one or two of the boys were admitted to the basketball or football team. The townspeople like to win, and some of these boys were too talented to ignore. One by one there was integration in sports.

And as for really getting to know any of these kids after that, we never attempted anything more than a classroom friendship.

Janet Ruth, Ada Lee, and I may have lived in the same town, but we lived in different worlds. When Janet Ruth and I crossed our boundaries, there seemed to be a safety net that we expected – and always found. It seemed to me that Ada Lee and her friends didn't have such freedoms. But I was wrong about them not having the protection and bubble we felt.

Ada Lee told me that as she and her friends look back, they felt that their parents worked very hard to form "a protective bubble that prevented incidents like this taking up space in their childhood memories; (their) parents and others tried to prevent any interaction with white adults that (might) be damaging."

Ada Lee also told me that many of the boys who entered in that first junior high wave ended up leaving school to join the military as soon as they could. Since they were not being given the opportunity to play sports in their new schools, and when they graduated, the prospects for jobs were limited, the military was a way out. There, they could play sports, learn a trade and hope, when their service was completed, to move to a place where the jobs weren't segregated. Many chose California.

When I thought about the injustices then, I likened them to the restrictions placed on girls and women. I didn't like it, and it didn't seem fair, but it was just the way it was. And you had to accept it. I had much to learn. I was a long way from being a freedom rider.

Epilogue:

Some forty years later in a supermarket in Bartlesville, my mother ran into Mrs. Milburn, who was in charge of the Y-Teen meeting that day. After a brief greeting, she reminded Mom of that incident so many years earlier. On the spot, she went on to express her remorse and shame for her conduct that day. Her actions had haunted her for many years, both for what she had done to the Black girls and for how she had treated me. She was very sorry. Mom was so surprised, but gratefully accepted her apology, as did I when I heard. Mom and I were deeply touched by her courage and change of heart.

The fact that this incident took place at the Y was ironic. Seven years earlier, the director had tried hard to integrate Y-Teens. At the same time, the long-time librarian pushed to integrate the children's story hour, developed friendships with two Black teachers from Douglass, and worked with a group of Bartlesville citizens (Bartians) to "promote improvements in the Negro community." This organized group included the Principal of Douglass and some of his teachers, and concerned citizens of the "Negro" community, including Ada Lee Bean's parents. There were also some whites, largely wives and a few husbands from the research department of Phillips Petroleum and a few others from Cities Service.

Their efforts were thwarted by a status-quo community who, with a technique borrowed from the McCarthy witch-hunts, attacked the group as Communist sympathizers. They chose Miss Ruth Brown, the 30-year town librarian as their scapegoat, accusing her of promoting subversive materials at the library. She was fired and ultimately left the Bartlesville community.

It was a black eye for this idyllic town, made national news and was the basis for a Hollywood movie starring Bette Davis, called *Storm Center.* The librarian's story is told in *The Dismissal of Miss Ruth Brown; Civil Rights, Censorship and the American Library* by Louise S. Robbins (University of Oklahoma Press, 1999).

My mother claims to have only a vague memory of this period, though she remembered that folks were perplexed when the librarian lost her job. At the same time, my brother had just been born, and we were moving to Philadelphia where my dad had been called up to serve in an armory during the Korean War. As she explained to me, "I just wasn't an activist."

Mom was ninety-nine when I asked her how she reacted at the time of the Y-Teen incident, and she responded that she just went on about her life and encouraged me to do the same. She refused to get involved in the gossip-chatter chain, and never passed on any of that talk to me. We would just be who we always were. But we did talk about the event many times in later years, and I always wondered about the Black girls involved.

It took nearly 60 years before I found Ada Lee and got answers to some of my questions. In 2017, I began exploring the White Pages on the internet. Using the name I knew her by, I found a female about my age, living in Oakland, California under that name. I tried the e-mail addresses listed but got no response. Then I wrote a letter and enclosed a photo of Ada Lee from a junior high newspaper I'd found in an old scrapbook. I enclosed my contact information.

A few days went by, and then on a Sunday evening she called. My husband answered the phone. He had an expectant look on his face as he handed me the phone, and I wondered if it could be her. Goosebumps rose on my arms when I heard her voice and words. It wasn't the voice I remembered, but from her first few words, I realized I had found the woman I'd searched for.

We were to meet in the spring of 2020, but the Covid pandemic thwarted our reunion. In the meantime, we have shared multiple phone calls and e-mails. And we've shared stories. She remembers integration as fairly calm, but also that she and her friends were never really a part of anything.

"We felt like visitors, she said, "Many of the boys who arrived had been athletic stars at Douglass – bringing home trophies and championships against other 'Negro Schools' around the state, but now they were not allowed to join teams."

When I asked her about that day at Y-Teens, she said that she had no memory of the incident. As I have done with my old friends, she has kept in touch with many of her Douglass classmates from Bartlesville, and when she asked some of them about that day, they couldn't remember it either. My guess is that the incident was a blip on their radar screens of injustices.

Ada Lee has told me of many events that far outweigh that day's drama, but it was my first personal experience with a bigotry that was dramatic enough to remember – and to begin an awakening. What she *does* remember about our culture is that she and her friends "didn't like [our] music and stars anyway – Rick Nelson, Pat Boone, and Tab Hunter." She and her friends ended up going to Y-Teens at the Westside Community Center, where Fats Domino was king! The Westside Community Center was their social center in a community that protected, loved, educated, and nurtured them in precisely the same way ours did. We just didn't *know* each other.

Following Page:

Pictures from the Gusher *newspaper, the junior high publication.*

Top: Caption from Ada Lee Bean: "I was offered the opportunity to be on the paper, but I would have to use my physical education period to do so. I chose to do it.

Middle: Patty Mac Sloan at the same time, second row, far right. Jill Everett is standing in the second row, second from left. My younger sister Pam is standing first row, far right.

Bottom: Janet Ruth is standing in the first row, fourth from the left...or right. Marie Charette is to her right. Virginia Smith is standing in the third row, far right.

Ohh...Venus

"Allemande left with your left hand, here we go with a right and left grand," sang the caller at our sixth-grade square dance. I didn't grow up square dancing, but when I tried it, it seemed fun, and a good excuse to wear flouncy skirts with multiple crinolines. Boys just wore those same Levis and white undershirts as always, but some did wear cowboy boots, instead of Converse sneakers.

Requiring partners, square dancing was our first experience with "toothy grins, and slimy hands," as Janet Ruth would later remember. And with these, the love bug showed up. It was hard to avoid. With all that right and left granding, you put your hand into the hand of every boy in your square as the music twanged, toes tapped, and skirts flew out and up, buoyed by all those petticoats we worked so hard to starch. Their worn-out elastic waistbands were seriously put to the test. Soon a cute boy caught your eye, and you worked harder the next time to get into his square before the caller began. Crushes were ignited. Later I'd confess to a friend that I thought I had a crush on Ronnie, and she better not tell.

"Oh, I promise..." And then, of course, she went to tell a friend (as I hoped she would).

"Hey Terri, did you know that Patty Mac likes Ronnie?"

"Really? How do you know?"

"Patty Mac told me. But don't tell, O.K.?"

"Oh sure," as she turned to head for our friend, Lee.

The whole "don't tell" chain was a ruse because everyone knew that a divulged secret was like freight on a train. It moved fast, and in no time, the message was sent. You'd profess outrage, but the hope was that the feeling was reciprocal now that the boy knew you liked him.

Square dancing was fun but short lived, and we had moved on by the seventh grade. Our parents came from the Big Band era of the 1930s and 1940s and loved dances like the foxtrot, polka, samba, and such. There was subtle, and not so subtle pressure to learn ballroom dances. We could go to the Civic Center, the YWCA, Charlotte Conatser's Dance School, or the country club. At one place or another you could learn the one, two, three of the very boring box step. For us, it was more limp hands and lifeless partners. The waltz *was* kind of fun, as was the cha-cha-cha and rhumba, but we were entering the era of rock and roll. What kind of beat was in that old-fashioned music?

Stooped shoulders, downcast eyes, and a halting pace spoke louder than any words. We abandoned conventional dance lessons and went to school at Dick Clark's television *American Bandstand*, listening to the rhythm and music of Elvis Presley, Jerry Lee Lewis, Ricky Nelson, Buddy Holly, Little Richard, Chuck Barry, the Everly Brothers, or the Big Bopper. We modeled our moves after the regulars on *American Bandstand* – Kenny, Arlene and Annette Funicello. We wanted to swing, twist, or stroll!

Girls definitely had more enthusiasm for dancing than boys. Those early school dances often looked as if someone had erected an invisible electric fence through the center of the room, dividing one group waiting...expectantly, patiently, from another group doing anything *except* dancing.

"Do you think anyone's going to ask you to dance?" I asked Janet Ruth at one dance we attended. In her usual dead-pan manner, she said, "Nope...it doesn't look that way...for anybody." But suddenly, we saw movement. William Cuthberton headed for Diane Ronaldson.

We knew they could dance, as they were often demonstrators at Conatser's Dance School. That must have given them the courage to lead the way, dipping and spinning, strolling and twisting until another courageous couple took the floor to challenge their skills. It definitely took some icebreakers to loosen up those boys.

By ninth grade, couples were pairing off, at least briefly. I liked Bill, but I also liked Bob, but Bob liked Liz, and David liked Susan, but Liz liked David, and actually I liked David, too. And so it went. Janet Ruth liked Will, but his dad got transferred and they moved after the ninth grade. Her first heartbreak. Dating was definitely a revolving door, but some attachments would actually stick.

In February of the ninth grade, Janet Ruth and I were invited to a Mardi Gras party at the Hillcrest Country Club. As was typical with many things in the town, it was no surprise to learn that Frank Phillips had much to do with the club's inception in 1926. In his early days, the only golf course available for entertaining business associates was nine holes out by the airport. Crude, with its tees and greens made of sand, it was hardly comparable to the eastern golf courses where Phillips had been a guest. He decided there needed to be a better course, and the result was the Hillcrest Country Club, a Spanish colonial structure with a spectacular golf course designed by Perry Maxwell, designer of Tulsa's Southern Hills, site of several U.S. Opens.

But Frank Phillips never really liked golf. It was too slow, and he was too impatient and headstrong. He preferred a horse ride for relaxation. However, he felt the club was good for business. Because of this, both Phillips and Cities Service sometimes offered employees company memberships making it easy for them to entertain clients. It was far more egalitarian than one might have expected, and at one point, even my dad got a membership.

So lucky for us, Janet Ruth and I were invited to a Mardi Gras dance there. She and I designed our costumes independently, and they were definitely independent. Janet Ruth showed up as a geisha with flowered pajamas and obi, orchid adorned ears, and scruffy slippers and socks. Whatever was she thinking? This was the only subservient role I ever saw her play.

Wearing black, and sporting Mr. Spock eyebrows (long before *Star Trek*, I might add), I came decked out with tin foil antennae, and metallic skirt and collar, my idea of a female alien. Sputnik was hot, and I guess I thought I might be. I'm not sure how much we danced that night; both costumes were pretty confining.

By high school, most of our dances were held at the high school gymnasium and called sock hops. We ditched our shoes under the bleacher benches as soon as we arrived and danced in our socks because the basketball court was sacred: no shoes ever if you weren't playing or practicing for the school. And by this time, sock hops were filled with shakers and strollers. I guess enough at-home mirror-practicing gave us all courage.

Occasionally, someone hosted a couples' party at their house. I remember one time when Bob Rumsford invited us to his home on Cherokee Avenue near Frank Phillips' in-town mansion. This was my favorite street in town, so I was excited just to be going.

After greeting his parents in the foyer of their home, we were ushered downstairs to a basement rumpus room, scented with the faint odor of mildew, reminding me of time spent in Aunt Didge's basement during tornado alerts. But with lights dimmed and music playing a current hit like "Come Softly, to Me," or "Venus," we were drawn gently into the mood for dancing with our dates.

Decorations and food at a venue like this were limited. Bob's mom had laid out snacks and cokes on a vinyl-covered table pushed against the wall beneath driveway level windows. That left room for dancing on the speckled linoleum floor. Some old sofas were pushed against the other walls, and a dark corner encouraged a little necking, but gatherings like this were pretty tame.

The Geisha and the Alien.
Photo Courtesy of Craig's Photography,
Bartlesville, Oklahoma

First dates. Above photo, 7th grade, and lower group photo, 15 year olds in 9th grade.

About half-way through this party though, Bob appeared with a light green Coca-Cola bottle to serve as the needle for Spin the Bottle. Sitting on the floor, we formed a circle, and the person who was "it," took the bottle, laid it down, spun, and waited to see where it stopped. There was a lot of giggling before the kiss was planted and the bottle exchanged hands. We must have had a girl/boy rotation as we waited, because I never remember kissing another girl.

Date nights were often going to the movies. Downtown, we had three theaters, the Lyric, the Arrow, and the Osage; the Hilltop Drive-In was east of town on Nowata Road.

The Lyric was well known for horror movies and, to me, for scurrying animals underfoot. Leftover snacks went straight onto the floor; no one thought to use a wastebasket. I'm sure it didn't make the owner too happy, but the furry little intruders from the alley were. One sighting was it for me, and I was done with the Lyric.

The Arrow Theater was on Frank Phillips, and it showed lots of western films. I lived in the west; I passed on most of them.

On summer nights in particular, we often headed to the Hilltop Drive-in Theater. For dates, it was Lover's Lane for the price of two movie tickets. And for groups of teenagers, it was a cheap place to hang out. One night we decided it would be even cheaper if we packed some of us in the trunk. It was Janet Ruth's idea.

"Whadiya think? Maybe some of us could hide in the trunk and then we'd only pay for the ones they saw in the car?".

"Great!!" said everyone, not really thinking it through.

"Who's riding in the trunk?" I asked. Then wished I hadn't.

"I dunno. Maybe we draw straws. Everybody in?" Janet Ruth said.

Well, I guess we all agreed, but I clearly lost, because the next thing I remember is climbing into that trunk. I didn't want to appear chicken but, though cars and their trunks were large in the 1950s and early 60s, they didn't even have the airholes of a school locker. We packed the seats up front, and then Janet Ruth and I climbed into the trunk, and the lid slammed shut over us.

At first we laughed, because we were doing exactly what we had dreamed up and were getting away with something, or would be. But then Janet Ruth and I stopped talking so much. The dark got darker, and the voices from inside the car sounded farther away. I'm not sure if I knew the word claustrophobia, but I developed a case about the time the car was checking through the ticket booth. My screams and banging gave us away.

The manager appeared, and demanded the driver open the trunk. *Thank God.* I think I would have gone to jail rather than spend another minute in that coffin, so I was out like a shot when the lid opened. We got a good talking-to but no criminal record. Although Janet Ruth swears they repeated the scheme successfully, it was a one time for me. I never seemed to get away with those capers.

My favorite movie house was the Osage Theater. It opened as the Odeon in 1913 "uniquely boasting of two firsts in the world" according to Bartlesville historian Bob Finney. With "shaded aisle lights to guide moviegoers to their seats and iced air, to cool the place," it was ahead of its time. But, by the late 1930s it needed renovation.

When that was completed in 1940, it was reborn as the Osage Theater. To celebrate the opening, Anna Neagle, a famous star of the musical, *Irene*, came to Bartlesville to premier the movie. It must have been some event. Finney went on to write in his Centennial article on Bartlesville that "well wishes arrived from Clark Gable, Lucille Ball, Henry Fonda, Tyrone Power" and others. Going to movies has always been popular, and our crowd, in our era, was no exception.

The love goddess showed up for me in the tenth grade, when I met my high school boyfriend at a school function. Our entire courtship centered on school, sports, movies, sock-hops and going out for a coke. It must have been enough. He would be my one and only.

Labels, Badges and Monikers

Growing up, my family and friends called me Patty Mac, but somewhere around the ninth grade, my friends and I chose to call each other by our last names. We never took a vote on this; it just happened. When I mentioned this to my adult friends, I always got a puzzled look; it seemed it hadn't been the custom where they lived.

Then I met Laurie. She grew up in Colorado riding horses with her brothers, rode her way onto a rodeo team in college, and then on to national horse-riding competitions as an adult. She and her mount disproved the common female stereotypes of that era, and her group of friends called each other by their last names. No wonder I liked her.

Thinking back, I realized that the boys in my school called each other by their *last* names. Paging through some old yearbooks, I noticed only surnames were listed under the boys' teams' photos, and though there were no female sports teams, pictures of coed groups and girls-only gatherings included both *first* and *last* names.

By our graduation in 1962, there was a girls' swim team, recognized in the yearbook as the "Wildcat Swimming Team." Most of those girls swam for the Phillips Splash Club and many were exceptional. My guess is that the school commandeered the eligible female Splash Club members to represent the high school. In doing so they created the first high school girls' sports team of my era. When their photos appeared in the yearbook, they were listed only by their last names, just like the boys. *Curious.*

Long before, coaches and the military realized that barking orders to Joe-Bob, Rodney, or D'wayne would not be as effective as "Hit the track, Wellston - Langford - Hewitt!" I mean, how could you shout?

"Gimme 10 laps, Arrn - old!"

If last names worked for the guys, I guess we figured they were good enough for us. And so Patty Mac became Sloan, Janet Ruth, Pickering, Virginia was Smith, and Susie was Reinfeld. That left Jan as Everett and Marie became Charrette. To this day, I still revert to those maiden-name monikers when we reunite, though most of us long ago shed them for those of our husbands. We weren't that modern.

New York City had the Jets and Sharks, but we had our own girlie-version of gangs costumed as high school sororities. Within a few years they would be banned at College High, but they were still popular when I was in school. Basically, these clubs were friendship cliques formed to benefit those already involved. Once you were a part of a sorority, you and other members could vote new ones in, but one couldn't ask to join.

There was one sorority in place when we arrived in the 9th grade. It included girls from various grades, but neither I nor any of my group were asked to join.

It was then that our band of "merry little women," as Pickering would later call us, decided we should come together, label ourselves and create our own club. Talk began at the lockers, and with the help of an older schoolmate, Dot Fossey, we met in Everett's basement to discuss how to proceed. Dot was happy to tell us how she and her friends had created the A.T.A.'s, her club. She listed the things we needed to do, we asked a few questions, and by the time she left, we were ready to begin.

Smith and I had already started one "clud" as we spelled it, in grade school, so we were full of confidence. For some reason, we felt secrecy was in order, so Pickering suggested that the next meeting be held in the attic of her house.

When we arrived, she led the way to her brother Cort's

bedroom on the second floor where the attic stairway was located. It was a vertical wooden ladder built onto the wall of his room, with a trap door in the ceiling for access. Pickering warned, "I'm just going to flip on this light, and then we can all climb up the ladder. Watch out for the floorboards. They're not all nailed down, and if you step on one end, the other might just flip up in your face."

Musty heat and dust assailed us as we scrambled through the opening, and our thoughts turned to the creeping-crawlies we might encounter. Bugs are the denizens of Oklahoma attics.

I looked right and saw a mound of roly-polies (pill bugs) already piled together as if awaiting a dustpan. But what made me really nervous was the possibility of meeting a lethal brown recluse spider. Some people called them fiddlebacks because the marking on their backs looks like a violin. They are easily identifiable. Furthermore, they liked to hide so you couldn't be sure if they were around or not.

Nothing caught our eye but a lot of cobwebs. But then again, those spiders were sneaky. Finally, we began to wonder if the meeting needed to be this much of a secret. *Who the heck was spying, anyway?* Whatever was settled, was settled. Mama Ruth had promised chocolate cake, and that sped up our agenda. We were down that ladder in no time.

There seemed to be no double-agents in our group so the next time we met in friendlier surroundings to complete the rest of our tasks.

Most of us were only vaguely familiar with names of Greek sororities and fraternities, but Smith brought us a copy of the Greek alphabet to help us name ourselves. Somehow, we decided we wanted to be S.H.E., so we had to figure out how to make it sound Greek. The written Greek letters do not always correspond to English ones so we had to work hard to come up with a Greek spelling for S.H.E. Sigma looks vaguely like an s, Eta appears as an H, and Epsilon looks like an E —

S.H.E. To celebrate, we had white sweatshirts made with S.H.E printed right over the spot where (as Janet Ruth would say) "our left tit should have been!"

That sweatshirt was fun, but since all fraternities and sororities had jewelry pins, we figured we needed one. Dot told us to go to a well-known jeweler in town called Duffenback and Derryberry. They sold fraternity jewelry as well as china, crystal, and silver to every new bride who wanted to register.

When we walked into the store, all the tables and nearby shelves were set with the place settings of choice for someone's upcoming wedding. That held no interest for us, so we headed straight to see Mr. Derryberry and have him help us to pick out something from one of his catalogs.

We poured through the books and settled on a silver shield, on which the letters, S, H, and E would be engraved vertically. A silver chain connected the shield to a torch which would be engraved with our graduation year, 1962. Our pin looked like warrior equipment. *What were we fighting against?* I could never have articulated anything then, but I could today.

Our motto was next, and Everett proposed, "Never do anything today that you can put off until tomorrow."

I'm not sure we all bought into that philosophy, but Pickering agreed, and that was settled. To this day, Everett regrets that she took that saying a little too much to heart.

Our meetings went from a basement to a creepy attic, and then onto the front porch of Charette's house. The secrecy issue seemed to have lost its importance. Her house was just two blocks from school, and with two older sisters, its front porch was full of teenage girls most days after school. It became the perfect meeting place for our club. Charette's mom worked for Phillips and was, at the time, the parent in charge. I guess she wanted her girls home after school – so we all dropped by, regularly.

There were now only two things left to do to complete Dot's club to-do list. One was to pick colors. *Didn't you wave colors as you went to war?* That happened by chance one day as we were sitting on Charette's porch and stoop. Smith noticed a flowering redbud tree blooming in the front yard.

"How about that pinkish-red color?" she said. We couldn't really give a name to it, but it looked pretty enough to us. Pickering, already having the eye of an artist, threw in white as a complement, and we all nodded yes.

Now the only thing left to decide was our honk, and that was probably the most useful thing we created. Soon, we expected to spend a lot of time trolling around in cars, going out for a coke. No one was old enough to have a driver's license yet, but we were hopeful that when we got ours, someone would have access to a car. We never expected anyone to actually *get* a car; few families had more than one vehicle.

As it turned out, Everett's mom let her borrow her car a lot to drive us around when she got her license. And since Smith's dad had a pick-up as well as a car, sometimes Smith would get to borrow his truck. Both held a lot of people, and with no seat belt requirements, you could stuff in as many as would fit. No one complained.

When it was time to pick up someone, instead of going to the front door, you banged out the rhythm of your club honk on the horn. Your friend and many of her neighbors knew someone was waiting.

Our honk went like this:
"Where-ev-er you are, on land or sea,
you sure-ly will find, an S. - H. - E.
We get a rou-ou-nd!"

By our senior year there would be 21 of us in our club. Meetings were held and minutes taken, but no one remembers any philanthropic or patriotic doings. We were straightforwardly self-serving and exclusive. And that is probably why such clubs were disbanded in future years. But like all teenagers looking to belong, these groups filled a need and promoted strong friendships among us.

We did have some boy-girl parties, but mostly we remember slumber parties, the fertile soil for our blossoming friendships and developing adventures.

Left to right:
Virginia, Marie, Jan
and Patty Mac

Charette's house where we spent a lot of afternoons.

Slumber Parties

Slumber parties. Well, there's a misnomer if there ever was one. My cousin Marilyn was thirteen years older than I, and by the time I came along, her dad, my Uncle Homer, had re-named these events slumber-less parties. If you went alone to stay the night, we called it spending the night, but if a bunch of kids were invited, it was a slumber party. Today kids call them sleepovers or sleep-aways. Frankly, they should just be called stay-awakes.

Many of my friends lived in small one-story houses with a central living space not conducive to hosting slumber parties which kept everyone in the house awake. Fortunately, a few friends had larger homes with "additions" or "rumpus rooms," (today's family rooms).

At the Reinfeld's house it was called the "new room." I first saw the new room when it was a few years old, and it remained the new room as long as they lived there. The Pickerings called their room the den, and at the Smith's it was the rec room. We were lucky to have so many friends whose parents had these extra spaces and who agreed to host these parties.

I remember one particular night when Virginia was hosting. All week at school, conversations began with, "Are you going to Smith's house on Friday?

I had spent the night there many times, and I really liked Virginia Smith's family, so I was excited about the party. We would have the rec-room to ourselves, and since it was located off the kitchen and downstairs from the bedrooms, I guess there was a chance for her parents to have some relief from the all-night shenanigans and laughter.

Friday night arrived, and so did we and our bedrolls. I don't remember that anyone ever brought a sleeping bag. We just assembled a log roll of blankets, pajamas, and pillows and tied them with string.

We piled into the house as Mrs. Smith, sporting a smile and an apron, met us at the door along with the aroma of rising yeast following her from the kitchen. Bess Smith was a real-life June Cleaver, the T.V. supermom on *Leave it to Beaver*. While other mothers, my own included, were embracing "new and improved" ways of cooking (using boxed cakes, frozen foods and T.V. dinners), Mrs. Smith continued to cook as her mother had. Cinnamon buns were a specialty, and we knew what that yeast smell implied. It was our lucky night.

Virginia had a brother named Owen who was two years older, and really cute, with a sandy-haired crew cut. We would have loved to spend time with him, but I think we were overwhelming. He absented himself as soon as we arrived.

Not long after he left, we heard the brakes of Virginia's father's road-weary pick-up as it squealed into the driveway. We looked out to confirm, and saw his truck, camouflaged with the bird splattering, red-clay dirt of Oklahoma. Mr. Smith was an independent oilman who spent a lot of time out on his leases checking his wells, and gathering dust and mud on his truck along the way. After greeting everyone, he came over to Virginia and me to begin his tease, "I checked in on your cottage today." We giggled and rolled our eyes, knowing what was coming. He loved to get our reaction.

It all started one day when we were riding with him as he checked on some of his stripper wells. Stripper wells are those see-saw pump-jacks which bring up small amounts of oil. We were all in the pick-up together, bouncing along roads on his lease when we saw an old shack nearby. Virginia and I began to make fun of it, making disparaging remarks such as, how could anyone live in a place like that? Immediately he said, "Why that's the honeymoon cottage I'm saving for you girls when you get married!" We groaned, and the joke began. Over the remainder of our school years, whenever it was appropriate, and sometimes when it wasn't, he would remind of his promise to follow-through on this proffered gift.

Even as a young teenager, Virginia was a gracious hostess. She had grown tall and slender with a lot more curves than the rest of us, which she wore modestly. She had shoulder-length dark brown hair, silky and thick, which fell away like a swing when she tipped her head. Sometimes she wore a single ponytail, but if she tried dog-ears (one on each side), we told her she looked like a basset hound. We never held back.

Most families had televisions by this time, but there really weren't many shows to watch. For hours daily, there was nothing but a "test pattern" on the screen. When we did watch a show, we planned ahead and gathered with friends and family to view it, almost like going to the theater. But I never recall watching television at one of these slumber parties.

This turned out to be particularly odd at Virginia's house, because in 1957, Bartlesville, Oklahoma was one of the towns chosen from across the country to experiment with pay-per-view television, called "Tele-movie." The Smith family TV was a market-research site. For a fee, one could view current movies on their own television in the comfort of their home. Virginia told us all about it that night, and pointed out the gizmo on top of the TV that made tele-movies work. But it was as relevant to us as giving a turkey to someone with a hot plate. I guess we could have watched a movie, but we never asked. This pay-per-view idea turned out to be way ahead of its time, failing here and elsewhere. That night, as on all the others, we made up our own entertainment.

Soon after we settled in, we unfurled our bedrolls all over the rec room, covering the carpet like a picnic quilt. Girls were draped on sofas, chairs and over the floor, chattering in little groups until Liz Black got everyone's attention. She had heard about a new trick where we could make ourselves faint.

It sounded weird, but we were intrigued and wanted to hear more.

"So the first thing you do is get down on all-fours, like a dog and begin to pant until you feel dizzy. As soon as that happens, you need to sit up fast and blow air into your closed fists until you pass out."

We made up our own entertainment.

This was even weirder, and an uncomfortable silence fell over the group until Jan Everett broke the spell and volunteered. She proceeded to get on all-fours just like Liz said, so Liz picked up on the action and began to repeat the rest of the instructions. Everyone gathered to watch. Rapidly, Everett blew air in and out, in and out, until she *was* dizzy, and sat back on her knees. Then she blew into her cupped hands, and before our eyes, she crumpled to the floor. We stood by, with mouths agape. Arms grabbed her as she swooned, and the blankets softened the trip to the floor, but this was a sobering sight. She came-to quickly and seemed O.K., but we didn't need a vote to make this a one-time adventure.

Sandy Tucker saved the day when Virginia's dog, Bootsie walked into the room – most likely checking out the hyperventilating commotion. When Sandy saw the dog she boomed, "Hey, this dog needs some more names!" Sandy was born on the fifth of July, and, as we used to say, "She was a firecracker that went off late."

Whenever she was speaking in a room, there was no doubting Sandy's presence: her voice carried everywhere. And it was difficult to ignore her request about the dog, because we had re-named *her* dog at the last slumber party.

Dog lovers seem to believe the more a dog is loved, the more names it should have. And we were all dog lovers. Sandy's dog, Tippe, was our first project, his new names coming from stories about Sandy's grandmother, Osa Mae Duran. I have forgotten the story details, but Tippe's new name may tell it all: "Tippe Cornelius Canoe Osa Mae Duran who sat upon a stool with a can of beer and a glass eye Tucker."

So, when Bootsie arrived, re-naming Bootsie seemed a good diversion from an emergency medical call, if the next hyperventilating victim didn't fare so well. We played with names, and soon Bootsie was re-christened "Bootsie Wootsie Woodle, Snookerdoodle Smith." The oxygen-deprivation episode may have made us less creative with her name.

Susie had a dog named Fizz, but we never touched his name. He had been owned and named by the Mercedes family, and when their boys when off to college, Fizz adopted the Reinfeld family who were neighbors. Fizz was a fixture at the high school and was often found wandering through the school hallways or following a gang of kids watching a football game. His full name was Gin Fizz. Who could improve on that?

Fatigue finally set in, and the bathroom became a rotating dressing room for changing into our pajamas. We were all modest, so we never undressed in front of our friends. In warmer weather, our preferred sleepwear were "baby-doll pajamas." These were made from pastel-colored, flowered cottons. The bottom half were bloomer panties and the tops were flared and sleeveless, often decorated with ruffles around the neck and even the armholes. Many of us rolled our hair in curlers, and then covered them with a patterned shower-cap. We were a veritable flower garden blooming in that room.

After we had climbed onto our bedrolls, and after the lights were dimmed, someone suggested a ghost story. All ears waited for Janet Ruth to volunteer. She could tell the best stories.

She began with an old favorite, which went something like this:

One night a couple was parked out on Lover's Lane necking and listening to music on the radio. Suddenly they were interrupted by an urgent report that an escaped convict was in the area. The announcer said you'd know him for sure because he only had a hook for a hand on one arm. *Well, that was scary.*

As the couple listened to the report, a chill came over them and spooked them both. The girl froze, but before either could speak, the boy quickly started the engine and gunned off into the night. His girlfriend was so thankful he did this without her begging him to leave, because that's what she was about to do. Enormous relief washed over both of them as they drove off the point, embarrassed by their fear, but relieved they were leaving.

The boy drove straight to town, to his girlfriend's house and driveway. He wasted no time in exiting the car to run around and open her door. But when he reached her side, he became numb. For...as he went to grab the door handle...he was horrified to discover a single bloody hook hanging from it...

Ooh...yuk...when were those cinnamon buns coming...?

Tornado Alley

A unt Didge was "bosomy." At least that's what my mom would say. I always blushed when she used that word. I just thought Didge was a little fat; but looking back at old photos, I realize Mom was right. Aunt Didge also had a large, toothy smile, and I adored her. In college she majored in Spanish and French, and as a single woman she went to Europe on her own. If she were alive today, she would be 119 years old; that was remarkable independence for her time.

Growing up, she and my Uncle Homer lived in a brick stucco bungalow on Johnstone, just down the block from McKinley School; I was always welcome to stop by and say hello. Their house had five steps up to the front porch which was enclosed with a low stucco wall capped with cement, convenient to sit on. During the summers before air conditioning, my aunt (who loved to play bridge) set up her card table on that porch. She put a fan on top of one of the walls, and strung an extension cord from the house for power. Then she put a galvanized metal watering trough (suitable for animals) under the table and filled it with water and ice. When her three friends arrived, they removed their shoes, took their place, put their feet in the tub, and played bridge while drinking Coca-Colas all afternoon.

When you entered their home, you went straight into the front room which was decorated in gray and pink. Aunt Didge loved pink, and even the air smelled pink. Uncle Homer grew all shades of pink roses in their garden, and when they bloomed, the house was filled with them. After they died, Aunt Didge took the petals, dried them, and created a potpourri which she kept in a silver ginger jar with holes in the top. She placed the jar in the front room on a bookshelf so that even in winter you could smell the pink roses.

A few minutes into any visit to Aunt Didge always brought to mind Coca-Colas. I would never have asked for one. It was not polite. But Aunt Didge never disappointed me; she always offered. The minute she did, I raced through the dining room to the kitchen and headed for the refrigerator. I knew exactly where they were kept – in a line, front to back on the left top shelf. When a bottle was removed, Aunt Didge replaced another at the back so that there was always a cold one waiting at the front.

Uncle Homer grew up in western New York State, became a geologist and came to Bartlesville to work for Phillips 66. Homer was slight of stature, wore wire-rimmed glasses and had short hair on the sides but tight curls on the top of his head, parted down the middle. He looked *detailed*. Which is to say, he looked precise about things. But he was also a jokester. As my dad worked for Cities Service, the rival oil company, there was always competitive banter. One Christmas Uncle Homer gave my dad a framed photo of the time and temperature sign prominently displayed on the Cities Service Building when he captured it reading "66 Degrees." Uncle Homer thought it was hilarious. He loved to play games and was as intense as his demeanor, but he didn't give a whit about winning. He did everything he could (even at his own expense) to mess up someone else who looked to be winning!

In the springtime, the season for tornadoes, we had a standing invitation to come to their house during a tornado alert. Built on a slab, our house had no shelter, but their bungalow had a below-ground dirt cellar, safe from tornadoes. One spring afternoon, the sirens blared.

"Patty Mac, go get Noche! The tornado siren just went off!" called my mom. Screaming yellow sirens were placed strategically all over town to alert when a storm funnel was spotted, and when this happened everyone kicked into high gear, or at least medium-high gear.

We'd been through this drill lots of times, but I had never experienced a tornado and did not really understand the implications of the threat. Nevertheless, I followed instructions and ran outside to call the dog. As I looked up, I saw dark clouds and a developing funnel hanging overhead. A certain quiet and calm filled the air that accompanied this sight; it was eerie and a little scary. Fortunately, Noche showed up quickly, and we all got into the station wagon and headed for my Aunt Didge and Uncle Homer's house.

"Come on, Noche, the siren just went off!"

Photos of Uncle Homer and Aunt Didge.
courtesy of Bartlesville History Museum.

After arriving, we hurriedly piled downstairs laughing and talking, and, once below ground, we found that Aunt Didge had already set up folding chairs along the wall and filled a center table with snacks, Coca-Colas and Grapette soda pop. This was party time for a kid, despite the fact that their basement smelled like the mildew and mold of the locker room at Sani-Pool. But with the radio plugged in reporting the storm, candles and matches lying unused until a power outage, and plenty of food and drink, we thought such storms were the next best thing to Christmas. Often driving over, we saw funnels hanging in the sky, but in those years, they never touched down. When the radio station finally reported an all clear, we headed for home. We couldn't wait until the next alert.

Over at the Pickerings, they headed for the basement in their own house, with no stench and a cement floor. Well, most of them did. Mama Ruth was terrified of the threats, and brought everyone downstairs with her. Mr. Pickering chose to get himself a scotch and water, then haul a lawn chair out onto the driveway so he could get a good view of the sky and funnel as it usually approached from the southwest.

Janet Ruth, never wanting to miss anything, joined her dad in the driveway for the show – the fomenting green clouds, yellowing sky and sudden calm and quiet. They planned to run for it if the funnel touched down, but otherwise the scene was too exciting to miss.

Big sky may bring Montana to mind, but there is plenty of big sky over Oklahoma for roiling thunderstorms to spawn tornadoes. Located southeast of Colorado and north of Texas, those two diverse climates collide over Oklahoma to cook up these storms. Warm moist air rising from the Gulf of Mexico at lower levels percolates with colder dry fronts moving down from Canada through the Colorado Rockies with different wind speeds and directions, creating the perfect recipe.

Since sometimes our family's reaction to these alerts was a little casual, my dad wanted us to realize how serious these threats were. When a tornado devastated Blackwell, Oklahoma, he drove our family there to show us what could happen. As we left, we headed to the car with the expectancy of departing on vacation, looking forward to car games and a hamburger stop.

It took about an hour and a half to make the drive west, long enough to play "cows and horses." It was our favorite car game where the driver and the left back-seat passenger were teammates, while the front-seat passenger and the right back-seater were on their own team as well. The kid in the middle could choose either team. To win points, any cow or horse or herd of cattle or herd of horses was valued at one point. If a fence separated these animals, then a single point was given for the group or single animal on each side of the fence. The winner was the team who accumulated the most cows or horses. But there was a monkey-wrench in the rules. If you passed a cemetery on your side, all your points were wiped out, and you had to start over. My dad was awfully good at returning home a winner. He knew the routes to all the cemeteries to wipe out his opponents at the last minute. The middle kid usually chose Dad's team.

Anticipation filled the car as we drove into Blackwell, a town of about 9000. Dad easily found his way to the devastation, and we saw neighborhoods disappear into piles of rubble. A pall came over our car. Every so often a house stood while every house around was gone – either blown away or left in ruins. A single china cabinet, its dishes unbroken, remained on the slab foundation of one home, while here and there a bathtub stood, indicating the presence of a home, now in pieces somewhere else.

When you have no cellar, one of the safety directives is to climb into a bathtub, and if possible, pull a mattress over on top. Suddenly we saw the efficacy of that idea. The sight of all this havoc was sobering to all of us. Suddenly those siren warnings did not seem so much like a call to a spontaneous picnic. After that field trip, when the sirens blared, we responded – fast.

Janet Ruth and I both remember lots of storm alerts, but fortunately for us, there were no funnels that touched down in our town during those years. The grounding of the storm funnel officially turned it into a tornado.

Local folklore credited Bartlesville's tornado protection to two large natural elevations bordering the west and southwest, the very directions from which tornadoes liked to travel. To the west was the Mound, standing 866 feet above sea level and largely devoid of greenery, looking like a giant pebble. To the southwest was Circle Mountain, our favorite destination for exploring. Only slightly taller than the Mound, but covering a larger base area, it too, supposedly served as a barrier wall to oncoming tornadoes. The idea we bought into was that the tornado would follow the contour of the land, come to one of these elevations, follow the land skywards and be launched over our little town, instead of blowing it away. Though this story appealed to our sense of security, no self-respecting meteorologist would endorse this explanation. Tornadoes can show up anywhere.

Thankfully, none of Janet Ruth's or my family have been victims of tornado destruction. Today more people are building or adding "safe rooms" onto their homes which can be below ground or even above ground, supposedly able to withstand the fierce winds. Sophisticated weather apparatus can alert people hours or even days ahead of a possible impending threat. It is probably no surprise that the National Weather Center is in Norman, Oklahoma, located centrally in the state, site of the turnpike of tornadoes.

The remainder of my Oklahoma family lives in Norman today. Up until the end of my mother's 100-year-old life, when an alert sounded, she poured herself a glass of wine and headed to the balcony of her apartment to watch the storms go by. She and Hank Pickering must be first cousins. I think she figured if she went out in a tornado, it would be a heck of a story.

Why Don't We Just...?

Contemporary painting by Janet Ruth
of an Oklahoma storm brewing.

Going for the Gold

Texas wasn't the only place with "Friday night lights." Custer Field Stadium and the bleachers behind College High School were packed with townspeople for every home football game, nearly always under the lights, and for away-games, the crowd became Wildcat roadies.

Winter basketball fans filled the indoor gym along with the smell of sweat and teenage hormones. The scene was intimate. The old gym floor stopped barely three feet beyond the sideline out-of-bounds, and the bleacher seats began at that point. Fans were parked shoulder to shoulder from there to the top row. No conversations ever took place without yelling. The electricity of those games still resonates in my arm hairs when I think of them. And the teams rewarded us: they were nearly always at the top of their conference, and sometimes even competed in state championships.

Track was less popular, but baseball could pull in a crowd. Younger boys played Little League and then, if they qualified, could go on to Pony League, and finally American Legion ball – at the Municipal baseball stadium adjacent to Johnstone Park, built for the Bartlesville Pirates, a class D affiliate of the Pittsburgh Pirates from 1948-1952.

If you were a girl and wanted to break a sweat, you could try out for cheerleading, twirling, or drum majorette.

Phillips Petroleum Company had long supported men's athletics. In the 1920s, Frank Phillips agreed to sponsor a company team for a group of male employees who loved to play basketball. Part of the National Industrial Basketball League (N.I.B.L.), and called the 66ers, they played against other business-sponsored teams all over the country. A legendary 66er, Joe Fortenberry, played basketball in the 1936 Berlin Olympics winning a gold medal. He was recently cited in the book, *Boys in the Boat*, notable for his height when the University of Washington rowing team met him in Berlin.

In the 1948 Olympic Games, Phillips sent their coach, Bud Browning, along with 66ers, Lew Beck, Gordon Carpenter, R.C. Pitts, Captain Jesse (Cab) Renick and Bob Kurland, the first seven-footer in basketball, to London, England where they won the gold medal. Cab Renick joined Jim Thorpe, Duke Pao Kahanamoku, and later Billy Mills as Native American gold medal winners.

The team fed the town's love of sports and provided an opportunity for company men to develop leadership skills. Future senior executives of Phillips, Boots Adams, Bill Martin and Paul Endacott, all began their careers playing basketball for the 66ers. Ultimately, professional basketball took over the sport and in 1968 the team sponsorship ended.

During the 1950s, Phillips created the Splash Club, a swimming program for sons *and* daughters of Phillips' employees. This was innovative. When the new Adams building was built, it included a gymnasium and a state-of-the-art swimming pool sophisticated enough to host A.A.U. swim meets.

My dad worked for Cities Service, which had no such benefits. Frankly, I was a bit jealous of the Phillips' programs. I'm not sure if I was interested enough to join the Splash Club had I been eligible, but I wanted the choice.

Janet Ruth and Marie both spent some time with the Splash Club but dropped out. When I asked Janet Ruth why she quit, she said, "*Well,* I realized I was never going to catch Marie Heff, and Annie Franz was catching me so my hopes for gold were fading. Besides, I was fourteen and discovering boys. I was tired of going out with wet hair..."

Marie's problem was sportswear. She said Speedo swim-suits were just too revealing for her blossoming body, and she checked out as well. So much for our Olympic hopefuls.

With few options left, we considered cheerleading. Guys liked cheerleaders, and the outfits *were* cute, so Janet Ruth, Marie, and I tried out and made the squad in the ninth grade. Our fame was short lived, though. Janet Ruth washed out in the 10th grade, I was demoted to alternate, and Marie moved away. The following year I didn't even make alternate. Jan Everett made the squad and lasted through high school.

Back at junior high, we did have girls' gym class, complete with uniforms – first cousins to the orange prison jumpsuits visible on highway clean-up trusties. Except they were electric blue, with arms and legs cropped. The suits were finished with sewn-in belt straps which hung from the waist, ready to be cinched together with a double-ring metal fastener after you buttoned yourself in. If you were lucky, this onesie was long enough and didn't give you a wedgie. And if you were really lucky, you never had an urgent run to the bathroom because there was no removing that get-up in a hurry.

Luckily, we never left school grounds in those uniforms. We did calisthenics and played "girls' rules" – half-court basketball against ourselves. Word was that full-court basketball was too much exertion for girls, and we'd run out of gas if we crossed that center line. I thought it was ridiculous then, and I can hardly re-count this to my granddaughters with a straight face today.

Our favorite gym activity was the trampoline, located on the stage at one end of the basketball court. The gym as a whole served as an auditorium for all kinds of programs and entertainment as well as for athletics. When the stage wasn't set up for the band or a play, they set up the trampoline. We could only use it at specific gym times with strict safety rules. One or two could jump at a time, but there had to always be a "spotter." We obliged; we liked that sport.

Actually, my favorite sports' activities were casual foot-races, called in an instant when a group was heading somewhere.

"Race you to the fencepost. Ready – set – go!" Usually, I was in the lead pack, and I loved that feeling. Maybe that was my sport.

I awoke to the Olympics in 1956 and found my heroine in Wilma Rudolph. She was amazing; I just wondered how she became a track star if her schools were anything like mine.

Finally, our chance to show our stuff in a track event came in May of 1959 when the "First Annual Jaycee Junior Champ Physical Fitness Meet" was held at Custer stadium. Both boys and girls from the seventh, eighth, and ninth grades were invited to participate.

"Hey, Patty Mac and Marie, ya' wanna sign up for the track meet the Jaycees are holding?" asked Janet Ruth one morning.

"Whadda' think, Patty Mac?" Marie said.

Here was my chance to be the Wilma Rudolph I dreamed of.

"Sure! Let's do it!" We all agreed.

Practicing never occurred to any of us, even though most of us had never even tried these events. We just thought you either had it in you or you didn't. The day arrived warm and dry, and after sign-up, girls outnumbered boys two to one (testimony to the fact that there were numerous sports venues for boys and nearly none for girls, I'd guess).

I'd thought I was nervous when I played the McKinley vs. Garfield softball game, but I reached a new level at this event. Nearly three years had gone by, but the cloud of possible embarrassment still loomed. There were even photographers on hand to capture any sports highlights – or disasters.

After a few instructions, the meet began: push-ups, 50-yard dash, baseball throw for accuracy (you can imagine where I finished), high jump, 200-yard shuttle relay, chin-ups, hop, step, and jump, broad jump and basketball shoot. We entered every event.

Well, the ninth grade Wilma Rudolph of the day went to Katherine Bailey, the only child and daughter of the high school principal. We knew she was smart and pretty, but now she was gifted athletically. Marie, Janet Ruth, and I filled in some of the second and third places. We partnered with Katherine to win the relay – against the only other team. I topped the chin-up chart – with two. I came in second to Katherine in the 50-yard dash – Janet Ruth in third. I did win the hop, step, and jump.

The event of the day, though, turned out to be the high jump. Janet Ruth and I tied for third while our friend Liz Black won. But Marie's jump, which earned her second place, provided the highlight photo for the sports page the following day. She was captured sailing over the pole, arms extended and balanced, legs bent clearing the pole, giving a full crotch shot of her short shorts, showing a teeny-weeny bit of her white underpants extending just beyond the shorts line. Janet Ruth and I failed to notice that detail. We made the background of the famous photo and were focusing on ourselves.

But no one else missed that little piece of underwear. It was the talk of the school. Word got back to Marie that her boyfriend did not like the picture and was going to break up with her. *How was she to blame?* We were all flying high from our successes in competitive sports and making the sports page, even though you had to look really hard to see Janet Ruth and me. This underwear flap was deflating.

A few days went by and a note arrived in the mail for Marie. Her sister Yvonne brought in the mail that day, and as she handed the envelope to Marie, she glimpsed the return address and realized that it was from Marie's boyfriend. Immediately, Yvonne tried to re-claim it, but Marie resisted, won, and headed for the bathroom. Theirs was a small house, the bathroom tiny but nearby. Unfortunately, it had no lock.

Marie headed there faster than her sister, making it through the door before Yvonne could reach her. Slamming the door behind her, Marie dropped to the floor with her back against the tub, and extended her legs to keep the door shut against Yvonne. She tore open the envelope, but Yvonne pushed the door with her whole body, and Marie weakened. Still, she was determined not to let her sister take hold of that note. Seeing no alternative, Marie *ate* the note.

It was a quick decision, and it meant she'd never read it — but neither would her sister, a victory of sorts.

Who could have ever imagined the problems girls would have trying to enter the world of sports? The guys certainly had it easier.

The famous shot. Credit: ©USA Network

At least I made it over the bar.

Woods, Lakes and Rocks

As Phillips Petroleum grew in Oklahoma, Frank Phillips opened a second office in New York City, nearer sources of investors and bankers, and soon found himself in the world of Northeast businessmen and tycoons. Often, he was a guest at their retreat homes in the Adirondacks, or on the beaches of Rhode Island or Long Island. In time, he too, wanted somewhere special to entertain, other than his mansion in Bartlesville.

After initial searches throughout the Northeast and along its seaboards, it finally dawned on him that what he loved and found so special were the Osage Hills. He had already built a humble cabin there as a quiet retreat for himself. In the meantime, his brother Waite had built a ranch retreat in New Mexico which was unique to anyone from the East, and was a place Frank enjoyed as well. After a trip to the Grand Canyon where he and Jane stayed at El Tovar Lodge, Frank realized that what he wanted for himself and his guests was a western lodge and game preserve right in his own backyard, reminiscent of those three places he admired.

In 1925 he hired Art Gorman, a local architect and contractor, and his log cabin began evolving. It was a sizeable home, but calling it the "cabin" seemed understated like the term "cottages" used for the Newport, Rhode Island mansions. His cabin, sited on a bluff overlooking Clyde Lake and fronted by an extensive veranda encouraged long, lazy views, and grew to be just the sanctuary Frank hoped for. The idea for the name of his lodge came from his longtime secretary and later treasurer of the company, Fern Butler. With woods, lakes, and rocks surrounding this new cabin, the retreat and ranch became known as Woolaroc.

As one enters the cabin, there is no vestibule; guests immediately enter into the grand two-story living room. It is lit by four magnificent former Waldorf Astoria antler chandeliers, the last of Frank's investment in the hotel before it was torn down, and its address taken over by the Empire State Building.

A large stone fireplace flanks each end of the living room, and an open balcony directly ahead and up the stairs overlooks the space. High stakes poker games took place up there with one local legend recalling that John Ringling lost his circus to Frank one night only to have it returned the next morning.

From the living room and left through a small breezeway is the dining room, large enough to host scores of guests with a décor reminiscent of Frank's mother's early dining room in Nebraska. Kitchen, bathrooms and bedrooms occupy the remainder of the house, but they were never open to the public. There had to be some good stories there as well.

The log walls are covered with western paintings, Navajo rugs, animal trophy heads, and horns. A Steinway grand piano stands in one corner, veneered in the same Arkansas pine bark that is used for the unique frames on most paintings at Woolaroc. This wood finish was developed and patented by Art Gorman and the ranch workers. The remainder of the room is furnished with Old Hickory-style Adirondack furniture similar to that found in the upper New York state lodges.

The log cabin was a perfect welcome for the olio of Frank's guests who visited. There were religious leaders such as priests, bishops, Cardinal Spellman and entertainers including Tom Mix, Rudy Valee, and Will Rogers. Politicians were popular guests and Harry Truman, Herbert Hoover, and Elliott Roosevelt were all invited. Alf Landon, who set a record loss to Roosevelt, actually announced his presidential candidacy from Woolaroc. And, of course, Frank's guest list included the head of any major company he ever dealt with and every cowboy he met, famous or not. It was a revolving door of visitors – just what Frank wanted.

Frank and Jane weren't alone in those beautiful Osage hills. With culverts, caves and limestone outcroppings, the area was a favorite hide-out for some local outlaws. As they were neighbors of sorts, Frank had numerous occasions to come face-to-face and even get to know some of these fellows, particularly Henry Wells. It seemed Frank had a kind of fascination with these bandits, perhaps stemming from his early banking days when he made his famous loan to Henry Starr. It was only natural that when Frank began hosting his famous buffalo bar-b-ques for out of town guests and locals, he wanted to include some of these rapscallions from the neighborhood.

He devised an event he called "The Cowthieves and Outlaws Reunion," managing to convince the law to honor a one-day amnesty moratorium for these renegades. Once approved, the good guys, the bad guys and those in between showed up to eat, drink, and be merry at Woolaroc together. At the end of the day, the ban was lifted, all bets were off, and the chase was on. It was a huge success and celebrated annually.

Animals arrived at the ranch about the same time as the first guests. Buffalo came, thrived and helped to re-establish herds all over the country. Frank's acquisition of exotic animals and birds was not so successful. Many arrived in poor condition or with illnesses, and coupled with extreme Oklahoma weather and local predatory animals, most did not survive. But Frank persevered to find those that did, and created the wildlife preserve he dreamed of, open to all who make the two-mile drive from the entrance to the lodge. Water buffalo, long horn and Scottish cattle, goats, peacocks, llama, ostrich, zebra, and, of course, bison roam today.

Frank and Jane Phillips' Lodge.
Photo permission: Woolaroc Museum, Bartlesville, Oklahoma.

Treasures from travels and gifts from guests accumulated, filled and over-filled the Lodge. Satiety arrived when one of Frank's airplanes named Woolaroc was returned to him following its famous 1927 win at the Dole Pineapple air race from California to Hawaii. Its flight followed Lindberg's by only a few months, and was great advertising for Phillips Petroleum and its aviation fuel. But with the arrival of the airplane back at the ranch, Frank was now forced to build a display pavilion. Soon art and artifacts filled the room around the plane, and the Woolaroc Museum was born.

The building of the museum has been ongoing with numerous additions. Frank chose to construct the exterior from local sandstone quarried from the ranch, but its magnificent exterior entrance was not created until 1945. Flanking the twelve-foot-high metal doors are two-story walls of mosaic glass tile images of Native American figures representing the five cultural tribes of the United States. The metal doors themselves are ornamented with eight onyx medallions whose etched designs were taken from the shell gorgets (armor) of an early Native American civilization uncovered at the Spiro Mound in east-central Oklahoma. Together with the mosaics, this entrance is a spectacular welcome to a museum filled with western paintings, sculpture, Navajo rugs, animal trophy heads, colt pistols, stagecoaches, pottery, baskets and of course, the airplane, Woolaroc.

Jane Phillips died in 1948 and Frank in 1950. By Frank's request both are entombed in a mausoleum on the property, along with an operating telephone. Several years before their deaths, Frank formed the Frank Phillips Foundation to run the museum, property and lodge, and to open it to the public when he and Jane were no longer living. And so it happened.

Janet Ruth and I were in the first grade in 1951, so we became part of the first waves of schoolchildren to enjoy this magical place. There was no admission fee for many years, but reality set in, and today one has to pay a nominal fee to the gatekeeper while listening to visiting instructions.

Woolaroc never lost its draw for us. As we grew older, it remained our favorite place to explore. And we never got into any trouble there. Well, they did have peacocks roaming free, leaving a feather or two around for the taking, to which we succumbed. That seemed acceptable. Other than that, there were too many legitimate things to see and do.

The Woolaroc Museum and mosaic tile entrance.
Photo permission: Woolaroc Museum, Bartlesville, Oklahoma

Woolaroc

Oklahoma winters can bring days of 15 degrees, snow and ice – or 72 hours later, 60 degrees, sunshine and warmth. But deciduous trees still lose their leaves, flowers die off, lawns turn brown, and Okies welcome spring like anyone else.

One day when everyone in the family was anxious to be outside, Dad suggested we go to Woolaroc on Saturday. I begged to include Janet Ruth, and after he'd agreed, I couldn't wait to find her at school to ask if she could go with us. She was as ready as we were.

The last time she'd been to Woolaroc was at the end of the previous summer at a Phillips company picnic. Throughout the summer, Phillips employees and their families were entertained at bar-b-ques alongside Clyde Lake Pavilion and other parts of the ranch not usually open to the public. Janet Ruth went every summer, and once again I figured my dad worked for the wrong company.

After picking up Janet Ruth on Saturday, we headed down Hillcrest to 14th Street. We left her neighborhood of large, beautiful homes and within three blocks, the still well-kept homes were much smaller. Quickly, out the window, the neighborhoods changed as if emptying ones' pockets. Beyond the tracks were the beginnings of "the West Side." Homes were humbler and some quite small, followed by the zinc smelters whose chimneys daily belched clouds and odors of mysterious waste. We avoided the factory by a shortcut onto a dirt road that connected us with Route 123, where we turned left and began the slow climb and twelve-mile drive out of Bartlesville into the Osage hills. Those twelve miles set the stage for our adventure.

First the woods of Circle Mountain appeared to our left as we climbed, and our town, if you looked backwards, became a silhouette against a bright blue sky with cotton-ball clouds. Fences separated ranches on our right and left, and when wild mustangs were later harbored on these prairies some 35 years later, we welcomed them as if they'd been here all along. The animals often huddled together, a dramatic sight when they stood motionless atop a prairie hill or raced across the land. Pump-jacks resembling iron see-saw horses, peppered the prairie ranches on the right. They could pull up a small amount of oil per day, only worth the effort if the price was right. At times they were in motion and other times not. You didn't need the New York Times to check the price of oil.

Finally, at the crest of one of the many hills along the way, we reached the sandstone entrance to Woolaroc. With a lily pond on each side, it stood just beyond the small similarly stoned gatehouse, a refuge from the wind, heat and cold for the greeter who laid out the ground rules for the drive in to the museum and lodge: "Stick to the speed limit, feel free to stop and watch, but no getting out of the car and no feeding or touching of any animal, and certainly, no souvenir collecting of bones." We agreed, though the bone collecting was a definite temptation.

As Dad drove towards the cattle-guard crossing just beyond the gate house, we passed the oversized plaster Indian giving us a big "How!" He was a little hokey, but nothing else was a disappointment on this two-mile drive in. The ranch still maintained a culled herd of buffalo, along with longhorn steer, elk, and antelope, almost all visible on any drive through. There were no barrier fences on this stretch of road, so often the buffalo sauntered in front of our car or paused, frozen, to stare curiously as we stared back. Stone Lake appeared to our left with plaster teepees showing through the scrub oak woods, looking authentic from a distance.

Culverts lined with sandstone bordered the road here and still held water from a spring rain. We got excited about the spillway crossing ahead, and sure enough, water from a pond to our left poured over the concrete dam, over our road and down another spillway to a stream below, where water buffalo bobbed quietly in the spillway water's swirl. Small sandstone guardrails directed us over the bridge, and even though the water was only 1 or 2 inches deep, we had the feeling we might get pushed on down the sluice. It was exciting to ford the stream in Dad's car, a thrill, rare in summer.

The Haunted Grove appeared around the next bend. Known for the number of animal skull and bones strewn throughout the woods, this was the place we were forbidden to loot. Native animals – with fur and without – often poached these remains, and Janet Ruth and I looked at each other when we saw how easily we could bolt from the car, grab a skull or two, and be back in "two shakes of a lamb's tail." Of course, it was never going to happen with my dad there. We just admired them from our window.

Next, we saw some of the penned animals: the miserable-tempered ostrich, a couple of ornery zebras, and some corralled buffalo. And just before the museum parking lot we passed the prairie dog village. There were more exits and entrances to this little dirt habitat than you could count, and just as one prairie dog head zipped out and back, another materialized from another hole like exploding popcorn. Our necks ached from trying to follow these little jack-in-the-boxes.

Finally, we reached the parking lot and hopped out. Mom and Dad planned to wander some of the hiking trails while Janet Ruth and I were eager to blitz the museum. With a "see ya," we raced up the stone steps towards the entrance.

Welcoming buffalo...

This is the rotunda where you enter the museum. In the summer with no exterior windows and air conditioning that could be 30 degrees cooler than outside, it produced a calming and reverence as if entering a cathedral. Photo Permission: Woolaroc Museum, Bartlesville, Oklahoma

The double front doors were enormous and heavy, but each of us took a handle, pulled, and stormed into the rotunda; we were immediately calmed. In summer, you were met with a blast of cold air probably 30 degrees cooler than outside. It was like entering the meat lockers at the Crystal Creamery and Ice House, where people stored food. That day the temperature change wasn't so dramatic, but the lighting always was. With no windows except for a dome ceiling skylight, which housed rotating pastel-colored lights, and a floor of "five-color terrazzo marble laid out in the design of a Navajo sand painting," the effect produced a reverence akin to entering a cathedral or a sanctified library. Even the two of us settled down.

A larger-than-life size bronze statue of Uncle Frank stood in this gallery, to which we gave a brief glance and then headed right, to the room of "exotic exhibits."

Lights were brightened in this room, and we bee-lined to our favorite exhibit – the shrunken heads – seven *real* shrunken heads. The Jivaro Indians of Ecuador had made them, presumably using the heads of enemy neighbors. They created these baseball-sized heads by first removing the skulls and then used a secret heating process to shrink what was left. Most had very dark skin and hair, though one was grey-headed, and another had brown hair. The eyelids were sewn shut with heavy lashes in place of eyes, and the crudely stitched mouths were patterned in a not-so-very-satisfied look. I guess I wouldn't look too happy either if I had had my head chopped off, emptied, and shrunk. We were mesmerized with the whole exhibit. We couldn't imagine going out in the jungle one day in South America and ending up dead, with our head shrunken, impaled on a stake, and then later displayed in a museum in Oklahoma!

These fellows were our absolute favorite exhibit. We kept trying to imagine going out for a walk, then getting killed, shrunk, and staked, then ending up in a museum a continent away.
Photo permission: Woolaroc Museum, Bartlesville, Oklahoma.

On a lower shelf in the far-right corner glass case was another favorite object d'art. We'd first thought the small clay sculpture depicted a couple of fighters. But then a closer look reminded us of a couple of dogs we'd seen once. *Yup, they were "doing it."* In missionary position. It beat any *National Geographic Magazine* naked-people-in-the-jungle photo we'd ever seen. From that day on, we never missed that little work of art on our museum trips.

This figurine was in a glass display case on the next to the bottom shelf in the corner, but we never missed it. Other than the girls' health film in the fifth grade, this was our sex education. Photo permission: Woolaroc Museum, Bartlesville, Oklahoma.

The next galleries were truly grand – in size and art. The ceilings soared over two stories and were filled with paintings from such Western artists as William Leigh, Charles Russell, and Frank Tenney Johnson. Janet Ruth's favorite was William Leigh's, "Vision of Yesterday," while I loved "Morning Sun" by Frank Tenney Johnson. Animal trophy heads (claimed to be from the early exotic animals that did not survive the Oklahoma climate) and Navajo rugs were hung alongside the paintings.

Remington sculptures and miniature pieces from the Pioneer Woman sculpture competition were also exhibited. Beside an old stagecoach stood a circular-glass diorama, which housed a pow-wow exhibit of Native Americans dancing before a bleacher full of older tribal on-lookers. A switch could bring the young dancers to life, drumming, chanting, and dancing around a sacred fire. There was always a circle of kids watching this. Us, too.

Our last stop was downstairs. We didn't care much for the guns, doll exhibits or even the "Woolaroc" plane there, but we couldn't resist trailing our hands along the Anaconda snake-skin displayed just above the stair railing. We had to see if we could caress it all the way to the bottom.

We did a whirlwind tour of that level before hunger took over. We headed outside to meet Mom and Dad for a picnic; in those early years you had to bring your own food. Later, a canteen opened serving Buffalo Burgers, their specialty – really barbequed buffalo.

A life-size buffalo taxidermy showed up one year alongside the canteen. When he first arrived, he was fitted with a vacuum tube from his mouth to somewhere inside to remove used pop cans. As soon as a kid's can-in-hand got to his mouth, it was rapidly sucked away! Many years later, my kids loved (and were terrified) of that buffalo. He no longer swallows cans, but he still stands as a figurehead, reminding us to dispose of our trash responsibly.

The Lodge wasn't open to the public in the early years, but when we were able to visit it later, we fell in love with that as well.

Woolaroc was, and is still, a special place to visit. Phillips company picnics continue to be held there, and thousands of people visit as outside guests. Annually, Bartlesville hosts a week-long Mozart Festival with concert venues throughout the town. The favorite one is the outdoor concert on the banks of Clyde Lake on a summer's night. And in the fall, the museum hosts a "Cowthieves and Outlaws Reunion," an event today, where the bad guys are known only to themselves.

When the museum began a docent program in the early 1980s, my mother joined the first class and guided there for twelve years. Well into their 80s, my parents continued to visit Woolaroc, often to just drive the roadway through the ranch, stopping for a Buffalo Burger half-way. Their dog, Daisy, enjoyed the prairie dogs the most, each trying to out-stare the other.

My niece Emily Clinton married Marc Claude in front of the entrance and doors to the museum, and the reception was held inside the great halls, a special day for our family and for the many guests who had never been to Woolaroc. Neither Bartlesville nor Woolaroc is on a thoroughfare. You have to work to get there, but you won't be disappointed when you do. Just ask Janet Ruth or me.

College High – Coming and Going

"Hail to dear College High, colors so bold
Bright banners in the sky of black and gold.
To you our loyalty never will die.
We're ever faithful to you College-High."

W e sang that alma mater with enthusiasm, gusto and no cynicism in 1959 when Janet Ruth and I entered Bartlesville's College High School. Built in 1940 on Hillcrest Drive in "streamline moderne," a late style of the art deco period, the main building is a two-story flat roofed structure, rectangular save for its north front corner, which is sleekly curved. It is finished in bright white insulated Dewey Portland cement. Surrounding buildings added in later years mirror the original.

When first built, the new school replaced a stolid brick fortress on Cherokee Avenue, which housed both junior high and high school students. With such a bold, modern style, the new school must have caused quite a stir.

By the time we arrived, the land around the school's footprint of at least two city blocks was largely devoid of trees, save for a signature elm. That gift from nature stood alone on the north end of the school, growing tall and broad, sharing water and sun with only the grass below. Its Y-forking branches invited explorers like Pickering and me to climb, but it was only a tease. The tree had grown too tall; its lowest branches were far out of reach. Nevertheless, we laid claim to that school's tree before we ever matriculated there. Only a minute's walk from Janet Ruth's house, in summer it provided a canopy we escaped to for a respite from the heat and sun. At night it was our meeting place where we sat and talked. And when it rained, we danced around that monument, our Stonehenge. Years later, at our twentieth reunion when Pickering and I were too cheap to buy tickets to hear Vince Gill perform at the football stadium, we and our husbands lay in the grass under the big elm to hear the concert. When we learned later the tree first fell victim to Dutch Elm disease and then to one of those glorious storms we loved, we mourned the loss of an old friend.

The name, Bartlesville College High or "Col High" was a mystery to us when we were students, but I guess it wasn't mysterious enough to investigate, because we didn't discover its origin until years later, when we learned that the school had originally housed the last two grades of high school and two years of junior college. When we thought about it at all, we figured the "College" part of the name was meant to serve as inspiration.

My friends and I had an easy transition to high school. We had completed our freshman year at the junior high, so we were already on our way with our courses and paths of study. And by that time we had grown quite independent and daring. Though there were still no women's sports or even girls' physical education, there were plenty of clubs, plays, and student government positions to engage us.

Our short stints as cheerleaders began to wane that year: Pickering washed out, Charette's life changed, and I was demoted to alternate. Actually, misbehavior had altered that. One Friday night as the buses were filling for an away-game, I boarded just as a couple of kids lit up (tobacco cigarettes, that is). As I walked down the aisle to find a seat, someone offered me a puff. All eyes were on me, so – trying to be cool – I leaned down, placed my hands on the cigarette while my gifter held it, and took a long drag – just as Principal Bailey climbed aboard for a head count. He didn't need a cig count. They mysteriously disappeared, and I was the single, guilty culprit.

"Off the bus!" he ordered. "And you are benched for the next two games." As I was an alternate, I was realistically already benched, but now there was no chance I'd be cheering. I'd never had the cigarettes, lit them, or passed them around. But I was busted, and no one was confessing, least of all Janet Ruth who just *might* have been smoking herself.

An art deco design referred to as "streamline modern."
Photo courtesy of Bartlesville Area History Museum,
Bartlesville, Oklahoma

While I remained in cheerleader limbo, Janet Ruth joined "Peppers," the pep squad who wore beanies. Really. They sat in a large group in front of the cheerleaders and made a lot of noise answering to the cheers. It was pretty effective unless you misspelled something. I did that once, as a cheerleader.

After several repetitions of "Beat Sand Springs!" as loud as we could make it, I took over the lead to spell it out...antiphonally:

"Give me a B!" I called.

"B!!" yelled the Peppers.

"Give me an A!" I continued.

"A?" they yelled, not quite in unison and perplexed.

"Give me an E!" I mumbled...the light suddenly dawning.

"E," they mumbled back.

"Give me a T," I finished. I gave up before "Sand Springs." It was probably fortunate I sucked that cigarette; cheerleading wasn't my calling.

By sophomore year our S.H.E. club was inviting more girls to join. We still didn't do much except wear our pins and have slumber parties, but it beat being a street gang, though some might have argued at times we were that.

Our sorority was pretty loose with no written records, but luckily for us, documentation came in the form of professional photographs taken by a man named Winston. He opened a photography business in Bartlesville, and early on, began to specialize in the lives of high school students. He was young and fun to be around, so he was welcome to show up for parties, proms, or anything else anyone thought worthy of a photo. And because he was professional, he could make himself an unobtrusive part of the group. You forgot about him, enabling him to snap candid moments in our teenage lives.

Our club now had a solid fifteen members so we felt we needed a formal photo, as well as those from casual moments. At an appointed time, fifteen S.H.E.s showed up at Winston's studio dressed in skirts and sweaters. But before we even had the proofs, we learned that Marie Charette was moving.

"Where?" and "Why?" we asked. All we were told was that Marie, her mother and two sisters were moving to Montana. Janet Ruth didn't even know why, and she was Marie's oldest friend. Montana sounded so far away, and we were devastated to lose our friend.

Their departure was swift, so swift we didn't have time to give her a party or a parting gift. But afterwards, the group gathered to choose a goodbye present. There wasn't much discussion before we decided to send her the photograph Winston had just taken of the club. Janet Ruth was put in charge of getting and sending it, and she did her job, but the rest of us never saw what she wrote to Marie at the time. Only many years later when we reunited with Marie did we learn the story. On the back of the photo, Janet Ruth had written:

Here's hoping you'll always remember us for sending you this free picture.
Love,
Sigma Eta Epsilons
P.S. If ya want a sweatshirt, you'll hafta pay! (ha).

Whoa. It seemed Mama Ruth's thriftiness was beginning to show up in her offspring. We never heard from Marie again, and to be honest, I'm not sure any of us ever wrote to her. We talked about her often, but after she made another move, we lost track of her. As the years went on, and we had our own reunions, we still spoke of her, remembered her, and wondered where she might be. Then, in 2006 when my husband and I were downsizing and going through old video tapes, we found one we had been sent from an All-Class College High reunion we had not been able to attend. We needed a break from the packing and pitching, so we sat down and watched it (for the first time) before throwing it out.

There in the video were Marie's sister Lucy and her husband, who gave their names and address in California. The video was several years old by this time, but we decided to see if we could locate Lucy, and perhaps Marie.

A call to information produced a phone number for Lucy, and I reached her on my first attempt. Fortunately, she remembered me, since she was only a year older. I began with the crazy story of losing touch with Marie after she left Montana and ended with Marie's contact information. I hung up the phone, took a deep breath and thought, *46 years had gone by, and I might actually get to speak to her!* And I wondered as I dialed, if I'd reach her on the first try as I had her sister.

I did.

Though she was, of course, taken aback by my call, we quickly picked up the old threads and tried to give each other synopses of the last 46 years of our lives. I included stories of Janet Ruth as well, and though we barely began, we each ended the call eager to renew our friendship. I promptly sent her all of our group's available addresses and phone numbers.

I certainly hadn't finished; my quest continued. Janet Ruth was living in New Mexico, and I called her right away. When her husband Tom answered, I asked him if Janet Ruth was home because I had some exciting news. That was all I said.

"Sure," he replied. "I'll go get her." He called to her, only telling her I was on the phone.

When she answered, I blurted out, "Guess who I just found?"

Without a second's hesitation, she said, "Marie!"

How did she know?!

I went on, "She lives an hour away from you in New Mexico." And the story spilled out.

Growing up, our lives were outwardly superficial, and our pranks often gently broke the rules. But we followed a pretty strict code when it came to nosing into someone's business.

No one shared any private family issues, even with our closest friends. We all knew Marie lived with her mother and two sisters, but we never questioned where her dad was. Later, when we reconnected with Marie, we learned their move reunited her family with their father, now living in Montana. As much as she liked us, she embraced her new life, and looked forwards not backwards. And with that crummy picture and a demand for payment for the sweatshirt, she might have thought us a bunch of tightwads. But she saved the photo with the inscription, which she sent to me some 60 years later when she knew I was writing this memoir.

Photo courtesy of Craig's Photography, Bartlesville, Oklahoma.

The Plains Picasso

I heard a lot of funny stories at the Pickering house, but this was one of the first. It gave birth to "Janet Ruth!"

Janet Ruth was only four years old and living in Houston, Texas with her brother and parents when she entered the world of crime. It was springtime and already warm, so everyone was enjoying the out-of-doors before the summer's oppressive heat arrived. Kids were playing and adults were visiting, when suddenly, a neighbor drove a brand-new car into his driveway.

This was an event. World War II had ended only a few years before, and new cars were just becoming more commonplace. Getting one was a big deal. Everyone stopped their chatting to walk over and check it out. The car was big and black, and prompted a lot of oohing, aahing, and questions before the adults finally tired and returned home. But the kids weren't tired and hadn't lost interest, so they stayed on. What held their eyes was the sheen – lustrous and reflective – and now that the parents were gone, they could get a closer look. It might have reminded them of the shiny paper used for finger painting. It definitely looked better than a chalkboard.

And then it happened. Someone – the who, long forgotten – got the idea to draw. Not having any markers on hand, the little artist picked up a rock and began to etch on the reflective surface. In no time, the rest of the kids followed suit with their own little rocks. The results were mostly the scribbles of little children, but Janet Ruth, the show-off in any group, upstaged them all by carefully, and precisely, writing her name. She got her friend, Mike, to get as far as the M, but no one else had mastered writing their name, and the "M" didn't indict him. This was her artwork, the owner's graffiti, and the Pickering's repair expense – the culprit was clear. When Janet Ruth's mother learned what happened, her disbelief and anger came out with the "Janet Ruth!" she bellowed throughout the neighborhood. As for me, her name became synonymous with the mischiefs and escapades we engaged in throughout our growing up. Now, my youngest grandsons refer to these tales as "Janet Ruth" stories.

By high school, Janet Ruth's urge to draw, paint, and leave a name behind blossomed. Everett, Reinfeld, and Marks joined her in Mr. Grace's art classes and they, too, were driven to "paint or write on unauthorized surfaces," that being the definition of graffiti. Most of the S.H.E.s weren't artists, but those who were, inspired the rest of the club to follow their lead. Whether it was a town roadway, or the local water tower, it seemed important to leave "S.H.E." painted all over town.

Some parents gave permission to paint S.H.E. on their home driveways, but the fun was putting it where it wasn't allowed. One such location, at 14th and Johnstone, seemed the perfect site for a street painting. It was a busy intersection and one where anyone going to town could see our handiwork, so our group began to plan.

It couldn't be done in the light of day; we'd have to do it during a slumber party. We decided Janet Ruth's house would be best since it was an easy walk to our target. And probably a full moon, or nearly full, would be helpful.

While we waited for the right night, Pickering, Reinfeld, Everett, Smith and I assembled the materials. We got the paint and brushes from Maltby Brothers Hardware, and then hid them in Pickering's basement.

The moonlit night finally arrived, and Pickering's unknowing parents agreed to host a few of us to sleep over. After settling into the den over the garage, we made a couple of sneaky trips to the basement to gather our gear. And then we waited for it to get dark, and for Mr. and Mrs. Pickering to go to bed. When the house quieted, so did we, until we had to stifle our giggles as we headed one by one out a den window onto a shallow roof with a short drop to the ground below. It was a warm night and with the moon our overhead flashlight, we made our escape. Carrying the contraband, we headed down Denver Road to Hillcrest and across 14th Street to the intersection at Johnstone, giggling all the way.

We arrived in less than fifteen minutes. It was a busy intersection, and it was going to be a great canvas for our club name, but it was going to take some finesse to get the paint onto the pavement. Smith and I set out the cans of paint, pried open the lids and laid out the brushes. We knew our job. The artwork fell to Reinfeld, Pickering and Everett. They set to work, but they would get one letter partly outlined only to be interrupted by an oncoming car. As it came closer, we all ran and hid in nearby bushes. Once the car passed by, we returned to our jobs only to have the same scene play out again. After Pickering and Reinfeld finally formed the bulbous letters, Smith and I began to fill them in. But again, we would barely start before we were interrupted. Nevertheless, this routine was making steady but slow progress when a call from a nearby house made us jump.

"Hey, what's going on here?"

We scrambled to hide when Pickering suggested, "Quick, pretend you're a bush!"

Well, not only was that way more creative than we could pull off in the few seconds wc had, how were we going to explain the paints and brushes in clear view? The voice got closer until he was standing beside the crepe myrtle better known as Virginia.

"What are you girls doin' here?" he yelled. Clearly, we hadn't fooled him with our bush disguises. And then there were those pesky cans of paints and wet brushes. And the art on the street. We hung our heads in shame and confessed our crime.

"You need to go home, get cleaners and come back here and scrub this paint off the street!" he ordered. And, of course, he wanted our names and addresses. He got them; we weren't good at lying. We were mostly good at dreaming up these schemes.

Defeated, we took our cans and brushes and headed back to Pickerings. Somewhat remorseful and definitely embarrassed, we hurried to their basement, found soapy cleaner, scrub brushes and a bucket of water and went back to the scene. We scrubbed. And scrubbed. Most of our art did come off, and I had heard about Depression curb painters who cut the paint so thin, the address washed off in the first rain. I was hoping for that.

Once again, we were repentant, but mostly for being caught. We'd try again. Our next canvas was the water tower farther down 14th Street. Water towers were popular paint targets; everyone got to see the artwork, and there was usually some admiration in the form of "How the heck did they pull that off?" We waited a few weeks to see if there were any more repercussions from our street painting adventure. Then word came that there would be a bunch of kids at the water tower one Friday night. It was beyond walking distance so this time we needed a ride to get there. Everett couldn't drive that night, but Smith was able to get her father's pick-up, and Smith, Pickering and I filled the truck and bed.

Arriving at the tower, we saw eight to ten kids milling around the base craning their necks through the moonlight to watch the activity already in progress. We knew most of the kids. Two boys had already been up the ladder to paint their club name, T.K.B., (Tappa Kegga Beer), onto the holding tank, and were on their way back down. Seeing that only made Janet Ruth ready to go. I, on the other hand, terrified of heights, didn't care how many "double dog dares" anyone hurled. Nothing would convince me to climb that tower. I was an aider and abettor only.

Water tower ladders are not easy to climb. For one thing, they never begin at ground level. I speak from the experience of one who watched; you need help to reach the lowest rung just to get started. Fortunately, there were a lot of willing boosters that night loitering at the bottom, so when Janet Ruth announced she was "goin' up," a couple of guys gave her a hand-stirrup-step to the shoulders of one tall boy, while others pushed her feet up, giving her purchase to reach the lowest rung. She then pulled herself up and was on her way, hand over hand, slowly up the ladder. Meanwhile, with my hands sweating, I covered my eyes, peeking occasionally to make sure she was still safe. *But what am I going to do if she slips?* I couldn't let my mind go there.

The climb continued, endlessly to me, and finally she ducked under the last rung and crawled onto the catwalk. She stood; a cheer went up, and a proud wave returned. But now what was she going to do? She hadn't brought any paint or brushes with her. *Darn!*

But suddenly ahead of her on the walkway, she got a surprise.

"Bonus!" she exclaimed when she saw that the guys had left behind paint cans and brushes. Clearly, they had thought through their plan, so now her mission was clear - get S.H.E. painted on that tower.

She was proud of her feat so far, but other feet - where they had been, and where they might be going — were inspiring her. Moving stealthily along the catwalk, she began her mural using the leftovers. Painting freehand, and as high as she could reach, she began to create the very large black footprints of a sturdy set of shoes, marching sideways, foot-printing the circumference of the tower until they reached the signature S.H.E. on the backside.

It took a while. I think I held my breath most of the time,

but finally, the deed was done. More cheers! Now the trick was to get back down. Leaving the cans and brushes, she headed to the ladder, turned, got on her hands and knees, and, holding the top rail, carefully reached one leg down until she felt the first rung, and then, stretching one leg after another, made her way down. I resorted to peeking through my fingers again, but finally, thankfully, she reached the lowest rungs, and the guys grabbed hold of her legs to drop her to the ground.

To be honest, I probably knew that this was a bad idea, but we were all proud of her creation and bravery. I couldn't be like her, but I could bask in reflected glory as her best friend.

Our graffiti days ended after this. Even Janet Ruth was not interested in topping the water tower escapade. It was clear she was going somewhere with all this creating, but that would be a long way off. In the meantime, she got better at choosing exploring venues that wouldn't land her in McAlester (the state pen).

The budding artist is on the left.

Mike

At College High, Latin was a subject taught to mixed grade levels, unlike most of my classes in which we were all the same age and year. Mrs. Ellsworth taught Latin I and Latin II, and every fall she hosted a Latin Club "Forum Dinner" in the Teacher's Lounge at school. Students in all her classes were invited, though it was an optional, after-school activity and one she suggested we attend in Roman dress.

I had begun Latin in 9th grade, so I was in my second year when I arrived at the high school. I liked Latin, and I liked dressing up and pretending I was someone else. The invitation sounded fun to me, but there was one problem: none of my friends taking Latin wanted to go to this function. Even Janet Ruth refused. It was optional, so she opted out; I would have to go alone.

I guess the costume part won out, because I dug around the house and found the best white sheet we had, wound it around me, threw the loose end over one shoulder, and then hopped in the car with my mother who drove me to school for the dinner. I felt kind of silly in that outfit, especially arriving alone, but inside the building, I soon saw a few other Romans headed for the teachers' lounge. I didn't dawdle; it was embarrassing.

The party started awkwardly, like our first dances, with girls on one side of the room and boys on the other. I was almost sorry I came until I noticed one upper classman, Mike Hewitt. I had known of him since the 5ᵗʰ grade at McKinley where everyone called him "Chicken," though I never knew why. (Apparently, when he first moved to town and played in his first touch football game, he didn't know to rush the passer. The following day, some of the boys on the teams labeled him "Chicken." He *was* tall and skinny with a buzz cut, but he didn't know enough to take offense, so the name stuck. Some of his friend's parents never knew him by any other.) I knew he was a good athlete and student, and at different times he liked Lucinda Cash and Regina Falcon – girls in his class. I thought I knew a lot about him, but I wasn't sure he knew anything about me. We had never formally met, but he looked like he was headed my way. My heart fluttered when I realized that this upper classman was coming to talk to me. Or it looked like he was, anyway.

He was, and he didn't assume I knew him and introduced himself.

"Hi, I'm Mike Hewitt." Actually, with his heavy Oklahoma twang, the Mike came out more like "Mahk."

"Well, I'm Patty Mac Sloan," I said as he smiled, showing his double-sided dimples. And then we talked – and talked – in a conversation that went on for most of the party. I really liked him though I have no idea what we talked about.

Maybe he liked the way I looked in that linen-closet toga

because by the end of the party, he'd asked me to the movies the following Friday, after we'd established there was no game that night. (Dating was always planned around boys' sports – football and basketball, mostly. If you weren't participating in the game, you'd surely be there watching.)

Friday night arrived, and I was excited to be going on a date with Mike Hewitt. He really was someone people looked up to – literally and figuratively. At 6'3" he towered over my 5'4".

For this first date, I wore a special outfit, a baby blue wool skirt and matching sweater set, store-bought. At the movie theater, we sat in the balcony.

What happened? Again, those memory tapes have faded except for the feelings. By the end of the evening I had a huge "crush" on him.

The following week he called me – once – to make another date. We never talked very long on the phone. My dad felt telephones were a business tool, not a social one, so I had no experience with chatty phone calls. And then, as telephone customs changed, Mike and I didn't. When it came to talking on the phone, I've had more conversation getting rid of a telemarketer than I ever had with Mike. When he called, we made our date, settled on a time, and said goodbye. We spoke in person when we saw each other at school, or on our dates, which were either a movie, a sock hop or just going out for a coke; there was little variation.

We weren't constantly in each other's lives, but we liked the times we were. Mike was busy with sports and studies, and besides studying, I was busy making sports out of adventures with Janet Ruth and my S.H.E. friends.

So, what did I like about him? Well, everything. I thought he was cute, had great legs, and I loved his double-sided dimpled smile. He was tall and thin, worked hard, and was smart. He had a buzz cut, and it would be a few years before I ever saw he had a great head of hair. He played football in the fall, basketball in the winter, and in the spring, he ran the hurdles in track, excelling well enough in all three to be recruited by colleges and offered scholarships.

But I also liked what he wasn't – macho, cocky, patronizing, a braggart or a greaser – a guy with a D.A. ("Duck's ass" haircut and sideburns).

Beneath the surface, what I *really* loved was that he was kind, humble, and generous. And he was spiritual. Despite my outward shenanigans with church things, I had a quiet faith and found strength in worshipping God. That was a significant part of who he was, too, though he didn't broadcast it. When he spent his post-high-school graduation summer working on a Mississippi River barge, he gave away his entire earnings to an orphanage in India. Our Presbyterian church had a mission relationship with them, and Mike felt they needed the money more than he did.

No one knew this. The conversation came out with me accidentally and with no fanfare. He was going to be getting a full scholarship to college, and his parents could afford to send him even if he didn't have the scholarship. What did he need the money for, he said. It seemed reasonable to him.

I couldn't imagine giving away my hard-earned money, but then our family never had any extra. He saw it as something anyone would do in his situation. It floored me.

When my younger sister began dating, she often went out with guys who seemed somewhat shallow, overly fun-loving, and not particularly serious about school. Since she was serious about school, I couldn't understand what she saw in those boys. When she did marry, a terrific guy whom I really liked, I finally asked her about some of those previous dates.

"Well I wasn't going to marry them!" she said. "They were just fun!"

As silly as Janet Ruth and I could be, I couldn't imagine wasting an evening with a guy who didn't seem to have any ambition. Good thing I met Mike.

Deep down we were both pretty serious and worked hard to succeed. Neither of us had any interest in drinking (then), though both sets of parents were social drinkers. I didn't like alcohol's effect on my dad; it made him testier, and I certainly didn't find that appealing. Mike didn't want to mess up his athletics, and he honestly didn't like the taste. There were definitely groups of boys who drank beer, but Mike wasn't one of them. Most of my girlfriends didn't drink either until our senior year of high school or college. Smoking was our vice, starting in our sophomore year of high school. It was a puff here and there, but it was the beginning.

For most of us, dating was pretty tame. Was there passion? Sure. But the fantasy of negligees and speedos was more tantalizing to us than "The Full Monty." "Necking" was popular. That could be defined as kissing, hugging and perhaps some groping hands above the waist, but there were strong social *governors* for many of us. Every year though, there were surprise pregnancies or girls who just disappeared for a while. Seeing the huge effect on a girl's life made pregnancy fearsome to me. My history of getting caught with my Janet Ruth pranks was enough to keep me celibate.

When late spring arrived, so did the high school yearbooks, where we spent hours writing in classmates' books. They were hardly the words of poets, just the embarrassing, hackneyed writings of high schoolers who cared about one another. I am still married to the one who wrote the following in 1961:

> *I once knew a girl.*
> *She could be happy; she could be sad;*
> *She could be silly and foolish: she could be serene and pensive.*
> *That is why she was what she was, and why I will never forget her.*

> *Love, Mike*

That same year I wrote to him:

Dear Mike,
There's not much to say to you compared to the beautiful words you wrote to me. You'll never know how much they really mean, Mike, we've had so many firsts together – I will never forget them. I have never met anyone like you and, I too, will never forget you.
Love, Patty Mac

By the time we wrote these notes, we thought we were saying good-bye. Those firsts? Well, it wasn't sex. But there was plenty of affection. He was always thoughtful, writing notes, letters and poems, making me feel special. Young as we were, I just knew there was something uncommon about him.

SHE-LES DES CHRISTMAS DANCE 1961

Patty Mac and Mike, ages 15 and 16 years old.
Photo courtesy of Craig's Photography, Bartlesville, Oklahoma

The A&W Root Beer Caper

“Hey, y’all, who wants to go out Friday night? Mama says I can have the car,” said Everett one day at school.

Mrs. Everett was always generous and let her daughter Jan use her car to ferry us around. Having prematurely lost her husband, she probably felt safer having Jan drive rather than ride with someone else. My later-in-life friend Alice Cronin was an only child with a widowed Irish mother. When Alice came of age to drive, her mother bought her first car and appointed Alice designated driver. Mrs. Cronin was a woman of few words, but her sayings made an impact. Every time Alice left to drive her friends somewhere, Mrs. Cronin warned, “Remember, the driver always lives.” I wonder if Mrs. Everett subscribed to the same adage.

I wanted to go out with everyone that Friday night, but my new boyfriend Mike had just asked me out for a date, and I wasn’t going to turn *him* down. Lynn Hobart had a date, too, so she couldn’t make it, but Pickering, Smith, Reinfeld, Sue Natare, Pam Oulde, Gerry Driver, Elizabeth Marks, Eileen Wafer, and Sandy Tucker all agreed. Everett would pick them up at Smith’s house so she didn’t have so many stops to make.

The night arrived and as soon as Everett had the car in gear in Smith’s drive-way, she began the familiar S.H.E. honk, certain to annoy the neighbors, and guaranteed to alert the pick-ups that their ride had arrived. In no time they ran out of the house and into the car. Bess Smith, Meredith’s mother, waved a good-bye and yelled, “Have fun!” No doubt there; they always did.

There was an umbrella of melancholy in the car that night because Sandy Tucker’s family was being transferred to New

Jersey with Cities Service Oil Company, a career advance for her dad, but sad for the rest of the family. We were all still reeling from Marie's move, and now another friend was leaving. Tucker was our friend with the big voice and the dog we called "Tippe Cornelius Canoe Osa Mae Duran Who Sat Upon a Stool with a Can of Beer and a Glass Eye Tucker." Her large presence would be missed. Anyway, they would have some fun that night before she left. Everett headed out – with nowhere particular in mind, as usual. And, as usual, someone suggested they go get a coke.

"Sure! I'll have a root beer," Tucker said, so Everett headed down Dewey across to Johnstone and all the way through town past the Osage Theater to Frank Phillips Boulevard where she headed east. The town was expanding in this direction with developments around and beyond a shopping center called Pennington Hills. Besides the A&W Root Beer Stand, a drive-in selling mostly hamburgers and root beers, there were many new businesses opening along Frank Phillips, some of which were getting a lot of attention. One place served this round, cheesy-bread thing called pizza. None of us had ever heard of it before, but we heard everyone who'd tried it, loved it.

However, all of them had already eaten that night, and they had no money for eating out, anyway. Probably that's why going out for a coke was so popular. It was cheap, and a great excuse to go somewhere and see who was hanging out.

It didn't take long to get to the A&W stand, and Everett rolled into one of the slots. The restaurant was in a small building where carhops brought the orders and picked up the food. The front door led to a walkway where cars parked on either side, protected by a metal roof. The place was busy, but soon a waitress came for the order.

"What'll you have?" she asked.

"Just a minute ... O.K., O.K.!" cried Everett through all the chattering. "What do y'all want?"

After a lot of, "I'm not sure...let's see...I don't know," three of the nine ordered a root beer. Everett relayed the order, and the car-hop left. Pam and Gerry hopped out to sit on the hood of the car to see, and be seen, I imagine. The rest stayed inside. After a few minutes, the waitress returned and hung the tray and three root beers by its rubberized hooks from the slightly-raised window on the driver's side. A similarly rubberized triangular brace underneath rested against the driver's door.

Everett handed out the three drinks, and the chatter continued while the drinks were downed. Nothing too interesting was going on, and six girls had ordered nothing, so they were getting impatient. The empty mugs were replaced on the tray, and Everett honked for the pick-up. Meanwhile, Pickering was hatching a plan. She and Elizabeth Marks suggested they could get into the trunk with their legs covered in ketchup, pretend they were injured, and they'd ride around town like that. Everyone loved the idea.

"But they haven't picked up the tray and mugs," whined Everett.

"Well, honk again," reminded Smith. So, Everett did, and when no one came, she honked again. Pickering used this time to get some ketchup from inside the stand, and by the time she returned, her friends were like racehorses at the starting gate.

Then a suggestion came from someone, another *who* long forgotten: "Phooey, let's just go. Throw the tray and mugs in the car. It can be a going away present for Tucker!" This was a cheap group.

Everything came into the car, and Everett wasted no time backing up, turning left out of the parking lot, and returning to town the way they had come. On the way back, she pulled into a Phillips' filling station (that's what we called gas stations) for the staging of the injury. Pickering and Marks climbed out of the car, covered their legs with ketchup and then stretched out in the trunk with the lid open to create the scene. Pam Oulde then asked the station attendant where the nearest river was. She wanted him to think that they had a body to dump, but their laughter gave them away. She returned to the car, and Everett took off down Frank Phillips again.

They didn't get far. The flashing lights of the police cruiser bore down on them quickly, and Everett had the sense not to try to outrun him. She pulled the car to the side of the road. Obviously, the two in the trunk stood out.

"What's going on here?" the officer asked after ordering all of them out of the car.

"Oh...*well*...not much," Pickering said. "Just havin' a little fun, I guess..."

"Uh-huh...I see...you been at the root beer stand?" The mumbling produced some yeses and some nos. "Really? A little confusion. Did you happen to take any of the mugs?"

"Oh, no, officer," said Janet Ruth as he shined his flashlight towards the back window of the Buick where the three mugs were lined up. And then he flashed the light through the open rear passenger window onto the floor, displaying the contraband tray.

"And...I see you got the tray, too," he said. "You all are going to be going to the police station. First, I want all of your names and addresses. Tomorrow morning you are to show up with your parents at the station for booking."

Everyone was stunned, and no one dared to speak. Quietly, they did as he asked, and then he barked, "Now, get back in the car and drive home – slowly." Silence fell as they closed the trunk and all crammed back into the car. They were busted this time for sure. No one had a lot to say on the way home; they were scared of what was going to happen.

"Did you happen to take any of the mugs? – and I see you've got the tray, too."

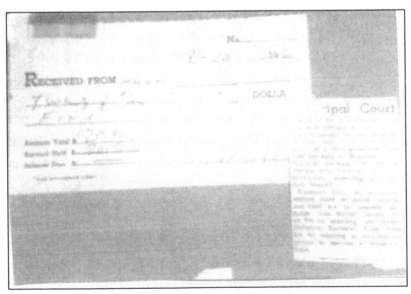

The receipt for Janet Ruth's fine — $20. To put it in perspective, my parents paid $80 per month to rent our house.

The owner of the root beer stand had had it. He was sick and tired of kids stealing his stuff, so he was pressing charges. Bad timing for my friends. Some told their parents that night and others figured they would break it to them later.

Janet Ruth tried the code of silence, but she couldn't sleep and finally woke her parents in the middle of the night to tell her tale.

Sue Natare was so ashamed and embarrassed to tell her mom that she was more upset than her mother when the truth came out. Her mother knew it was very unlike her.

Virginia Smith's parents were reasonable, like they always were, and allowed their sensible daughter a little slack. It was unlike her as well.

Gerry Driver was in such big trouble that she had to "mow the lawn for a year."

Everett's mom was disappointed too, and that shame was enough for Jan.

The following morning, we were all to meet near my house, at 18th and Dewey, for a bike ride to Circle Mountain. Eight o'clock sharp. We did this on a lot of Saturday mornings, and usually five or six girls came. This Saturday, Lynn Hobart arrived, but no one else showed. This really wasn't like them. *Wonder what's going on?* Then Virginia came riding up on her bike, looking very serious, and shared the story. This was just like her. She was concerned we'd all be wondering where everyone was, so she came over to tell us what had happened. She was in trouble, too, so she couldn't stay; she had to go to court with the rest of them.

We were speechless. None of our pranks had ever really gotten us into trouble. First, we felt bad for all of them. Then, we were selfishly relieved that the two of us weren't there. Like me, Lynn Hobart was on a date. Years later I learned that when her parents found out what happened, they knew that if she had not had a date, she would have been there...so she still got punished!

As for me, I dodged a bullet – thanks to my new boyfriend. But I have to admit that when enough years had gone by, those of us who were not there were sorry we'd missed such an infamous night.

At the police station and court room, they were booked and told their stories. The judge listened. The two perched on the hood of the car got off because they weren't in the car when the "decision to flee with the goods" was made (they must have had a good lawyer). The rest paid a fine and received a petty larceny record. That was the *really* bad part. We heard that it might keep you from being president, or something.

You know how we loved publicity. Well, this made the paper, but I'm not sure it was quite what Pickering had in mind.

Many years later, quietly, Virginia's father was able to have the petty larceny records expunged. We don't know how he did it, and for a long time he didn't let anyone know. He wanted that *governor* on all of their behavior. He just never felt the crime merited the punishment...

Moving

I wonder if my parents had a charge account at Millstead Moving; we moved so often. I have moved a lot during my married life and vividly recall those relocations. However, though I can remember all our houses as a child, I have no memory of the moving days and all of the chaos. I just remember being there.

During the summer before my junior year there was more talk of another move, but with real excitement. We kids were not a part of the search; we were just informed one day that we'd bought our first house! Over the years, every time we moved into a rental house, my folks cleaned and painted, Mom made curtains, and both parents planted flowers and even a tree once in a while. They made the place look so good it often prompted the landlord to sell, and we were forced to rent a new house. I am sure one could have argued against going to so much trouble when it was only a rental. But it was our home. And when my parents did those things, they made the house ours – a welcoming safe haven.

It taught me a lot about nesting. Even if I am staying in a place for a brief vacation, I buy plants, rearrange furniture, and try to make it mine. And no matter how long one might live in a home you own, the minute you move out, it becomes a house again. I find it pretty easy to make a nest wherever I land.

I would like to say I was thrilled when I saw the new house, but I wasn't. Located on a corner lot in a development off the Nowata Road, it was a single-level, L-shaped, brick ranch-style house with an attached garage, like hundreds of others. It was boring. And besides being ordinary, it was well outside

183

of town. That was the worst part. I couldn't walk to anything, and I no longer lived near any of my friends. I'd have to take a bus or have my mom drive me to school. I think I acted like a brat and demanded rides from Mom; I felt bus transportation was beneath me.

The inside of the house was gloomy, probably because the windows were shadowed by aluminum awnings, designed to reflect some of the summer heat, definitely keeping the house cooler — but dark. It didn't help that the interior walls were forest green, the only real color coming from the flowered draperies, similar to the ones Janet Ruth's mother was always threatening to make into a dress for her. They were ugly, whether they were hanging alongside our windows, or on Janet Ruth.

But there were some things I did like about the house. I liked the blue spruce growing in the front yard. It was full grown and would have made the grandest Christmas tree. And I liked the room my sister and I would share; we'd each have our own closet, and maybe it would be easier to hide my favorite clothes so she couldn't borrow them. But there was so much space she could easily see what was available, so we continued to fall into those clothes-sharing fights. And it seemed we would still share that iron bed, though by this time we had mastered the corpse-at-the-viewing sleeping position. We were pretty careful not to cross that center line.

My brother got his own room, larger than ours and with an outside entrance. We were never offered it, probably because of that escape route. I'm sure it wasn't the best feature for two teenagers, but he was still a little kid when we moved in; I guess they figured he wouldn't wander. Years later, my teenage brother made good use of that exterior door.

I tried to be happy about the house. For once, no one was going to make us move, I thought. Dad had been trying to start a new business — again — and I hoped that this one was going to work.

At the beginning of my junior year, we moved into our new home, school began, and Mom drove me there daily. Janet Ruth and I dove into school clubs, supported the guys' athletics, and anything else the school offered, absent girls' sports. She and I both tried theater that year. She won a part in the All School Play, *The Remarkable Incident at Carson's Corners*, and I was cast as a secretary in *The Broom and the Groom*. No Tony awards came our way, but it fed our love of drama. Drama seemed to follow us anyway, or we created it when it didn't.

That year, the class ahead of us welcomed the first American Field Service exchange student, Akira Yamasaki from Japan who lived with the Cuthberton family. He was popular with the entire student body and seemed to love our school.

I was fascinated with his opportunity, and being the exploring person I was, I decided to apply for the A.F.S. (American Field Service) summer program offered through our school. I filled out the forms and after a few weeks, six finalists were announced: three girls and three boys, and I was one of the girls.

My excitement was short-lived. A polite letter soon arrived bringing the news that my childhood friend, Terri Constable, was to be the representative to go to Berlin the following summer. Terri and I had been friends since we were little girls, so I was happy the winner was someone I liked a lot, though I was very disappointed.

My friend Lois often says, "Man plans, and God laughs." Before I could get too sad about not being selected to go to another country with the AFS program, the moving conversation began again at the dinner table. There were never family discussions about what was going on; there were only announcements. With complete disbelief, I heard the words that my father was taking a job in Calgary, Alberta, Canada, leaving to begin the new job in November, with the rest of us to follow him at the end of the school year.

Why Don't We Just…?

This was a fate worse than death. I was going to miss my senior year and be the new kid in school in a foreign country. *Hadn't I just applied to a program to do that?* Well, this wasn't the same. This was for the whole school year. I had to talk to Janet Ruth.

When I saw her, I wailed that she was never going to believe this, but my parents were moving to Canada, and I had to move, too!

"What! You're kidding…right?

"No, I'm not. They're serious. My dad will be leaving for Canada in November."

It was all I could do to keep from crying – and I don't cry easily.

Janet Ruth immediately settled into one of her think-up-something modes, and comforted me with a, "Don't worry, we can make a plan." I knew about her plans, and they were always fun, even if bordering on illegal. This was really serious. We could go over things on Friday night when I would stay over. *Maybe she really would come up with something good.*

In the meantime, all I could do was to imagine what this change would bring. *What am I going to do? I can't leave everyone…and school…and Mike. This is just like what happened to Marie and Sandy. I never thought it would happen to me! I just move around town.*

Friday took forever to arrive. It was unusually warm that fall night, and as Janet Ruth and I were talking in the Pickerings' den, we realized it had begun to rain. Warm rains were like a magnet to us. After a quick, "ya' wanna go?" we opened our escape-hatch window from the den, slid onto the roof on the low side, and dropped to the ground. Though we liked being in the rain, we chose the short-cut through the back hedges, past the Merrifields to get to the elm tree at the high school. It was our conference room.

Oklahoma rains are rarely drizzles. They are downpours.

186

No matter what protection you might think you have, you become as wet as standing bare in the shower. We did, and we loved it. We ran in circles around the tree, the drenching like an embrace that felt free, unleashed and forbidden. We laughed as we each saw our image in the other – wet Nero hairdos as the rain pelted our hair forward into our eyes, and our shirts outlining every curve we owned. I felt far away from the reality of the move.

But Janet Ruth had a plan and moved to the tree trunk to sit down. I followed. She started with, "I've been thinking. Do you even think you can graduate in one year if Canada has different requirements? I mean, would you have enough time to complete all their courses?"

"I never thought of that. And I bet my parents haven't either. Wow...keep talking..."

And then, carefully, she proposed the idea of my living with her and her family for the school year. I was speechless and just smiled. The news was just too good. *But could it possibly happen?* There were so many "ifs." First, her parents had to O.K. the whole idea before we even asked my parents. Meanwhile, should I plant the, "I might not be able to graduate in one year" seed in my parents' mind to make them more receptive to the idea of my living with her – *if* her parents agreed. We definitely had some work to do.

Janet Ruth didn't waste any time approaching her parents. Fortunately, I had been at her house so much that I had come to know her family well. I really liked them, and I felt they liked me a lot. That was a good start. She began the wheedling. Later she told me what her opener was.

"Couldn't Patty Mac just come live with us next year? We can pretend she's our foreign exchange student!" She *was* good. I never knew what worries or arguments her parents presented. Janet Ruth's older brother Cort was away at college so that was one fewer kid in the house. I am sure the fact that my high school boyfriend would be 200 miles away in college was also on the plus side of the equation; *still*, it was a lot of responsibility. But they agreed. Soon they talked to my parents, and I talked to my parents, and Janet Ruth talked to my parents, and I spoke to the Pickerings. Everyone agreed to the plan. My dad, who always said no, said yes.

It was a miracle.

I think I felt like I *was* going to be a foreign exchange student. My summer would be spent in Canada, and then I would be coming back to Bartlesville for my senior year. I wouldn't be leaving my friends, and even though Mike would be away at college, he could come to Bartlesville for visits. Once I knew this was happening, I relaxed and enjoyed my life again.

I was in love as much as any high schooler could be. But I think we were different from typical high school sweethearts. We weren't "love-struck," and in each other's lives constantly. We each spent significant time studying, participating in activities and enjoying our friends in addition to being with each other. I just knew he was special.

What I couldn't imagine then was that I would never live with my family for more than a summer for the next three years. And after that, I would never again live closer than 1500 miles away. This decision to stay behind turned out to be a very large fork in my life-road.

Our brief home. I think what I didn't like about it then was that it was dark...and far from town and my friends. But I did love that blue spruce!

Morning News

Everett got her Mama's big yellow Buick for Friday night's slumber party at Pam Head's. No one else's car could fit nine, and Everett's large trunk had plenty of room for our bedrolls. We could toss our wallets onto the package shelf, located below the rear window and behind the back seat. It was a great place for storing small stuff like comic books when you were on vacation.

As soon as Everett got to anyone's driveway, she gave the S.H.E. honk:

"Where-ev-er-you-are-on-land-or-sea

you-sur-ely-will-find-an-S.-H.-E.

We-get-a-rou-ou-nd!"

We were always ready and came running.

Pickering's mom drove her to Head's house earlier that evening because they were already out doing errands. While they were waiting for Everett's carload to arrive, Pickering, Pam Head, and her brother Jack played around with a football in the front yard. Jack was a big guy who was a notable tackle for the Col-High Wildcats. He'd heard that Janet Ruth was athletic, so he began kidding her to see what she could do as they tossed the ball back and forth. Pickering caught and returned it every time. He booted it. She booted it. Pam Head tried, but wasn't so hot. Pickering's shots were taking flight.

Then Jack challenged her, "Hey, Pickering, how about seeing if you can kick that ball over the house?" He was sure he had her this time.

"Oh, O.K.," she said, never missing an opportunity to take a challenge and possibly show off. Jack handed her the ball, and she stood in front of the house and then punted it, up and

190

right over the top of their house. Jack was speechless. Janet Ruth shrugged and smiled.

Jack had been sure she couldn't do it, so with lingering doubt, he ran to the back of the house to confirm the kick. And there was the football – right in the middle of the backyard. Good thing for Mia Hamm that Pickering didn't show up in her era.

We missed the show, though the legend began that night. Jack told the story for the rest of his life.

Meanwhile, the rest of us had been hatching another plan while picking everyone up. Susie Reinfeld wanted to go bushwhacking. None of us knew exactly what that meant, but Reinfeld's older sister had done it and gave her the idea.

Reinfeld began, "Sooo...first, you have to pick a night where there's some moonlight – like tonight – 'cause we'll be driving around in the dark. Then we all pile into Everett's car, and head out to Dodie's Dump and start driving around. My sister says lotsa kids go out there to park." (Parking involved necking – and who knows what else.) Once we get on the dirt roads, we need to shut the lights off so no one will see us coming. Then when we find a parked car, we roll up behind them, flash the lights and honk the horn! It'll scare 'em to death!"

"It'll scare us to death, too!" I said.

"Then we have to turn around real fast and get out of there before they know what happened," she said. By this time, everyone was laughing, and wanted to do it.

After Everett and the rest of us got to the house, Jack took the stage to tell us about Pickering's football feat, which amazed us too. But being narcissistic teenagers, we were honestly more interested in our next adventure. So, when Jack finally left the room, we filled Pickering in on our idea to go bushwhacking. She loved it. We couldn't announce that plan to Mr. and Mrs. Head, so once we'd greeted them, someone suggested we go out for a Coke, and they told us we could go.

Most of our friends' parents were really reasonable; I guess that's why they agreed to host slumber parties in the first place. And the Coke-outing usually worked to get us out of the house.

With our enthusiasm about Janet Ruth's kick, and in our haste to get into the car to leave, we forgot to off-load our bed-rolls from the trunk. We'd be sorry about that later.

Everett headed out of town onto Route 75 towards Tulsa to the turn-off for Dodie's Dump, a country road. Reinfeld was in the front seat giving directions and after a few miles, or-dered, "Slow down, the turn's coming up." Everett slowed and made the turn from the highway onto the dirt road, which immediately turned hilly. With up and down elevations like a piece of ribbon-candy, our drive began to mimic a roller-coaster ride – if you gave the car a little gas. Everett wasn't shy, and once we made the turn, she took off, giving us a slow chug up the hill aping a coaster climb, and then accelerating just before reaching the crest to produce that exhilarating, stomach dropping, slightly airborne feeling you get as you de-scend the first rollercoaster fall. We screamed, but not con-vincingly enough for her slow down. She gunned the engine again for the next climb – and the next. This kind of ride would continue until some kid threw up or the driver tired. We managed to avoid vomiting, and Everett finally slowed because Reinfeld reminded us we had to look for a turn-off to find parkers. So, Everett did, and we found an off-road and headed down it. Finally, we were in bushwhacking mode. The car quieted as the lights dimmed to nothing. It was dark and the moon wasn't completely full, but there were enough moon-light and stars out to keep us on the road. We accustomed quickly to the night, and everyone began looking for a parked car. Everett edged along, all of us excited and wondering how this would play out. Time and the car crept on, but we couldn't find a single parked couple.

Finally Smith said, "We better watch the time. Mr. and Mrs. Head said we should be home by 11."

"Ohh...come on...go a little farther!" Reinfeld urged. But we knew we had to be on time. Everett wavered as disappointment washed over the rest of us. The night had been a total failure; suddenly, Everett called out, "Hey! What's that over there? See? On the side of the road."

"What is it? It's huge!" Nancy Lord said.

It didn't look like a body, but it was big. Everett inched up beside it and then backed up to shine her lights on it. To our shock we saw that it was a very large coyote. And a very dead one. We hopped out of the car to take a closer look.

We could almost see the lightbulb flash over Janet Ruth's head when she said, "Hey, I've got an idea...why don't we pick the thing up, put it in the trunk, and take it to someone's house and put it on their front porch?"

The laughing started about the time she got to the part about picking it up, and finished with whoops at the thought of unloading it on some unsuspecting victim. This was better than bushwhacking.

Then Virginia Smith, our voice of reason, spoke up, "How are we going to pick it up?"

"*Well*, we could use some forked branches like spatulas," Nancy suggested.

"Good idea," Smith said. Everett opened the trunk to get ready for our treasure, apparently not noticing that our slumber party bedding covered the bottom. Meanwhile the rest of us were out collecting forked branches in the dark.

When we had a few, three of us made the first try to scoop up the creature. No one wanted to touch it, so we approached the remains as carefully as we could. All of us shoved our forked branches under the carcass and with a...one! Two! Three! We heaved together. One fork held, but the other two snapped, causing us to drop our quarry. I fell to the ground laughing so hard I wet my pants. That was a first, but it wouldn't be the last; I was worthless from that point on.

A second team made another attempt with the same results. The branches we found weren't strong enough to support this rigored animal. At this point, Nancy Lord took
charge: she grabbed the coyote by the tail and dragged him to
the trunk. Then with a little help from a couple of others with
branches, she flipped him in – and on top of – all our bedding.
Oops. Too late now.

But she had landed the fish. Her dad was a doctor, so we
figured she must have inherited the immunity-to-blood-and-
guts gene. No one else had that kind of courage.

We closed the trunk, and though we were disgusted we had
thrown him on top of our bedrolls, we had a more pressing
need: we needed to figure out where we would leave it.

Someone suggested Gerry Driver's house. She was a friend
who couldn't come that night, and her house was close to
where we were, and was on the way back to Pam Head's. That
seemed a good idea.

There was still the problem of how to get the carcass out of
the trunk. We'd worry about that later.

We were foiled by Gerry's getting out of a car from a date
just as we rode up. Stymied, we just did a drive-by. I don't
think she ever heard about the prize she might have gotten
that night because we never told her. (But she knows now.)

Smith reminded us again that it was getting late, and wondered what we should do. We had to get rid of the stiff in the
trunk.

I finally piped up and suggested, "Why don't we go to Pennington Hills Shopping Center and put it in front of one of the
stores there? We could get a newspaper, roll it up, put it in its
mouth, and prop it up like it was delivering the morning paper."

"So, who's got a newspaper?" Head asked.

"Uhh, how about we pretend we're on a scavenger hunt and
get one from one of those houses?" I said pointing to the neighborhood. I'd come up with a plan, such as it was, and no one

had an alternative, so we headed out.

We stopped at the first house with lights on, and sent Everett to the door to request the daily for a scavenger hunt. It worked; no one could refuse that adorable girl. We drove away laughing.

The parking lot in front of the strip mall was empty, so we got as close to the walkway as we could. Once again, all eyes turned to Nancy Lord to get the animal out. As deftly as she heaved it in, she flipped it out by the tail and then marched down the walkway, dragging the coyote by its tail. We were doubled over.

We decided to drop it off in front of Peters, a general department store. Nancy Lord was grateful to make the deposit at their front entrance. Then it was someone else's turn to deal with the set-up.

We took turns trying to push it into some kind of sitting position, but I think it was more propping than flexing that finally got it there. The coyote kept slipping down, and we were laughing so hard we could hardly concentrate. Its mouth was already open, so it was easy to slide in the rolled newspaper. Finally, the coyote was set, and we were sure this scene would make the front page of the Examiner-Enterprise.

We had focused so intently on the problem of disposing the coyote, that it took until the last leg of the ride home when someone reminded everyone we had dumped its body onto our bedding. A huge groan echoed through the car; no one wanted to share a pillow with the remains of a dead coyote. I think we borrowed some bedding from Mrs. Head, but I wonder what excuse we used. We couldn't all have forgotten our pillows.

Well, our delivery *dog* didn't make the paper. Maybe that was a good thing; we weren't up on dead animal ordinances, and we might have crossed the line. But we made our curfew, and had way more laughs than scaring parkers.

Life Without Father

Dad's new job brought excitement into the house. He was to be general manager of a Canadian hydrocarbons company in Calgary, Alberta. It was definitely a promotion, and though this wasn't his own business, he would run the day-to-day operations. And he would make more money, though no one spoke specifics about that around the kids. He left in early November to begin this new chapter of his life, and ours.

When he arrived in Canada, he stayed in a hotel temporarily, but soon began to look for a rental house, when it seemed our recently purchased house in Bartlesville wasn't going to sell quickly. It had been for sale awhile before we bought it, and Mom and Dad hadn't had the opportunity to fix it up before we left. The buyers hadn't lined up before, and they weren't again. The only option was to rent out the house in Bartlesville, with Dad renting one in Calgary.

We missed Dad that fall, but life was busy, and fairly calm without his outbursts, so the weeks passed quickly. But as Christmas approached, we looked forward to his visit home.

Christmas was Dad's favorite season. It was really the only time we got gifts other than our birthdays, which for Pam and me came in January and were somewhat anti-climactic. But at Christmas, Dad was the ultimate Santa, typically surprising us with something we never knew we wanted as well as a couple of things we did.

My excitement at this largesse required more self-control than I could muster. When Christmas morning arrived, I was often awake at 4 A.M – ready to go. That was unacceptable. My parents compromised on a 6 A.M. wake-up for them. Of course, that didn't stop me from waking earlier; I just had to entertain myself after I did. Naturally, I woke up my sister, and she and I played cards by the clock, watching the hands endlessly circumnavigate the minutes until they aligned precisely at 6 A.M. Then we raced to awaken Mom and Dad.

When I was seven years old, and a firm believer in Santa Claus, I got my most memorable gift. I liked dolls, and I had already put one on my wish list for Santa, when, about three days before Christmas I decided I *had* to have a Mary Hartline doll. Mary Hartline was a real person, a circus majorette. She had become famous first as a radio, and then a television star. She was so popular that a doll was created in her likeness, and suddenly, this was the toy I wanted more than anything else.

Christmas morning arrived with loads of presents – but no Mary Hartline doll. I still remember my disappointment, but I didn't want to show it because Santa brought another doll and so many other things. Still...

We opened our gifts, and unloaded the stockings before we finally gave into hunger and breakfast. We'd had an early start. And then the doorbell rang. *Who would be coming by on Christmas morning,* we all wondered. "I'll get it," Dad called, and rose to answer it. Before we could imagine too much drama, he was back in the kitchen with a wrapped gift in his hands.

"Who was that?" Mom asked.

"That was one of Santa's elves. He was delivering something that Santa Claus forgot to leave for Patty Mac."

I couldn't believe my ears, nor my good fortune to be the one with the extra present. I was so excited I tore it open where I was standing, and when I lifted the lid, I was speechless to discover a Mary Hartline doll... I'm not sure any other gift in my life ever topped the thrill of that one, and the way she showed up. I kept her for decades. Dad loved making gifts a complete surprise and an extravagance. The very best of him came out at Christmas.

A Christmas Card for Dad from me. Inside, the card read:
Here's Dad on Christmas Day, it's tough
He gets the bills, We get the stuff.

I only spent a few months in our new home, but I have nice memories that Christmas – sitting around our first fireplace, the wood ablaze and warming the five of us as Dad talked about Calgary and what our new life would be like. I distinctly remember being lectured on how to behave when we arrived.

"We will be guests in their country, so we should never be critical or compare it to the U.S. in front of other people. Remember, we chose to go there, and if we don't like it, we can come home. The Canadians are going to remember that, too."

I figured I could do that. I really wasn't going to be living there, anyway; I'd be living with Janet Ruth and the Pickerings. I still didn't quite believe it at times, but Mom later told me that Janet Ruth had done a great job convincing Dad to let me stay with them. He liked her as much as I liked the Pickerings.

There were no conflicts that holiday, and soon Dad headed back to Calgary. Our life resumed in January and with it, a newly predictable and calm rhythm, which agreed with me. Every new thing I wanted to do or try wasn't met with Dad's worry-driven forecasts of disaster. Life with Mom was so reasonable. I liked going to her, telling her what I wanted to do, discussing it, and moving on. It seemed sane.

My birthday was in January, and I wanted to host a slumber party. I never wanted to have one with Dad around as I wasn't sure whether he'd have one of his outbursts. Now was my chance. Mom said yes, and I was able to host the second slumber party of my life. We didn't have a rec room, but we could use the living room to bed down. Mom could cheerfully deal with the all-night shenanigans, and my brother Chip promised not to streak the event as he had at my first slumber party when I was thirteen.

The third week in January (my birthday week) is often the coldest week of the year. Even in Oklahoma it can be cold, icy, and raw, so no one was interested in any going-out-for-a-Coke plans that night. We made a fire and sat around talking. Suddenly Pickering had an idea, "Hey, Sloan, let's get your mom to take a picture of us. We can borrow some of her cigarettes and pretend we're smoking. Think she'll do it?"

"Maybe. I can ask." And I did.

Since we really wouldn't be smoking, Mom agreed and handed out the cigarettes. By this time some of us were already in pajamas and had curled our hair in rollers for the night. I completed my look by caging those curlers in with a shower cap. After all this, I slept on that creation; it was a peculiar kind of torture. If you were in prison and someone made you do this, it would probably be considered abuse. Frankly, it was surprising that some of us agreed to a photo with this look. I guess the idea came about too quickly, with no time to question.

We gathered as if we were on risers, with some sitting on

the floor, others kneeling, and the last row standing, cigarettes dangling from our lips. Just before Mom took the picture, Janet Ruth suggested that we all flip the bird at her, and we obliged. Mom laughed between snapshots. When we saw the finished photo, we laughed even harder. At least two of the girls didn't know which finger to advance to officially "flip the bird." This snapshot became one of our most famous S.H.E. photos.

Some of us didn't even know which finger to advance to "Flip the Bird." Patty Mac is second from right, top row and Janet Ruth is the first one on the far left, middle row.

Meanwhile, at school I was enjoying following Mike's sports. The Wildcat football team, all white except for Don Watson who joined the team that year, had a fairly successful season with only two close losses until a famous game against Tulsa Rogers, the number-one ranked team in the state. It was one of two games left in the season, and as it progressed, Rogers was pummeling the Wildcats. With two minutes left in the game, and after Rogers had scored to make the game 40-0, the Wildcats had the ball on their own 35-yard line, fourth down with two yards to go. It looked grim. The team huddled and quarterback Bob Blaker called, "Punt formation!"

"What?!" halfback Bill Dutcher said. "We're not going to go for it?"

To which, Blaker replied, "Do you want to lose 47 to nothing?!"

The score stayed at 40-0 and was a record-setting defeat as the worst home loss ever. Five-thousand onlookers visually recorded this rout. Fortunately, the team's last game was a win.

By winter, football was history and a good basketball season was underway. As a sophomore, Eugene Edwards joined Larry Geary as the second African American on the team, but by Eugene's senior year he was the only Black member and one of the best players. One Examiner Enterprise newspaper sports story quoted, he could "wipe the boards clean" with his rebounding. The remainder of the players included Mike Hewitt, Bill Dutcher, Bob Blaker, LeRoy McDonald, and Stan Ogle. The basketball team's games packed the gymnasium. They had a respectable record early that winter, but as the season progressed, they continued to improve and came alive at the regional basketball tournament. After losing twice to Tulsa Edison in conference games, the Wildcats beat them in the regional finals, advancing to the State AA Basketball

Championship in Oklahoma City. Double-A included the largest schools in the state, so this was The Big One. Four teams would compete in this tournament.

Janet Ruth and I wanted to be a part of this event, but Oklahoma City was 150 miles away, and required a hotel stay. I had never done anything like this, and it would be an expense. But with my dad's absence, I only had to navigate my mother's concerns, and I was able to go.

The games were held in the Memorial Auditorium at Capitol High in Oklahoma City. When we entered the auditorium on game night, we were awestruck; it was a theater. Tiers of seats overlooked the stage, which was now set up as a basketball court for the event. Temporary, but sturdy baskets anchored the ends of the stage to create a court, but it never lost its theatrical feel. We were used to being spectators sitting only a few feet from the action.

Mike later told me that even the floor felt different that night. He felt he should be in a play rather than racing up and down a stage with a basketball.

The fans' energy filled the auditorium, and the noise, already making it difficult to hear, set the tone for the excitement to come. At 7:30 P.M., we took our seats and squirmed our way through the first game between number two seed, Norman High School, and number three seed, Shawnee High. Norman High won easily.

We were up next, seeded number four against state number one ranked Douglass High School, the all African American school in Oklahoma City, heavily favored to win. We knew we were lucky to be there, and we were aware that we were the lowest seed. Our hearts beat fast, our palms were sweaty, and we were nervous just thinking of our team and what they were going through. We knew them all, and hoped they could pull off a miracle.

Douglass took the lead in the first half, and Mike, who was later reported in the newspaper as "not locating the basket at all during the first half," finally got himself together in the second half. But others were playing well that night. Singly, Eugene Edwards rebounded over half the balls. Bill Dutcher, Stan Ogle, LeRoy McDonald, and Bob Blaker handled the remainder. Still, Douglass led the entire game. Then, during the final seconds, Mike sunk a 25- footer to go ahead by one point and then made two free throws with twelve seconds left in the game to clinch the win. Everyone was in shock. After playing so well in season, and so poorly that night, Mike says he was so relieved to have finally contributed. Later, when Bill Dutcher praised Eugene Edwards for his phenomenal rebounding that night, he said, "Eugene, I've never seen you jump that high before!"

To which Eugene responded, "I never needed to."

The finals were held the following night, Norman High versus College High. Perhaps it was the *let-down* after the *high*...or that Eugene fouled-out in the fourth quarter...or that Norman High was just a better team, because they won the championship. We were disappointed, but we were still ecstatic to have beaten the number one seed to make the finals. Water balloons rained from the hotel windows that night, and Janet Ruth and I returned to Bartlesville, proud to have witnessed the historic event.

Those Wildcat boys would relive the games well into their elderhood, guessing and second-guessing that with rule changes like three-point shots, and a shot timer to eliminate stalling, just who *could* have won that night. Again, sports seemed to provide the forum for boys' bonds of friendship, and I envied that. Our friendships came from our slumber parties and adventures, but they would never get us admission or scholarships to college.

I missed my dad that winter and spring. But I didn't miss our clashes, and I felt free and grown-up. He might have let me go to Oklahoma City for the basketball tournament, but it probably wouldn't have happened without a lot of drama. My mom had rules, but they were simple, logical, and reasonable; they made sense. The real miracle of that spring was Dad's approval of my living with Janet Ruth's family for my senior year. He had said yes and was standing by his word.

Home Coming and Coming Home

Making a home is like building a nest – you squirrel around, fluff up some stuff, and create a spot to make a home. If one place doesn't suit you, you find another. The summer before my senior year, I found myself living in Calgary, Alberta in my first two-story home, the kind Ruth Pickering liked, where "nice people went upstairs to bed." I liked that too. A bedroom on the second floor felt private and removed from the comings and goings downstairs.

Pam's and my shared iron bed went with us, but our room was larger than any previous one, with windows high enough for privacy, yet accessible enough to watch the sweet peas climb the backyard wall that separated us from the elevated yard, and the home of the Schulz family next door. From our dining room window, directly below us, we could all stand and chant the family mantra, "Just look at those sweet peas!" The northern light lingered on those summer days and with never a blistering heat, those sweet peas grew and bloomed as we had never seen, blanketing the retaining wall that held back the Schulz's property next door.

We lived on Stanley Drive near the Elbow River. Our baby blue house sat on the slope of the street and lot, giving us three stories at the back but only two visible from street side. The neighborhood, like others in Calgary, was full of houses painted in nursery colors similar to ours. Had we lived in Quonset huts, we might have looked like a carton of Easter eggs. Calgary winters were long and colorless, so before the flowers came out, we all had colorful houses to cheer us in anticipation of spring.

That summer, I had my first real job in the men's department at Eaton's Department Store: folding, stacking, unstacking, and trying to sell merchandise. One of our featured items was a pricey waterproof woolen sweater made by a Canadian Indian tribe. That it was water-resistant, was intriguing to me, so I tried to intrigue customers into buying it. One day a gentleman with a British accent did take an interest,

"Please...tell me more about this waterproofing. It just looks like a heavy wool sweater to me."

"Well ..." I explained, "It seems this particular wool has some persistent oils left in the yarn which have the effect of repelling water. I don't think this is going to work in a downpour, but it is supposed to hold up well in a drizzle."

"That should work well for me, as I do live where it drizzles. Is it dear?" But my ears heard "deer."

"Oh no, sir – it's 100 percent wool!" And then he began to laugh. His laughter prompted my elementary French to kick in and remind me that the literal translation of *tres cher*, "expensive," means "very dear." Laughter covered my embarrassment, and he bought the sweater. It was the most entertaining day of my retail career.

Meanwhile, letters began to arrive from Mike. Soon after his high school graduation, he began his summer odyssey working on the Mississippi River. Though he had no experience, he was hired by Phillips as the lowliest deckhand on board a barge and tow boat, hauling specialty petroleum products up and down the Mississippi River. He was paid $15 per day.

His commitment was for three months with no days off, working two shifts: 6 A.M. to noon, and 6 P.M. to midnight. Sleep took six hours, which left six hours in the afternoon with nothing to do. His only reading material was a copy of *The New Testament*, which his mother had given him when he left. He'd been sure they'd have a television to watch on his off hours, but once aboard, he learned that televisions were banned, because they interfered with the boat's radar. And though he shared a room with another college student, they worked and slept on opposite schedules so they literally "passed in the night," with no shared time to get to know one another. The only things he found to pass the time, besides work of course, were writing letters and reading the only book available to him.

The crew worked hard, and Mike tried to, but for these men, this was their life. There was no leisure time, and the job demanded physical skill, on-site problem solving, and courage. It made them tough. Mike wasn't that kind of tough.

He vividly recalled an episode with a galvanized bucket. The container was particularly valuable because it was zinc-coated and wouldn't corrode. Over and over, Mike heard the admonition, "Don't let anything happen to this bucket. It's the *only* one we have."

And then his next letter arrived:

It's very lonely here, and I'm pretty much looked down on. I guess I deserve it, because I'm a greenhorn when it comes to tools and fixing things. My dad wasn't a handyman, and I didn't learn anywhere else. The very first day they asked me to get a crescent wrench, and I didn't know what it was – and my job is basically to help get what anyone needs or wants. That was a terrible start. I also clean up bedrooms, change beds, and wash down the decks of the barges, particularly after there has been a spill which happens pretty often.

We have one galvanized bucket with a metal handle. It's pretty big, and when we need water, we just dip it in the Mississippi off the side of the barge. When I clean up spills, I first use soap on the area to scrub it; then I dip the bucket into the river to fill it with water, and then rinse off the spill throwing the water out towards the side. Usually it takes four or five times to get it clean. Every time I throw the water out towards the side, I tell myself, "Don't let go of the bucket, don't let go of the bucket." Then I must have forgotten that part – and I let go of the bucket. It shot right off the side.

The current was moving in the same direction as the barge, but not as fast so the bucket bobbed backward, and it had hit the water upside down so it was bottom-up as it was moved along. I started running – and reaching – and it wouldn't come near. I was never so panicked in my life. I had just about given up when a river current changed and moved the bucket just close enough to be within my reach, and I got it! I'm not sure if anyone saw all of this, but at least I didn't have to report an overboard bucket.

Letters and work were not enough to fill his time, so with nothing else to read, Mike started reading *The New Testament,* right at the beginning. His letters relayed what beautiful words he found there and how much it was helping him cope with his confinement and loneliness. He kept reading. And he kept writing.

The regulars on board had a slightly different schedule and worked 30 days on and then 30 off. Crew transfers were made at ports-of-calls where the provision boats brought food and supplies and removed trash. Mike watched this coming and going every two weeks. After six weeks of this life with six more to go, the barge arrived in St. Louis for provisioning and a crew change. When Mike saw the provisions boat heading their way, he knew he was going to be on it heading back: his break for freedom.

The captain didn't argue. There were no farewells, and Mike was going home. There was a train from St. Louis to Kansas City, then one to Bartlesville. He briefly thought of spending the night in St. Louis to see the Cardinals play; they were his team. But when he hit shore, he kept right on going to the train station.

That summer and those letters and his honesty, his weaknesses and sensitivity, only made me love him more. Despite his accomplishments in some areas, he was a very *human* being. I was happy to know I could go back and be near him.

Meanwhile, I was having the summer of my life, and I felt a little guilty. I saw the Canadian Rockies for the first time, witnessed my first rodeo – the Calgary Stampede – and loved the Canadian people. All this inspired Janet Ruth and I to concoct a plan for her to visit Calgary. My family and I were taking a driving vacation to Minnesota to visit one of my mom's sisters and her family, so we thought Janet Ruth could fly to Minneapolis and meet us. And because our family car would only hold five people, the two of us could board an overnight train to Calgary for the return while the rest of my family would make their way home in the car. After a two-week stay in Calgary, Janet Ruth and I would fly back to Oklahoma to begin our senior year. Our families liked the idea and agreed to the plan.

We were excited about the train trip: meals in the dining car with white tablecloths and silver served by our own personal waiter, watching out the window for Canadian Mounties and Indians riding along the way, and views of majestic mountains in the distance.

We must have cut class during Canadian geography.

In Minneapolis, we picked up Janet Ruth at the airport and headed directly to the train station for our overnight ride. With screeching train wheels, steam whirling like dry ice from a witch's cauldron, fresh and stale food smells assaulting our appetites, and passengers, conductors and engineers scurrying around like cockroaches with the lights suddenly turned on, the scene provided a lot more drama than the airport.

Then the call came, "All aboard!" We hurried to our car. We were on a budget so there was no Pullman car for us. We'd be sleeping in our seats, and we went aboard and found two.

209

"Good evening, young ladies," said the conductor knowing that we'd be sitting up all night. "How about a pillow for 35 cents?" We hadn't figured on paying for pillows, and since we were each carrying a raincoat, we decided we'd save our money for dinner and tuck in with our coats.

We sat down, imagining dinner in the dining car, just like in the movies. But then we discovered a further wrinkle in our economy seating. Since we didn't have reserved seats, it was squatters' rights in that car. If we left, someone could take our seats. We were prisoners.

We rationalized that the dining car was probably too expensive anyway; we'd just eat in our seats. The next time the conductor came by we asked him what we could get.

"Bananas," he said.

"Bananas?"

"Yes, Miss. Bananas. The rest of the food is offered in the dining car."

Oh, shit! I thought. We liked bananas, sort of ...

"Oh, O.K.," Janet Ruth responded. "We'll take two." That barely filled us up, but we were tired, and the movement of the train was beginning to rock us sleepy. So, with darkness and half-full stomachs, we settled in, our faces jammed against our raincoat pillows. We fell asleep thinking of the fantastic sights we'd see in the morning.

The sun woke us early and when we saw each other's button-marked cheeks, we broke out laughing. Then, the scenery registered. There was nothing but plains to see as far as we looked. We might have been traveling across Oklahoma. The transcontinental highway paralleled the train tracks to the north unless it swapped sides and ran south of us. We saw plenty of silos, but no Mounties, mountains, or Natives.

Our sweet conductor showed up, offering us more bananas, and registering the reality of a twenty-four hour banana diet.

"Sure, we'll take four." We were starving, and they seemed our only option.

There was no such thing as "take-out." It was either eat in the dining car or bananas. Worse was the boredom we were facing. We made bets to see if the Sloan family station wagon would appear, rolling along the highway.

Until then, we had not talked with anyone but the conductor. I'm sure my dad warned us of speaking with strangers, but we had to find some entertainment. So, inspired by our high school foreign exchange student, Janet Ruth took on the role of "Yan" from "Feenland." And she never gave it up. I don't know where she came up with her stories, but we began meeting and chatting with all our neighbors who were clearly enchanted with this charming girl from "Feenland." They probably caught on, but were as bored as we were, welcoming the whole scheme as theater. It worked. We laughed and talked and ate bananas all the way to Calgary.

My family's neighbors in Calgary, Herb and Rosemarie Schulz, met us at the train station as the rest of my family hadn't completed the journey. We had traveled through the night, but they needed to stop and sleep, arriving a day later.

Whenever my family had houseguests to ferry around to local sights, we refer to the adventures as "Vista Tours." Janet Ruth's "Vista Tours" included touring the rodeo grounds of the Calgary Stampede and renting inner tubes to "tube" down the Bow and Elbow Rivers. The highlight, though, was the trip Dad planned to Banff, a mountain village in the heart of the Canadian Rockies.

We all rode together through the spectacular mountain passes we thought we would see on the train. Dad surprised us by taking us to the Banff Springs Hotel, one of the grand Canadian Pacific Railway hotels built across Canada when the rails were laid in the 1880s. It looked like a castle, with stone turrets, grand ballrooms, formal lobby and dining areas, and mysterious hallways and stairwells to catacombs below. They definitely interested us, but not as much as the pool did.

Janet Ruth hadn't quite gotten over her success with "Yan," so she brought her out for our hotel stay. She was still carrying on when we went to the pool, and I was getting a little tired of this charade. So, when, to my surprise, I met a boy who said he *was* from "Feenland," I saw the chance to *out* her, and told him about my Finnish friend, Yan. He was cute, so Janet Ruth was eager to meet him – only to be stopped short when he declared he was from Finland. At which point, she yelled "See ya!" and dove into the pool. I fell over laughing, and Yan was gone for the rest of the trip.

That weekend, we rode the gondola to the top of Sulphur Mountain for the panoramic view, saw Mounties on horseback, and even espied some Canadian Indians before we returned to Calgary. Two weeks went by quickly, playing, and then packing me up for a year away. After our low-budget ride to get there, we now looked forward to the antiseptic airport departure on Braniff Airways and Sky Chef meals. We wore our best dresses for the flight; I even wore a Frisbee-style pill box hat to complete the outfit. It seemed flying and church required the same clothes.

The Pickerings met us in Tulsa, and drove us to Denver Road in Bartlesville, my new home for the school year. There, for the first time, in my shared room, I had my own bed, a twin, which I dutifully made every day. It was upstairs, along with the rest of the nice people in the family.

Maybe the hat was supposed to help us in take-off...

A gondola ride in the Rockies.

Settling in

"Sloan, you take the bed by the door. Mine's by the window - the better to see old Sherman Mueller when he undresses at night," said Janet Ruth as she nodded towards his house next door. His bedroom was on the second floor, opposite ours, across a driveway.

"What! You're peeking at him through the window?"

"Well, yup – sort of. You only see him from half-way up in his undershirt, but it's kinda funny."

"Ya know, Janet Ruth, windows are two-ways, and he might just be peeping at you, too!"

"Ooh..." she said. "I never thought of that." So over the year, we had a few peeps at him, and most probably, he at us, when we forgot to lower the shade.

Janet Ruth shared part of her closet and a few of her drawers, and we began our lives as sisters. Her real sister, Sherry, who was 8 years younger, had been living in that room, and I was now sleeping in her bed. She moved to the sewing room, a euphemism for a room only slightly larger than a closet. I never heard Sherry complain about getting the boot, and she was fun to have around, but I have to wonder if she didn't protest. I do think she took a lot of notes about the stuff we did. She could probably write her own book – or blackmail us.

In many ways the relationship between Janet Ruth and me mirrored Mike's and mine in that we were not always together. We were in different clubs and activities, took separate classes and studied independently.

Janet Ruth recalls, "You took all the hard classes, and I took the easy ones. You were preparing for life, and all I cared about was art."

I think a better description might be, she took what she loved, and I took what I thought I should.

Home, where nice people go upstairs to bed.

By the time we arrived for school, football season was underway. The players began training before school started with brutal "two-a-days." I never witnessed one of these practices, but they were legendary endurance workouts held twice a day in the Oklahoma end-of-summer heat. And what was really horrific was that drinking water was discouraged and seen as a sign of weakness.

In fact, guys were labeled "sissies" if they drank much. My friend Bob Rumsford once got so thirsty he sucked up the sweat from his jersey. I guess this treatment toughened the guys up, but I'm surprised there wasn't an epidemic of heat stroke. It didn't seem to deter boys from wanting to play, though; football was *the* sport to play.

Besides football players, cheerleaders, and the pepper squad, there was one other member of the football scene: "Willie Wildcat," the team mascot. His job was to rally the Pepper squad and get fans to scream, yell and cheer on the team during games.

Historically, the role had been given to a senior boy who put on a papier-mache wildcat headpiece and a tawny-colored jumpsuit, complete with tail, for all the football games. At the end of the season, that boy handed down the costume to a willing guy in the class behind him.

During our junior year, Pat Petersen was Willie Wildcat, and at the end of the season, instead of asking some junior guy if he wanted the job, he approached Janet Ruth. This was unheard of, but things were changing.

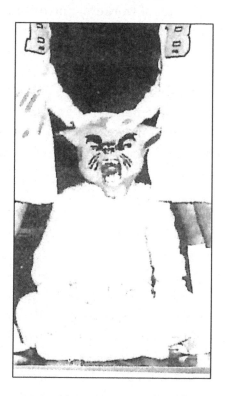

Janet Ruth as Willie Wildcat.

217

Janet Ruth didn't waste a minute before saying yes. She was at home with a job description that included showing off, inciting the crowd and annoying the band. I was no longer a cheerleader, but now a beanie- wearing Pepper. Frankly, I didn't think that was nearly as much fun as what Janet Ruth would be doing.

Homecoming was the highlight of the football season, and soon plans for class floats were in the works. Our senior class design team came up with a four-footed wildcat, made of chicken wire and black crepe paper, about ten times life-size. The woodworking guys at school built the frame-and-chicken-wire-form a few weeks early, but we didn't fill in the crepe paper until right before homecoming weekend. Because it was time-consuming to weave the paper in and out of all that chicken wire, it took a lot of workers, and all the time, we were worried about rain-storms which could destroy our work in minutes. Luckily, fall was not the rainy season.

As a senior girl, I felt a heightened interest in the nominations for the Homecoming Queen, to be chosen from the senior class. I cannot honestly remember if I thought I had a chance to be a candidate. I was a normal seventeen-year old awed by such events, and I did have a lot of friends on the football team which chose the three nominees. From those three, the student body elected the winner.

It was possible to be nominated. But did I see myself as "queenly?" No, not really, although, when I was five and at a May Day festival, my name and that of a six-year old boy were drawn out of a hat to serve as King and Queen of that May Day celebration. We sat on cardboard thrones made from old Sears washing machine boxes, and I loved that throne.

The highlight of the fete was a dance around the Maypole, braiding it with colored streamers. Everyone was asked to join in the dance, but I wouldn't budge from that throne. Finally, someone's mother came over to personally invite me (she probably thought I was shy). Not a chance. I was certain that if I vacated that throne, some other little girl would take it over. I guess I did like being a queen.

Homecoming Queen nominations were to be announced on a particular day, but there was no news when that day arrived. There were just some rumblings that something was amiss. It piqued our curiosity, but before we could wonder very long, the candidates were presented: Everett, Marks and Sloan (me): three close friends, all members of S.H.E.

It felt odd to be competing against my *sisters*, and my other friends felt awkward supporting one or the other. No one was outwardly saying to any of us, "Gee, I hope you win."

That would backlash. We really had no experience with competing against a friend unless it was in the classroom. And that we did. But it was private, quiet, and the results were largely unknown. I found the situation very uncomfortable, and I think my friends did as well.

The school vote was taken soon after the nominations were announced, and when the count was in, I was elected. Of course, I was thrilled, but because my two friends hadn't won, the honor came with mixed emotions. I felt it, and so did my friends. Once again, no one could be too excited for me without hurting someone's feelings. On top of that, I was disappointed not to be able to share the excitement with my family or Mike. Half the fun of having something special happen is sharing that good news, and I didn't really feel I could.

Those feelings turned out to be short-lived. When the Pickerings heard, they whooped it up, and I began to get excited. I called my parents, and they promised to send money to buy a homecoming dress. That alone was a big deal.

And then the following day the doorbell rang, and when I answered, a floral delivery man presented me with two arrangements from Mike. He'd heard the news at college and sent flowers - one bouquet to me and one to Janet Ruth, celebrating Willie Wildcat and Homecoming Queen. Suddenly, this was fun.

Homecoming day began with a late afternoon parade through the downtown streets of Bartlesville. Highly polished convertibles of all makes and models appeared, on loan from local families and car dealerships, to ferry the Homecoming Queen and her court as well as the Yearbook King and Queen, Key Club Sweetheart, Trade and Industry Sweetheart, Band Queen, and sophomore, and junior attendants and their dates. There was a lot of royalty that day.

Smaller floats on pick-ups celebrated high school clubs, and bands played between the parade entries. But the parade favorites were the class floats, designed to inspire a win.

Our black wildcat float, reminiscent of our mascot Willie, turned out to be an angry cat, ready for the kill. Good luck if anyone thought Janet Ruth was going to scare any team into losing, but she might make them laugh and lose their concentration.

Our senior Wildcat float ablaze at Homecoming.
Photo Permission: Craig's Photography, Bartlesville, Oklahoma

The final parade loop ended at Custer Stadium. Hundreds of football fans filled the bleachers and stands, except for a roped-off area in the bleachers for the honorees. Unbeknownst to me, Mike had raced from his Friday engineering lab to his car to make the 180- mile drive from Norman, Oklahoma to Bartlesville that night. Cutting it to the minute, he parked, headed for the closest gate, but found it locked.

The final part of the parade was taking place around the track encircling the football field, so he stopped and watched through the mesh of the chain-link fencing. As my car circled past him, I heard my name called from outside the gate.

Even through the noise of the crowd, I recognized Mike's voice, and I saw him smiling and waving. I was so surprised, and smiled and waved a vigorous thank you. I never imagined he would come to the game and see my night of juvenile glory; once again, I realized how special he was.

The Homecoming ceremony with co-captains Bob Woody and Harry Brookby, and my escort Bill Owen. Photo Permission: Craig's Photography, Bartlesville, Oklahoma

I don't remember learning what was "amiss" about the nominations at the time, but I did learn about it later. Apparently, when the first vote was taken, one of the Black girls was selected to be one of the three nominees.

Coach saw this nomination as an insincere act and refused to accept it. He demanded a re-vote, which was presented a day later. I do not know whose name replaced hers.

It is uncomfortable to think about the behind- the-scenes reality of that event. It was racism, for sure, though we had no name or understanding of what was really happening. Given the era, it was likely a challenge to the changing times, though I cannot answer for those who participated. Nearly one hundred years had passed since the Civil War, but Whites and Blacks were still a long way from being treated equally.

The Yo-Yo Girls

Located just two minutes from Janet Ruth's house, the high school became a magnet for some of our brief adventures, especially after school when we were bored. Late one afternoon when we were walking around outside the gymnasium, we discovered a basement window that was ajar. The glass was intact, but the latch was broken.

"Hey, Sloan," Pickering said, "maybe – with a little push – this thing might just open all the way."

"Really?" I said. "And then what?"

"And then what? We're goin' in!" And she pushed the window open, slid through the sluice, and dropped to the floor. I couldn't say a word; I could only follow her. So I squeezed through the window and dropped to the floor just behind her.

"We're in!" we exclaimed. "Yahoo!" *Now, what are we going to do?* There was no plan. There never was. Adventures naturally led from one thing to another. So, we went exploring.

Just outside the room we'd dropped in to, we found a flight of stairs leading up to the gymnasium and stage. This was familiar territory, site of basketball games and student assemblies. When the stage wasn't in use, students could use the trampoline stored there, as long as they followed certain safety rules. Usually lots of kids were hanging around, so you were lucky if you got one turn. We never felt we got to jump enough. Now, when we saw the trampoline just sitting there, we began to think of endless possibilities.

"Hey, this could be fun," I said.

"No kidding."

We hustled up the stairs onto the stage and climbed one at a time onto the trampoline. At first, we took turns bouncing and spotting for one another as we had been taught. But we became bored with that routine and decided double-jumping would be a lot more fun. We both piled on and jumped until we'd had our fill.

And then, always the worrier, I whispered, "I think I hear something!" We paused and heard nothing more, but we decided we'd stayed long enough, so we jumped off and headed back the way we'd come. We found the little room and its window with the broken latch, found a piece of furniture to stand on to reach the window, and one by one climbed out. Then, carefully and gently, we pulled the window closed, making sure it didn't re-lock, so we could re-enter another day.

Though the school day had ended, football practices continued until early evening with Assistant Coach Sid Burton directing workouts on the playing field behind Custer Stadium. The stadium stood between the field and the gym house, but Coach Burton still had a view of the upper windows of the gymnasium building. As it was late in the day, the sun was falling lower in the sky, producing glare, so when Coach Burton glanced towards the gymnasium windows and caught glimpses of a couple of flashes, he chalked it up to the fading light and went back to his scrimmages.

We repeated our break-in and trampoline workout on two other occasions, once with our friend, Gerry Driver. That day Coach Burton again saw a couple of flickers in the high windows but disregarded them. But not the third time; a cloudy day with no glare couldn't play tricks on his eyes.

There were only the two of us merrily bouncing when we began to get a bit edgy. We kept hearing noises, prompting us to leap from the trampoline, jump off the stage and find some place to hide nearby. After a respectable wait when nothing happened, we'd re-appear and resume jumping. But when we heard noises for the third time, Janet Ruth bolted for a storage closet, but I was getting cocky. We'd done this so many times, and they were always a false alarm, so, I took my time, got down from the trampoline and walked to the edge of the stage to re-claim my sneakers. As I bent to collect my shoes, a man appeared before me, and the shock sent my arms and sneakers straight to the ceiling. When I came to, I realized it was Coach Burton.

"Uh, oh," I confessed, "We're not supposed to be in here, right?"

"Right." he said. I wasn't sure where this was going, but he seemed really serious, and I knew I had been caught, and I had no intention of being the only culprit. With no hesitation, I ratted out my buddy Janet Ruth, yelling for her. She didn't answer right away. I guess she wasn't convinced she'd be caught. But when Coach Burton called, she reluctantly came out of hiding.

The coach was a young teacher, but as such he still commanded the same respect and deference from us as from one much older. He played the role well. In his most officious tone, he said, "You girls know better than to be breaking into the school. What's going on here?"

"*Well...*" Janet Ruth began, "we were just walking around the school when we went by the gymnasium and saw this broken window and got the idea to come in and look around. And then the trampoline was just sitting here and no one was here so we decided to have some fun jumping. Really, that's all we did."

"Have you done this more than once?" he asked. We figured he already knew the answer, so we confessed to the other trips.

"We're really sorry, honest. We didn't mean to cause any trouble," I said.

Coach Burton was popular with all the kids so regaining courage, Janet Ruth continued, "By the way, howja know we were in here?"

"Well," he said, "I was out on the football field holding scrimmages, and one day when I looked back towards the gym, I noticed some flashes in the high windows above the stage. At first I thought it was from the setting sun and light. Then one day it was cloudy, and I could see that those flashes were a couple of heads popping into the window frame on each bounce, and then disappearing. It looked like a yo-yo. I figured it was a couple of kids on the trampoline."

We all laughed, and we both apologized, but once again, the regret had more to do with being caught than the act itself. After all, the window was already broken, and we were just having some fun.

But he made his point, and we promised to "never do this again." And from that day to the day we graduated, whenever we saw Coach Burton he would quietly give us a knowing look and then carefully and slowly bob his head up and down, up and down. He knew. And he knew that we knew. So, we kept our promise. Sort of.

It was our twentieth high school reunion, and though we were no longer kids, we had a lot of clear memories of our time at College High. But much had changed since our departure. The population of the town increased enough to need a second high school, called Sooner High. Then, after a few more years, the town decided to reunite the schools under the name of Bartlesville High School. The teams would be called the Bruins, and we learned that all the memorabilia from College High, now stored in the gymnasium basement, was to be thrown out. We were horrified.

"Well, I wonder whose idea that was?" I said. "They could have made a lot of money auctioning off those old trophies and sweatshirts to people like us, instead of just throwing them away."

Janet Ruth began to wonder. "Do you suppose that window is still broken? We just might be able to get in and save them some trouble from tossing all that stuff," she said.

"Janet Ruth, are you kidding? When you're eighteen, this might be funny, but when you're thirty-eight they call it breaking and entering!" I said. My admonition went nowhere. The Pied Piper was at it again, and she had a cadre of abettors on board to try the window with her. I could only imagine the headlines in the newspaper announcing our arrests. But I hung around. I had to see this in person.

Janet Ruth led the way to the window, and in no time, the almost-broken window was open, and three of the courageous S.H.E.s were down the chute and into the bowels of the t-shirt and sweatshirt storage bins. Nervous minutes went by as we awaited their return, but soon they came back, laden with arms of booty emblazoned with College High's name and logo.

The rest of us immediately regretted not taking the plunge. Spoils in hand, we drove to Smith's house where the culprits shared their haul. We donned the shirts, and, in Virginia's front yard, created a pyramid of girls, climbing on one another's backs – at least for one level. Just as we were trying to complete this feat, Principal Bailey drove by. Someone recognized him and his car. It was unbelievable.

Oh my God. I thought. *We are going to be busted again.* But no, only a great friendly wave came from our old principal. Our caper had succeeded. Once again, Janet Ruth had led her "band of merry little women down the rabbit hole."

I was able to find Coach Burton in 2015, and asked him if he had any memories of our trampoline prank at the high school so many years ago.

"Oh yes," he replied, "It was a funny look from out there."

The Foxes in Charge of the Henhouse

Up until now Janet Ruth's and my rap sheet might read something like this: vandalizing tractor (her crime), causing a racial disorder (my crime), breaking into church camp sacristy to taste wine (our crimes), aiding and abetting illegal climbing and painting of water tower (our crimes), graffiti painting of public streets (our crimes), smoking on school property (my crime), trying to sneak into movie drive-in without paying (our crimes), breaking into high school to jump on trampoline (our crimes), and theft of three root beer mugs and tray (her crime). Further misdemeanors might include egging neighbors' houses and mail chutes at Halloween, and the minnow bucket episode one Friday night.

Jan Everett and Virginia Smith ended up being our usual drivers all through high school; Everett always used the big Buick, but Smith drove her dad's pick-up truck. If there were more than three of us going when she had the truck, some sat in the truck-bed unless it rained or was cold.

On one such night when we were out cruising with the truck and a bed full of girls, we stopped at a light and a convertible filled with four guys pulled alongside. Immediately, they began heckling us. We didn't think it was funny, but we were stuck at the light so we couldn't speed away – yet.

But then, two of us sitting in the truck bed caught sight of Mr. Smith's minnow bucket sloshing with leftover pond water and dead bait. Without thinking, I got up, picked up the bucket, and dumped it over the side of the truck onto the heads of the boys, and all over the inside of their car.

They went nuts, but we were saved by the green light, which we raced through while they scrambled in their seats.

228

They never caught us. Later, when we realized our good luck in getting away, we chalked that up to another one-time adventure.

Our Halloween pranks were pretty mild, and not really creative. Lots of kids egged houses or slid the egg slime through the mail chute. We only did that a couple of times. I think it hit too close to home after having to clean-up at our own houses when someone egged us.

Once we stole a horse. Actually, "borrow" is a better verb. Mr. Mule had a small farm and paddock behind the high school, and the area beyond was woods and wetlands, leading to the meandering Caney River. It was a great place for a little horseback ride, though neither Janet Ruth nor I had had any training. You might recall I formally met Janet Ruth when she was recovering from a broken wrist suffered during a ride. Now recovered, she was ready to try again. I liked horses, wasn't afraid of them, and I had ridden a few times when I had the opportunity. Mr. Mule, better known as "Old Man Mule" rented out his horses for rides, but once again we had no money for such extravagances. We thought we'd just borrow a horse for quick ride.

We waited until we were sure he had gone out, then got a horse that looked calm, and we took turns riding him through the woods. It wasn't as much fun as having two horses, and it was a little nerve wracking waiting your turn, hoping Mr. Mule wouldn't show up while you were on guard-duty. We *almost* pulled it off. We got the horse back to its stall, but we think Mr. Mule must have gotten a glimpse of us running off.

We didn't actually figure that out the day of the ride. About two days later, I was out with the whole Pickering family and when we returned home, we found a handwritten note taped to the front door of their house. There was some reference to our having ridden one of his horses, but that came after the first part of the note which read:

"I raped at your door several times with no response." And

229

then the part about how we took his horse followed, but no one could read it because we were laughing so hard from visualizing him raping the front door. We dodged another bullet, and gave up horseback riding.

During our pranking years, the town of Bartlesville passed a city ordinance creating a Youth Court for teenage traffic-offenders. Provided there were no physical or property injuries, youthful offenders could opt to come before a court of their peers. The Youth Court judges would then hear and rule on the cases and appropriate subsequent punishment, such as theme writing or attending traffic safety classes held by highway patrol officers or the local police.

Students could choose to stand before the Municipal Court and pay monetary fines; punishment in Youth Court was more personal pain and annoyance for the teenager, but you didn't pay any money.

Court was held twice a month, and the number of cases heard varied between five and fifteen. The judges could assign the length of a theme, but the final papers were sent to English faculty at the high school to review. I'm not sure the kids liked these options, but the parents did. It was definitely cheaper, and according to an article entitled "'Braking' Traffic Violations" in the November 15, 1961 edition of *Scholastic Teacher*, the program reduced teenage traffic offenses five to ten percent during its two-year existence.

Youth court officials were elected by the high school students during fall student body elections, and I was stunned to be elected one of three judges. We heard cases, decided innocence or guilt and imposed fines. Janet Ruth was elected bailiff who kept order in the court as commanded by the judge and could make an arrest (at least in municipal court). Somehow, our past had not caught up with us or, maybe we were thought to be pushovers. Somehow, we were now part of the law. *Amazing.*

Jan LeFevre and Johnnie Draper were the other two

elected judges during the term I served. Oddly, the attorney for the prosecution was David E. Kiley, and for the defense attorney was David C. Kiley. (This is starting to sound more like a TV show, but it's the truth). Connie Alan was the clerk, administering oaths and keeping court records. Positions were held for six months, then rotated or moved out, when new students took over.

"Next case, please." I wonder what that guy did?
From left to right, Judge Jan, Judge Johnnie
and Judge Patty Mac.
Credit: © USA Today Network

One memorable case involved a boy charged with speeding through a school zone. His clever defense attorney was able to prove that the offense occurred on a Saturday, which was not, in fact, a school day and therefore, the defendant was not guilty. The judges concurred.

Judge LeFevre had a pretty clean record with respect to scrapes with the law, but later she admitted to me that she participated in repeated beer cannings during those years. She and her friends made night-time trips to the alleys behind the 3.2 beer stores to collect the beer can trash, which they artfully stacked as a pyramid on someone's porch or front steps. She cleaned up her act when she was elected to the court.

LeFevre provided some interesting quotes from two news articles. She recalled the trickiness of dealing with close friends in the court. That was soon resolved when she quoted, "We have established standard sentences for various offenses. In this way, we avoid partiality." That was easy. But she went on to say, "The one thing we all think about is the day *we* might get a ticket."

Luckily, we didn't. One other local newspaper article quoted a judgment I made during a session: "The court suspends your driver's license for two weeks. If you do not turn it over voluntarily to this court, then your case will be referred to municipal court for proper action. They might take it away for two or three months."

Apparently, this was the most drastic action the court had ever taken since its inception in 1960. I wasn't re-elected. My children and grandchildren had a lot of laughs when they heard this story. They think that I came into my own early on, and my classmates never realized they were voting for "The Hammer."

Pontiac Guy

It was springtime of our senior year, and we were walking from downtown back to Janet Ruth's house. Everywhere we went, the greens of spring were breaking through the straw mat that was left when winter killed the lawns. And that reminded us of Harold Beach. Harold was a funeral director, and a part of everyone's life, even if you never signed on. If your picture ended up in the paper, you'd likely receive a laminated copy from Harold, compliments of Harold and his funeral home. And he kind of seemed like Harvey, the invisible rabbit – he turned up everywhere, and he knew everyone.

We thought of him when the grass turned green because the grass in front of his funeral home was *always* green. Or had been for the last few years. Maybe because winter in Oklahoma can become colorless with no leaves, flowers, or lawns to mow, and little or no snow to turn things into a wonderland, Harold decided to spray-paint his front yard green.

And it wasn't shades of green; It was one solid bright green, Irish green, or Kelly green, my mom might say. It was hilarious. I guess he couldn't stop trying to make dead things look good.

That morning we headed on down Johnstone towards Dewey. As long as we were enjoying spring, we decided to detour by Mr. Bryce's house to check out his iris, something I'd been doing since I was little. His garden, once a tennis court, now blossomed with flowers all year, but they were particularly stellar during iris season. Their unique aroma, stately carriage and dramatic purple, yellow and white created a sight and smell worthy of a detour. Once we passed his house on Dewey, we headed back to Cherokee, towards Pickerings' house on Denver Road.

We weren't in any hurry, just talking and walking and enjoying the day, when a guy in a Pontiac slowed to our curbside. It was a busy street so we were not used to cars stopping, but when we saw the car pull over just ahead of us, we thought he might need something, so we stopped.

Since it was a warm day, the passenger side window was already rolled down, and the man leaned into it to begin asking for directions. We were happy to oblige. Pickering ran to his car, popped her head through the window and quickly froze her eyes to his, as she had briefly glimpsed his completely exposed *paraphernalia.*

Assuming he was unaware and not wanting to embarrass him, she continued with the directions he supposedly needed, careful to appear unphased. I stood behind her on a slight hill, so from my angle, I had a bird's eye view of his equipment, and no need to look him in the face. I was frozen in disbelief.

Something told me this was no accident, but it was a first, so who knew? He could have been in a hurry getting dressed that morning, with no one around to give him the X-Y-Z (eXamine – Your – Zipper) code. And Pickering didn't quit. She finished with the directions and backed away from the window as he took off. We barely held our laughter until he was out-of- hearing.

"Did you see his weenie?" asked Pickering.

"Of course, you idiot! How come you kept giving him directions?" I said.

"You think he knew?" she asked.

"Yeah...well...maybe?" I wondered aloud. We were only a few blocks from Janet Ruth's house when this happened, so we were still laughing and joking as we walked through the door.

Mama Ruth couldn't help but hear us and wanted in on the fun. For a second, we debated if we should tell her, but it was just too funny not to share, so we recounted meeting Pontiac guy, coloring the story with our guess he had been clueless about his exposure.

Well, Mama Ruth wasn't clueless. She wanted to call the police!

"What?! Come on, Mom—don't call the police," said Janet Ruth. Even though we were eighteen, Mama Ruth told us everything that could have happened, that guys like that are perverts, and that we needed to be careful about approaching an unknown guy in a secluded place. And on and on. So, she won, and she called the police.

Old Officer Cronin showed up, and after telling us how lucky we were, he went through his drill, asking for descriptions: of the guy, of his car, his license plate, and the direction he took when he drove away. Fortunately, he didn't ask about the offending weenie. Janet Ruth later confessed she could have described that better than his face.

Prom Night

Proms, like other larger-than-life occasions, don't measure up to one's fantasies. Instead they involve a lot of drama – like not getting invited, getting invited by the wrong guy, having Pepsi spill down the front of your dress ten minutes before your date is picking you up, having a miserable time, or – perhaps – having the time of your life.

When one of my daughters was a ninth grader, a senior boy invited her to a prom. I thought she was too young to go and wouldn't let her attend, arguing that she had many years ahead of her. But she and her sister ended up at a high school that didn't host proms, so neither ever went to one. I still hear about that.

And when I was a high school junior, I was no different than any other American teenage girl; I eagerly looked forward to the prom. It was called the "Junior/Senior Prom," and though both grades could attend, it was tradition for the junior class to be in charge of the theme and decorations. I helped that committee some, but I was mostly focused on going with my senior date, Mike Hewitt. Janet Ruth went with her good friend Doug Pennie.

The prom was held in the school gymnasium, on the basketball court. Each year, the junior class spun magic to turn that arena into a romantic setting. Our year Janet Ruth, Jan Everett, Susie Reinfeld, Suzanne Larry, and the rest of their art squad worked hard to come up with a theme: they decided on "Fanta-Sea."

At the entrance to the gym, they created a giant clam shell to frame the door opening, which spat out the glamorous couples into an undersea world of fish and mermaids painted onto murals wrapping the room. Once inside, large fishing seines filled with colored glass balls hung here and there among the murals, and the ceiling was lowered by draping crepe paper streamers to mime the slope of a circus Big Top. You definitely felt you were under...something. It felt magical.

I bought and wore a baby blue dress with spaghetti straps while Mike wore a white sports coat and a pink carnation, which I discovered stunk and looked phony. I have disliked them ever since.

Mike and I began the evening at a classmate's pre-prom party where the ever-present Winston the photographer took photos. We ate a little, then headed to the school. And as for the evening, I clearly remember the décor and mood upon entering that transformed sports arena. It seemed a lot more glamorous than a function hall.

At the end of the evening, we did go to a post-prom party, literally changing into casual clothes in the locker rooms of the gym before we left. The after-parties were private and were as varied as their hosts. Some served beer, others had no open drinking, and somehow there were always some who secreted their forbidden alcohol wherever they went. But for the most part, there wasn't drinking. Neither Mike nor I had any interest in alcohol then, and if you weren't interested, no one gave you a hard time.

It was a fun evening, but the conversation and dances have washed away with the last of that crepe paper. It would be my senior prom that holds the memory tapes which have not faded.

It began in the fall of my senior year. Mike was away at college, and I was happily enjoying school, living at the Pickerings, having fun with my friends, but not dating. Actually, Mike and I had agreed to date others, if we had the chance. We were mature enough to realize we were living in two different worlds, and it would be stupid to become a hermit. But for me, dating someone new hadn't happened.

I always had friends who were boys, and that fall I made some new ones. Martin Blair was one such boy. We seemed to enjoy one other's company a lot, laughing and chatting in a class we shared. Then one day, when the subject at hand had nothing to do with what was coming next, he asked, "So, would you like to go to the prom with me next spring?" His invitation was such a surprise, and I was so taken aback, that I paused briefly, but my mind quickly realized, there were only two possible polite responses. "I'd love to!" or "Sorry, I already have a date." But it was October. Now, really, could I have possibly responded, "I already have a date?" Of course, there was a third response. "No, I don't want to go with you." But that wouldn't have been the truth either. I liked this boy; I just hadn't come to think of him as a possible date.

So it was, "Uh, oh...that would be great...sure, I'll go."

But then I began to wonder...and question...and feel a little locked-in. *How did I get into this?* It was a long way off. I put it out of my mind. Sort of.

Months went by, and closer to the prom, two different boys asked me to go with them. Of course, I had to refuse. Do I remember who asked me? No. And it really had nothing to do with the people. It was the *option part.* I just remember that I felt trapped. As the prom date neared, I became more and more annoyed at being committed to this arrangement.

Meanwhile, the pre-prom and post-prom party invitations mushroomed. They sounded great, and I knew they were the most fun of the whole event, anyway. Often the pre-prom ones were girls-only, so it would be fun for sure. Linda Morningside was having a "Hic" party with fake champagne. I'd focus on that.

Scenes from Fanta Sea.

"Fanta-Sea" prom night with Mike, his senior prom.
Photo courtesy: Craig's Photography, Bartlesville, Oklahoma

The totally non-alcoholic, all-girls, pre-prom "Hic Party."
Photo courtesy: Craig's Photography Bartlesville, Oklahoma

As Janet Ruth and I talked about what we would be wearing to the prom that spring, we both decided we were a little fat. I guess we weren't the only ones worrying about weight, because all the girls seemed to be talking about weight loss, and they were all talking about diet pills. According to the gossip, all you had to do to lose weight was to take these pills, and suddenly you didn't eat so much, and the weight fell away. We had no idea what they were made from or how they worked. We didn't care. The whole thing sounded good to us. The only complication was you couldn't just go to Nutter's or some other pharmacy and buy these pills off the shelf. You had to get your doctor to write a prescription. So, we both called our family doctors who willingly agreed to write an order for the pills we wanted.

And it worked. Our appetites reduced and so did we, like magic. Within a short time, we had both reached our goal of

241

losing five pounds. But then a couple more pounds came off. We felt great, and were all set to look our best at the prom, but we were kind of hooked on the pills, afraid if we quit taking them, we'd blow up again. We decided to keep taking them until they ran out, and if we lost more weight, we'd have some spare pounds to play with as we went back to normal.

Finally, prom day arrived. I have a picture from the pre-prom event where Martin and I looked like we were enjoying ourselves. Afterwards we changed into our prom clothes which, for me, was the same dress I wore with Mike.

As for the post-prom party...we never got there. By the time Martin and I were headed for the prom itself, I had become quiet, sullen and was making no effort to be pleasant. The months leading to this night had provided plenty of time to convince myself that I had been trapped into going, losing all my options, and I had worked myself into a first-class snit. The reality was I was angry with this lovely boy for asking me early.

When I was young and took on one of those moods, my parents called me "Pouty Mac," and I was sent to another room to re-group, and "when I could find Patty Mac, I could return."

That evening, I'll bet Martin wished he could have done that. I'm not sure we made it even half-way through the evening. I only recall that Martin suddenly said in a mature, certain manner, "I think it's time to go home." And I got it. And I knew I was to blame.

It was a quiet but short ride to the Pickerings, quieter than at the dance, because now it was just the two of us. I guess I said good-bye; it's a blur in my memory. Fortunately, the lights were on, and the door unlocked so I could quickly enter. I walked right to the kitchen and found Mama Ruth and Mr. Pickering at the table playing Scrabble.

I didn't have to say a word; they knew instantly something was wrong. Since there was always something tasty cooking on the stove with Mr. Pickering, he was quick to offer me something to eat. I sat down, and soon confessed the whole juvenile, embarrassing story. I was sad though. Even then, I realized that I had brought the whole fiasco on myself.

When I was through with my tale, Mr. and Mrs. Pickering immediately regaled me with prom night disaster stories from their high school days, and soon we were all laughing. We stayed at the table a long time, mixing stories with Scrabble, and long enough for Janet Ruth and Doug to return home to change their clothes for an after-prom party. They invited me to come with them, but I was done for the night. I stayed home and went to bed before Janet Ruth returned. I remember thinking as I fell asleep, *do these events ever turn out like the movies?*

Martin was a perfect date, and in later years I learned that it was quite traditional to ask a prom date in the fall for the May event. Of course, there are legions of stories of miserable evenings from keeping those promises while finding other loves along the way. Often, dates would ditch the actual prom date and take another to the after-prom party. But I was unaware of these things at the time, and it probably wouldn't have made a difference.

I never apologized. I don't know why. Embarrassment, probably. We graduated within a month, I made my move to Canada, went off to college, and never returned to live in Bartlesville. I did return for some reunions, but it was the twenty-fifth before I saw Martin again.

I really wanted to apologize to him then, but I couldn't bring myself to do so in such a public forum. There has never been an appropriate place, but I never stopped regretting my behavior that evening. So, this late-in-life memory of the story will have to be my public "mea culpa." However, his reaction just might be, "Patty Mac, who?"

Pomp and Circumstance

"So, who do you think you're going to room with at O.U.?" I asked Janet Ruth one night as we were settling in after lights out.

"Marks and I are talking about it. We're both going to be art majors, so she won't mind having that art crud around all the time," she mumbled as she drifted off to sleep.

Most of our friends were going to the University of Oklahoma or Oklahoma State. Once you knew where you wanted to go, you just filled out a form. There was no wondering whether or not you'd be admitted; it was automatic – if your grades were decent, you got in. But where was I going to go to college?

Since money was an issue in my family, I knew I needed to find a college closer to my home, which was now Calgary. I knew little about colleges in general, and certainly none in particular. The only school I ever visited was the University of Kansas during my junior year, when Mike was interested in the school. I was able to stay with my cousin Nancy who went there, and Mike was invited to stay at the Sigma Chi House where they were hosting their "Sweetheart of Sigma Chi" dance. We were both invited.

The University of Kansas was located in a hilly area of Lawrence, where the roads and streets were lined with marching umbrellas of elm trees. With the school's ivy-covered brick buildings, it rivaled any Ivy League campus I would come to see. I was completely taken with the school, and there was still the party ahead.

After arriving, Mike and I separated to get dressed for the dance. I got a chance to visit with my cousin, while the Sigma

Chis were trying to impress Mike, hoping he might choose the University of Kansas and then, perhaps, them, if he elected to "go through rush" (the process for joining a fraternity or sorority). Everyone had their best face on. When it was time for the party, Mike came to pick me up, and we went back to the fraternity house together.

The house was a grand three-story brick home, where we were not directed inside, but to the back. As we turned the last corner, our mouths dropped. A waterfall cascaded from an upper-story window and flowed into a man-made pond below. The members had used the driveway to the under-house garage in the rear as the walls and floor for this water feature. The house wall provided one side, a stone-retaining wall bordered the outside and the garage door itself had been closed tightly, creating a well. Then the entire basin was lined with a rubber matting and filled with water. A hose from an upstairs bathroom fed the waterfall which now spilled into the pond, alive with real swans.

An intimate ballroom was ahead, the tennis court now a dance floor. Christmas lights were strung along the top of the chain link fence surrounding the court, shimmering candle-flame lights, and crepe-paper flowers grew from all the openings in the chain-link fencing. It was a Cinderella scene, and I took the bait. I just couldn't get the school out of my mind; I wanted to go there. But my family's move changed everything.

Unlike Janet Ruth and Elizabeth Marks who both knew they were artists, and that art was what they wanted to study, I didn't have an inner passion for anything. I just knew I needed to major in something where I could exchange my diploma for a paycheck.

When I was eight years old, a family friend noticed my oversized hands and remarked that I would make a good physical therapist. At the time I watched a lot of polio telethons where, against background music serenading, "Look for the Silver Lining," I watched physical therapists in therapy pools working with children who had contracted polio. I cried through these dramatic scenes, which captured me like the Kansas experience, so beginning at the age of eight, whenever anyone asked what I wanted to be when I grew up, I declared, "A physical therapist." I never wavered, though I'd never been to a physical therapist nor known one in my entire life. I did like biology, but my career research was definitely light.

The guidance counselor at College High tried to be helpful, but in reality, she knew little beyond the schools of our state, Kansas, and Texas. My parents were in Canada, and had little experience with colleges elsewhere, so it was up to me to figure out where to go. I approached my research based on physical therapy programs, and the University of Washington in Seattle came to the top of the list. I applied there and nowhere else. It cost money to apply to schools, and "U-Dub" seemed like the best option. I just figured I would be accepted. Fortunately, I was, but I never visited nor knew anyone at this school of 25,000, its population rivaling the entire town of Bartlesville. What was I thinking?

After college acceptances came in, my friends and I began looking forward to moving on. My prom night behavior was still weighing heavily on my conscience, so I focused on graduation. Friends began planning before and after commencement parties. Bartlesville was definitely a town that used about any excuse to host a party. We sent engraved graduation invitations to relatives and close friends. These were mostly not-so-subtle hints for graduation gifts; we definitely didn't want to miss out on that.

Our farewell assembly took place three days before commencement. Student awards, scholarships, and acknowledgement of academic achievements were presented and announced. I still have the assembly program from that day, which I read with renewed interest as I wrote these stories. I was impressed by the nine merit scholarship finalists and the twelve "commended" scholars that came from our class. Janet Ruth and I were not among them. But Allen Zbruz was. He was in my kindergarten class and could read anything put in front of him when he was only five. The teacher was always bringing people in and then giving him *The Tulsa World* to read. We were all impressed.

Carol Hoops was named, too. I remember that she was constantly reading – in lunch line, in between classes, and in classes, if she could get away with it. It really was no surprise to see their names. It made me appreciate the education I received from College High, and the importance of becoming a reader.

I was surprised when I read through the assembly program and saw the awards made to five Black students in our class. I had no idea what any of these awards represented then or now, and when I tried to find mention of them in the yearbook, they were noticeably absent. But there in our graduation program was listed the "Oklahoma Federation of Colored Women Award presented to Nadine Haley, the Porte Soir Club award to Val Gene Conley, the Alice McCrary Foundation Award to Maxine McDade, the N.A.C.W. Award to Wilma Jean Nash and the Luvinia Brown Renaissance Club Award to Carlene Robinson."

In researching some of Bartlesville's history, I found in the *Centennial* publication for the town's birthday, that several of these clubs were mentioned in the section recalling the African-American community throughout the town's one hundred years. As reported by Josie Marie Oulds, the organizations named in the awards were instrumental in "attempting to secure life, liberty and the pursuit of happiness within the African-American community." As such, they made awards to worthy students at graduation. It had now been six years since Jane Morrison, the first Black student, had entered College-High. She "recalls racial taunts and how she was ex-

cluded from the Prom, the YWCA and some restaurants during band trips."

By our year, some small inroads were being made, such as
the presentation of these community honors, but that's as far
as it went. No one made any effort to explain to the mostly
white student body what the awards stood for, nor did they
honor the students' successes by reporting them in the yearbook.

Graduation day came, and my parents arrived to witness
the pomp and circumstance ("ceremony and fuss") of this high
school finale. I was rarely homesick during the year, but this
was an important passage, and I wanted my family there.

Before their arrival, Janet Ruth and I began dreaming up
an after-graduation getaway, but when I presented the idea
over the phone, my father wouldn't agree. I begged and
begged, but he was not going to let me take off for the Ozarks
to party with my friends. I hoped that when my parents arrived, he might have weakened, but he was as stubborn as
before, and my mom didn't jump in to support me either. Janet Ruth and I were disappointed, but, looking back, I have
to admit that Dad was probably right.

Janet Ruth and I wore our gowns and mortar boards
proudly that day. We were instructed that the skull cap portion should sit on the top of our head so that the mortar board
was flat. The tassel should hang to the right until we were
presented with our diplomas, at which point we could move
the tassel to the left. I loved the ceremony of the event.

We stood for numerous photos that day, with various
groups, but my favorite picture was the re-gathering of my
kindergarten class. We assembled to stand in the same spots
we took for our kindergarten picture. Incredibly, of the fourteen five-year-olds from Horace Mann, only one student and
the teacher had moved on by our high school graduation.

On May 27, 1962, just over 400 students graduated from
College High. There were tearful good-byes, though most of

my friends would not be leaving everyone for good. This time I really was leaving, and going to a school no one knew, least of all me. This reality was only beginning to sink in.

Janet Ruth and I celebrated with our families, went to some parties and finally headed back to the Pickerings', where we said good-bye to my parents for the evening. I would see them the next day when we would pack up to all fly back to Calgary. Janet Ruth and I weren't quite ready to go to sleep, so we headed for the den over the garage to hang out. Pretty soon, we heard footsteps coming towards us from the living room.

"Hey, Babe," called Pop Pickering to Janet Ruth, "whatchu guys doing?"

"Oh, just talkin', Dad. Come on up."

"I got a little surprise for you two," he teased. That perked us up. *What could it be?* And there it was in his chubby little hand...a six pack of 3.2 beer. Six bottles. For the two of us.

"I thought you might need a little preparation for college. Better to get your first tastes at home than at some frat house."

We were stunned. That would not have been my dad's graduation present. Pop Pickering winked, and then went to bed.

There was only one thing missing – the opener. Janet Ruth knew exactly where it was located in the kitchen drawer, so she was gone for only a minute or two. She returned with a big smile and expertly popped the top off of two beers. We toasted and took a big drink. I had never drunk alcohol before, except for a taste of our family doctor's Christmastime bourbon-laced eggnog that he served my sister and me when we were five and seven. Janet Ruth claimed she hadn't either.

Whoaaa...bubbly...different, and without the burn of the bourbon. The second sip went down easier and by the third, we were sailing.

All through high school, whenever we got together with

those who participated in some of our pranks, we loved re-living our nights and tales. I think we had as much fun in the story telling as we did when we lived it. Plied by our 3.2 beer we began recalling all our adventures and explorations throughout our friendship. The "Pontiac pervert" was fresh in our minds as he had shown up only a few weeks earlier. That brought howls of laughter as we recalled how we thought his exposure was an accident. We took another sip. And that led to the coyote night story. And breaking into the high school episodes. Another sip. Which, of course, reminded us of break-ing into the sacristy at church camp for wine. By this time that beer was finished. We burped a few times before popping the lid off the second one. We knew we were saying goodbye. That led to the story when I met her after her broken arm episode with the horse. We didn't talk about the softball meet-ing. That was my memory, which had etched itself on my brain in a singular way.

Those diet pills were still reducing our appetites, so we were soon feeling bloated and dizzy. And who knows how they chemically combined with the beer? I saw the room lurch about the time my stomach did and crawled to the bathroom. Janet Ruth doubled over in laughter, but she was soon right behind me. We lost those beers. Over and over and over. We were drunk on three bottles each of 3.2 beer.

Hoping for relief, we made our way to bed, though that brought no comfort. I felt I was on a tilt-a-whirl ride. The bed spun while I tried not to. Sleep finally came, and then so did the morning – with two hangovers.

I don't know if Pop Pickering knew the results of our par-tying. He probably did and was laughing himself to sleep. Years later we learned that Mama Ruth was well aware of those nights we snuck out through the den window and thought we were getting away with it. Not much got past those two. They just seemed to know when to keep quiet.

It took about thirty years for me to develop a taste for alcohol. During college, I still had no interest in drinking. The memory of that misery was fresh, and I was not one who liked feeling out of control. That night probably saved me from a lot of trouble.

But the real fuss after all that ceremony was saying good-bye. And what did it really mean? At that point, we had no plans to see one another. Janet Ruth and I accepted that. Mike and I accepted that. We were all young enough to know that we didn't have much control over the next phases of our life and "pretty much" did what we should. We were governed by a lot of "shoulds."

It would be decades before I would see the movie *The Best Exotic Marigold Hotel*, but we already believed in their famous line, "Everything will be all right in the end. If it's not all right, then it's not yet the end."

One night during our senior spring, when we were talking about my leaving again, I told Janet Ruth that I bet someday I would marry Mike Hewitt. Not soon. But one day. Deep down, I never really thought that this *was* good-bye. To her or to him. I just had a feeling...

No shenanigans for this finish line.
Photo permission: Craig's Photography, Bartlesville, Oklahoma

U-Dub

Following graduation, I returned to Calgary with my family and found a summer job working for Royalite Oil Company. It was almost impossible to escape a life not connected to oil. Though my job was only slightly less boring than selling men's clothing, I did learn to type. I never took typing in high school, but with my mother's old textbook and a lot of practicing "the quick brown fox jumped over the lazy dog," I learned to type, and was a whiz at filing. I'm not sure that's something to brag about, but I like making order out of chaos, and I don't think many others did. The summer went by, and soon I was leaving for college.

At that time, the University of Washington (U-Dub) required two trips to campus to begin school: one for orientation and registration, and then a second one two weeks later to move-in. For students who lived in Seattle or a short drive away, this wasn't a hardship, but it was a burdensome expense for my family.

Mom and I decided that for the first trip she and I would travel the 700 miles to Seattle on a Greyhound bus. We thought it would be fun and a lot more scenic than Janet Ruth's and my banana-fueled train ride across the Canadian Plains. This time the trip would take us through the Canadian Rockies, and we figured we'd see *something* exciting.

Unfortunately, much of the trip went through the night, and the interesting scenery turned out to be the variety of passengers in our motor coach. The standouts were a group from a British Columbian religious sect who recently made national news when they burned a barn as a protest against materialism. Newspaper headlines blared that the group was naked or partially-naked throughout the protest; I guess they took their anti-materialism literally, but they were clothed on the bus. Being a newshound, my mom recognized the bearded men and scarfed women from newspaper photos. She and I tried to eavesdrop on their conversations as we attempted sleep, wondering if a commercial bus would be their next target. Apparently, they had places to go because nothing happened.

We arrived in Seattle and took a taxi to the Y.W.C.A. for two nights, another economy measure. We never stayed in fancy places (except for the Banff Springs with Janet Ruth), but none of the other places smelled like Mr. Clean. From the moment we entered the front door of the Y to check-in with the lady manning the front desk, we could identify that smell throughout the hallways and then our room and bathroom. The place reeked. We didn't know if the assault was prevention or a cover-up. But the Y was a great location, enabling us to walk anywhere we wanted, so it was a sensible decision. I learned early-on to be sensible.

The sprawling campus was in the middle of the city, built to accommodate the 25,000, many of whom were day students. This was my first time to actually see the school, and I was somewhat overwhelmed by its size, coming from a town no larger than the university. But the tour guide knew how to impress us, and led us to Frosh Pond, where we could see Mt. Rainier rising in the distance. At that moment I found a beautiful school awaiting me. The remainder of my registration took place at the administration building. I recall a lovely woman there who did everything she could to make us feel welcome and make the process easy. But I never connected with any incoming students or faculty or had any orientation. We left to return to Calgary the second morning.

Two weeks later, I flew back to Seattle for the move-in and to participate in "rush," the process of joining a fraternity or sorority. Because of the school's size and my desire to be part of something smaller, and because I came from a place where this was a popular thing to do, I wanted to join a sorority.

I spent my first few days in a dorm with other incoming freshman women who were also "rushing." The format was to attend parties at different "houses," where we had superficial chats with girls following song and dance sketches that were supposed to convince us that these were *our people.* I liked them all, but I finally found two where I particularly liked a member. I was about to select my first choice when my dorm advisor convinced me to opt for my second. She had taken a liking to me, and I to her, and I suspected my second choice was her sorority, though she couldn't say so. After I was formally invited to join, I found out that it was.

Because of a housing crisis, the university ruled that out-of-state incoming freshman could live in fraternity and sorority houses if they had space. I qualified, and immediately moved into the Kappa Kappa Gamma house, with an instant group of friends from my pledge class and upper-class members. Every pledge was assigned a "big sister" to help guide them into this college world. Mine was Katy Blackman, who became very special to me. It was a good start.

All over campus, gardenia vendors sold flowers, and girls bought them for their hair. I fell in love with the custom and the flowers. Every few days, I spent fifty cents to buy a gardenia and bobby-pinned it behind my ear. The sweet scent was intoxicating, and it was difficult not to want to touch the flower to bring it closer. But that little flower doesn't want to be touched. It reacts with a bruise as if it had been punched with a fist, its creamy petals darkening, leading to an early death. I felt as fragile as those flowers. I bought an Army-green canvas book-bag, filled it with my books and papers, slung the strap over one shoulder, and was ready to go. It was probably the closest I came to being a flower child. I was trying to fit in.

Though I loved my sorority, my roommates, and my pledge

class, it wasn't enough. Seattle winter settled in, and Mt. Rainier disappeared behind a blanket of fog and rain for the remainder of my stay. I grew up in the Sun-belt and living day after day in a cloud was depressing to me. At times, I actually wished for a downpour. That was the rain I knew. In Seattle, it just drizzled constantly.

I ran out of diet pills, and I was no longer having my period. Though I had no understanding of drugs, I now believe I was in withdrawal from those pills. They were amphetamines.

And I was homesick. When I'd left home a year earlier to live with the Pickerings, everything around me was familiar, and I was surrounded by people I knew and loved. At U-Dub, not only was there no one familiar around, communication was limited. Phone calls were expensive and an extravagance, used for holidays or emergencies. And there was nothing familiar about where I was. I went to parties on houseboats, drank coffee at dark coffee houses, and I was making new friends, ones I really liked, but it didn't seem like home. I even went on a few blind dates, but I always compared them to Mike, and found them lacking. I had no anchor.

During that first term, I had a 7:30 A.M. English class studying *The Heart of Darkness* by Joseph Conrad, and mine felt darker than his book. As I soloed across campus to class through the fog and constant drizzle, my footsteps the only sound, I was brought to a low I had never known. I discovered pizza and ice cream, and soon none of my clothes fit. I wrote home about my sadness, homesickness, and missing Mike, drawing teardrops where I signed my name. (I was always dramatic).

I did like my classes, especially French and anthropology, and we completed our first term before the Christmas holiday. I was so happy to go home for this first visit back to see my family. But, despite no homework or finals hanging over my head, I carried a low-level feeling of dread at the thought of returning to Washington. I just wanted the cloud to lift from the weather and my spirits.

Luckily, I was to fly back; that alone was exciting. I dressed up for the flight, took my seat by the window, and dutifully listened to the welcome and safety instructions by the "stewardess." The captain, too, greeted us as we prepared for takeoff. All went well, and I spent most of the trip happily reading and dozing. When it became dark, I was aware we should be landing soon, and I looked out to see the lights of a city, presumably Seattle. I wasn't sure what I'd see, as flying was new to me, but I imagined I might see runway lights. Yet all I saw were city lights, over and over. Minutes went by as we seemed to be circling over Seattle. The other, more seasoned passengers began to get restless and questioned why we weren't landing. About that time, the captain came on the loudspeaker. In a calm voice, he began to explain our situation: there was a problem with the landing gear. They needed to use up our remaining fuel, so that they could perform a foam landing. I listened quietly and knew that didn't sound good, but I said nothing. None of the passengers around me said anything either. We all waited for what was to follow.

After circling a bit longer, the captain came back on to tell how we should position ourselves for the landing. I didn't know enough to feel panicky or terrified or perhaps I was numb. I felt confident that whatever needed to be done was being done, and we just needed to follow instructions. That's what I tried to do.

We were told to lean forward with our arms against the seat in front, and then to rest our heads on our arms as we landed. We all did as we were told, and the plane began its descent. I prayed. Everyone around me seemed to pray.

The next thing I remember was a thud and rolling down the runway just as I remembered from previous flights. Over the loudspeaker, the captain dropped his crisis-calm, and in a celebratory voice reported that at the last minute, the wheels had descended! Everyone cheered.

When we looked out of the window, we saw ambulances, foam, and firetrucks all around us. Everything was in readiness for our potential crash landing, which miraculously did not happen. I lost my breath a little as I viewed our surroundings, and the reality of the situation began to register. As the passengers continued cheering, some of the young men carried the stewardesses off the plane on their shoulders. Suddenly, everyone was talking to everyone else.

An older man across the aisle befriended me to offer reassurance and celebration of our good fortune. Since we were so late, he wondered if I could use a ride somewhere; he had his own car at the airport. All my life, I had been told never to get into a car with a stranger, but he didn't feel like one. We had just been through a near-tragedy together. It seemed like the right thing to do, so I happily accepted.

We retrieved our luggage, and I followed him to his car where we began the drive to the university and the Kappa house. He was very chatty, and asked me lots of questions which I answered, happy to get my mind off what we had narrowly missed. I didn't know my way around Seattle, but I had a sense of how long the ride should take, and after a while, it seemed we were having a repeat of the plane ride; we should have arrived at the school by now. When I finally asked him, he said, "Oh, I thought you might like some dinner, first."

And then my radar went off. He wasn't taking me home; he had other things on his mind. I went into overdrive telling him my friends knew when I was arriving and would be expecting me. They'd be worried about my late arrival. They might even call the airport to find out what happened and send the police out looking for me. Well, it worked. Reluctantly, he made some turns and took me to the Kappa house.

I was so relieved to have first escaped a fiery plane crash, and then a possible abduction, I was happy to be back.

Going Our Ways

Despite my low-level depression during the first term, I had done well academically, and upon my return, I had escaped a plane crash and abduction. Of course, I was happy about that, but it was short-lived. Very quickly, I ran into a buzz saw. Through a placement test, I tested out of one math class only to be put into a trigonometry class that turned out to be a repeat for everyone but me. The very first day, a gangly, bespectacled student entered the room, tripped over the wastepaper basket, and then took his place at the podium. *Uh...oh...he's the teacher.* And then he began to teach – quickly. I was met with a subject that held little interest for me, seemed to carry no relevance, and was difficult to learn at the speed he was teaching. I found it difficult to stay focused, and I felt overwhelmed. My instructor, who was young, kind, earnest and just out of college, was willing to give me extra help, but I felt like I had a mental block that just wouldn't absorb this branch of mathematics. The more I tried and sensed I was failing, the more panicky I felt. Running away seemed a good option.

I went to the administration building to try to drop the class, and found the lovely woman I met when I first arrived. She invited me into her office to chat and listen to my story. She was sympathetic, but in the end, she encouraged me to keep trying. Reluctantly, I agreed. And then she said, "Maybe you need a little change of scenery. I'm going to Victoria, British Columbia this weekend. Why don't you join me?"

I was very surprised, but I was drawn in by her kindness and attempt to help me out of this dark time, so, I agreed. I don't recall a lot of that weekend, but I do remember that during dinner the first night, she told me stories of some of her homosexual friends. I only remember that I was shocked by her tale, and reacted as such. And that was the end of that conversation. Nothing happened, and after we returned, I never saw her again. Many years later, I have to wonder if she was probing my gender orientation. For all my explorin' adventures, I never explored that.

I finished the trimester, and with the help of the trigonometry instructor, I made a C. I was never so happy to receive such a grade, and I had never made a C in my life, or even many B's. When the term was officially over, I received a call from the student/professor, who asked me out on a date! I was as shocked as I was with the administration lady. Who ever heard of dating your teacher? I politely declined. *Thank goodness the grades are posted*, I thought.

Throughout the winter when I felt so low and was so afraid of failing, I had fleeting thoughts that it might be better to be dead; I couldn't see a way out. I never really thought about actually killing myself, but death seemed to provide a way to deal with all the difficulties. It isn't easy to write these words, especially over such a trivial thing as a class grade, but many things were feeding this depression. And I had no one to talk to; I was afraid to share any of my worries with my new friends; it felt shameful and weak, and I had never even shared many personal things with Janet Ruth or any close friends. But when I had those thoughts of death, I tried to put them out of my head; I could acknowledge their craziness.

Unlike today, there were no counselors for students, or if there were, they weren't readily available. Mental illness carried a stigma, and I saw that it was something to hide.

My parents were aware of my depression, and during my break between winter and spring terms, they allowed me to travel by bus to San Francisco with two of my Kappa friends. The bus trip covered 800 miles one way, but it would be worth it. Mike was to be in California at the same time, running in a track meet at Palo Alto against Stanford and San Jose State, and I could meet him there. I couldn't wait.

My friends and I sunbathed on the beaches, and I got the worst sunburn of my life, exposing my Seattle-hibernated skin to that California sun. But those eight hours in the sun were the happiest I'd been in a while, and the following day, I would get to see Mike.

Through letters we arranged that we would meet at the stadium where the track meet was being held. When I arrived at the campus, I was in awe. As beautiful as I thought the University of Kansas was, I was completely taken-in by Stanford's Spanish architecture. The red-tiled roofs, sandstone buildings, and arched walkways were as romantic as this meeting. Immediately, I began asking directions of anyone I met as to how to get to the stadium. I found my way along one of the arched walkways, and then I saw Mike coming towards me. I couldn't believe it. It was like in the movies, both of us running as soon as we caught sight of the other.

After all that preparation, we only had a short time to talk and walk before he had to prepare for the meet. Given that we seldom spoke on the phone, most of our sharing was through letters. Now that we were together, we just tried to catch up with the stories of our lives. I know I told him how much I missed him, and hoped he felt the same. He must have because I was happy after this brief reunion. He re-joined his team, ran his races, and we both returned to our lives. What I remember most is that when I left, my feelings for him had not changed. He was everything I remembered.

The third term began with more new classes, none of which seemed overwhelming, but I had trouble concentrating. I couldn't seem to focus and get organized. I had dreams of failing over and over. And then I got a phone call from my mom.

"Patty...Mac?" her voice quavered, and my stomach lurched. Something awful had happened, I just knew it. I thought of Dad.

"What's wrong, Mom!?"

"Aunt Didge died. She was in the hospital for asthma treatment, and the morning she was to be discharged, she went into a coughing spasm and had a cardiac arrest." She was 61 years old.

I was bereft. Both my grandmothers had died either before or just after I was born, so Aunt Didge had always filled that role. For most of my life we lived in the same town, and she was my "grandmother" who showed up for school events, who spoiled me and loved me. I lost the Didge who gave Pam and me Cokes and Grapette every time we visited, the Didge who threw the best tornado-alert parties in the world, and the Didge who showed up every Christmas morning at 6 A.M., when she knew she could come in and see the surprise on our faces at what Santa had brought.

I couldn't go to the funeral. School was in session, and the flight was too expensive. Money always seemed to throw a monkey-wrench into my needs. My friends at school were very sweet, but they couldn't really understand my sadness at losing my aunt. They didn't understand how important she was to me; I felt alone in my grief. Once again, I had moments of thinking it would be better to be dead than alive. I was miserable, and I knew I needed help, but I didn't know how to find it.

A week went by, and in desperation, I called my parents to see if I could come home. As the phone rang, I anticipated the conversation to follow. I was sure they'd say, "It's only six weeks until the end of term. We just paid the tuition. Can't you just stick it out?"

Those six weeks might as well have been six years. *How could I explain?* But before I could even try to make them understand, I realized I didn't have to. They told me to come home. There were no questions asked, no recriminations — nothing. I couldn't believe it. I hung up, packed my things, and left.

Leaving the University of Washington was my first big failure, and it was hard for me to accept that I could not rise above dealing with the difficulties I was experiencing. I was giving up. But I had never felt so happy and relieved. I felt I could give in to all the sadness I was feeling without having to *produce* at the same time. I wasn't capable of doing both.

I wasn't sure what to expect when I got home: maybe Mom and, especially, Dad, would regret their decision. But neither one did. I found the same acceptance and welcome that they gave me over the phone. (In later years, I asked my mother about this time, and she said she had read an article about young adult suicide. It made her think, and she told her thoughts to Dad.)

But they had no professional guidance either. They asked me very few questions when I returned, and appeared content to let me be. They didn't suggest any outside help, which I would have liked. But it wasn't commonplace in our world. It was expensive, and it still carried a stigma. I felt it was shameful enough quitting school and wasting tuition money; I would just get a job.

It took a few weeks at home before I could set out to look, but when I did, I headed back to Royalite Oil Company.

Meanwhile Janet Ruth's freshman year seemed to be everything she expected. She and Elizabeth Marks headed off to the University of Oklahoma, art school, and Herrick House to live as roommates during their first year. Piled high with their belongings, Elizabeth drove Janet Ruth to school in her yellow Fiat which miraculously made the 180 miles, only to die in the parking lot where it remained for the duration of the year. Like me, they chose to rush, and each pledged a different sorority. Unlike me, they continued to live in the dorm, which was customary, and moved into their respective houses when they began their sophomore year.

Both loved their art classes and their social lives. Within a few months, each found a special boy. Janet Ruth met Vince and fell in love. He was from New Jersey, three years older than her, handsome, funny, and fairly cocky. She had never met anyone like him. She was used to being in charge, but not anymore. She was moving into unknown territory.

Janet Ruth and I wrote letters during that freshman year, but infrequently. That first year of college consumed each of us, only in very different ways: Janet Ruth was moving forward, while I was overwhelmed by the obstacles I found. And without Janet Ruth, I had no one to make me laugh.

Destination: University of Oklahoma

Office work at Royalite Oil Company was the perfect job for me at that time in my life – mindless and routine. My colleagues couldn't have been nicer, but their conversations about babies, Pablum, and potty training didn't interest me in the least, and the prospect of an office career was chilling. *Did I want to go back to school?* Maybe. Did I want to be with Mike? Most definitely. That meant going to Norman, Oklahoma and the university there. It had been four months since I left Seattle, and it was now August; classes would begin soon.

My mental health was slowly returning, but I was fearful of falling back into depression. *Would re-entering school with all those stresses bring that darkness back?* I had a lot of questions and worries, but with the fear of a forever office job breathing down my neck, I felt like a runner about to be lapped. I wanted to do other things, and that meant I needed to return to school. I decided to apply for late admission to the University of Oklahoma in Norman. Other than my C in trig, my grades were A's and B's, and I dropped out before I flunked out that last trimester at U-Dub. I was accepted.

As a transfer student, I wasn't automatically able to live in the Kappa house, though I was welcome to attend meetings. I had to live in a dorm instead, and by this point, the most desirable dorms had long been filled. It wasn't a surprise that I was assigned to the least favorite one on campus. My old friends groaned when they learned where I would be living, but I couldn't get hung up on that; I knew I was lucky to be there at all.

My reunions with Mike and Janet Ruth were all that I

hoped. I met her new boyfriend Vince, and Mike seemed happy at my return (though I learned 50 years later that he'd had a date with his old girlfriend the night before).

And then a gift landed in my lap. Sorority and fraternity rush ended, and the Kappas found there was an extra bed in the house. Transfers weren't usually candidates to live-in, but they decided to invite me. I knew several members from Bartlesville, so I imagine they put in a good word to make this happen. It was completely unexpected, made me feel very welcome, and confirmed my decision to transfer.

I dove headfirst into my science classes and labs, even taking an extra-credit hour every semester to make up for my early freshman departure. It was in one of those classes that I ran into one of my Bartlesville childhood friends, Terri Constable. Sometimes, when she and I were six or seven years old, we would gather up the stuff of our lives we no longer wanted, put it on a card table alongside the curb, dress up as washerwomen (that meant stuffing our shirts to create a hefty chest) and try to sell our stuff. I was always looking to make a nickel, and I think I had some marketing sense with that washerwoman schtick. Later, in high school, Terri was my friend who was chosen to become our school's foreign exchange student to Berlin. Now I learned that she was one of the sixteen students in the O.U. physical therapy program. It was one more welcome home gift.

Janet Ruth and I began to drift apart. It wasn't intentional, and it had nothing to do with how we felt about one another. We belonged to different sororities and lived in their respective houses. And we were each doing what we set out to do: become a physical therapist and an artist. And then there were our boyfriends. Young men, not girlfriends, were our priorities. Janet Ruth and Vince were close to another couple, so we didn't double-date, but when she could borrow her brother's car, she'd call me to come by, go for a Coke and catch up. But as with any real friend, time can go by and life can intervene, and when you connect, it seems no time has passed. No one needs to offer any explanations, excuses, or apologies. You're together, you're in the moment, and you cherish those moments. That's what we did.

For his first two years of college, Mike lived in Jeff House, the athletic dorm for wrestlers, swimmers, track-and-field men, and baseball and tennis players. My (now) brother-in-law, Gary Clinton, describes his Jeff House room as "only slightly better than a prison cell." Washington House, the residence hall for basketball and football players, was definitely a step up, but life was "Animal House" in both places. The bathrooms were so disgusting that Mike used the library. When an opportunity presented itself, he moved out with a track teammate, Harold Close, and rented a small house at 621 Jenkins. He was living there when I arrived.

Harold was a distance runner from Dayton, Ohio who was on scholarship along with Mike. I liked Harold a lot, and as I hung out there when I could, we three became good friends. He was majoring in business, but, by his own admission, was performing at a mediocre level. Once, Harold was taking a class in which all the students were doing poorly. In frustration, the professor announced that the next quiz would be written, answered, and graded by the students themselves. Mike and I were totally intrigued with this crazy teaching experiment and couldn't wait for the ending.

"So, what did you do?" Mike asked after Harold turned in his exam.

"Well, I made up a test, answered the questions – and then gave myself a C," said Harold.

"What...a C! Why would you do that?"

Harold deadpanned, "I never made higher than a C in my life. I figured why should I start now?"

For Harold, majoring in business was like "trying to put socks on a rooster." After he graduated and joined the Army, he discovered he had an aptitude for languages, and became an interpreter. Then he served in the Peace Corps in Africa, and began establishing track programs wherever he went. Over his life, he has been a teacher, a social activist, and a mediator.

Academically, Mike was doing well in chemical engineering, but his fit wasn't much better than Harold's. Mike's dad was a chemical engineer, and through high school, Mike was good at math, physics, and chemistry, so it seemed logical to follow his father's path. But as Mike progressed through the program, he found he really didn't like engineering. By that time, he was far too invested to change majors, so he decided to stay the course. It was the path of least resistance, though I'm sure most people wouldn't consider engineering a least-resistant path. A summer job at Exxon acquainted him with students who had been engineering majors who went on to get a master's in business. Suddenly, he saw a way out, and that became his goal.

My adopted pledge class and sorority were a good fit. I was lucky to have found a home in yet another huge (though not quite so large as U-Dub) university, and this time I had some old friends and Mike, which made a big difference.

My most challenging class was comparative vertebrate anatomy, where we dissected and studied both a dogfish shark and a cat. Since this study would lead to the dissection of a human body later in my major, it was an important class. Some of our exams were lab tests, where we moved from station to station identifying anatomical parts of the animal. In order to review information, I felt I needed the animal with me, but once out of the lab, it had to be kept frozen. When I saw an old freezer in the basement of the Kappa house, I got a brainstorm, but I needed to speak to our house-mother.

"I know this is a crazy idea, Mrs. Widener, but I'm taking a biology class where we dissect animals, and sometimes I need extra study. It's kind of tricky to bring them home, because they need to be kept frozen after they've been out awhile. Then I saw an old freezer in the basement and thought maybe I could use it for my cat this semester."

"A dead cat? That's what you'd be bringing here?" she said.

"Uh...yeah. It'd be all wrapped up, and I wouldn't ever bring it upstairs. I'd only study in the basement, and then I'd store it in the freezer until I took it back to the lab."

"Hmm. This is very unusual, but I see your dilemma. I just want you to promise that you'll only have it in that room. It's only for one semester, right?"

"That's it," I said. And she gave permission.

I kept my promise. The cat never did come upstairs, but the smell of formaldehyde did. It filled the freezer room, and it permeated me. I tended to do my work in the late afternoon, so I arrived for dinner smelling like *eau de chat mort*. I was definitely persona non grata at the supper table.

When the course ended, and I was left with the picked-over remains of my cat, I decided to prank the student-houseboys who worked in the kitchen. After clean-up from dinner, all the trash was taken outside to a dumpster. A metal door kept the contents from being rifled by raccoons and other invaders, so every time something went in, the door had to be opened and then shut. There was a sill just inside the opening to slide the bags over, and I decided to perch my little companion there. At this point there were no cozy remains to this drafted lab animal, only a picked-over carcass and skull with its mouth wide and open – and angry. I enlisted Ellen Roberts and a couple of other new friends to help stage the tableau, bringing back memories of the coyote night adventure. I handled the cat, and my audience provided the enthusiasm. Then we headed for the evening meal.

Once dinner was over, and clean-up began, it didn't take long before we heard the yells and laughter from the guys in the kitchen, who burst into the dining room looking for the culprit. I wasn't hard to find. Everyone knew of my little side-kick that semester.

"Sooner Scandals" was an annual musical revue put on by students. Anyone could participate, and sororities and fraternities often performed skits. One evening, in preparation for a solo in our skit, the Kappas held singing auditions. I was upstairs laughing and talking with friends when the director came by looking for volunteers to try out. In a weak moment, I decided to audition. I had no idea what to sing, but I had recently heard a silly, bawdy tune by B.G DeSilva about a mermaid who "lost her morals down among the corals," and I impulsively chose that song.

And then...I got the part. Panic set in. I had never sung a solo, and I couldn't believe they'd chosen me. Frankly, I don't think I was very good in rehearsals either, but we were all saved when I developed appendicitis and had my appendix removed the week of the show. The understudy went on.

I'm not sure I ever sang such a song again, and I have to wonder what made me sing it then. I know I wasn't drinking.

When the sorority elected officers in the spring, I was elected pledge trainer for the following year's pledge class. My job was to guide and instruct in the ways of Kappa and being a "young lady."

At a reunion many years later, one of my former pledges came up to me and recalled that I had taught them to "smoke with manners": allow a man to light your cigarette if possible, and never walk and smoke at the same time. If you have to walk across a room with a lighted cigarette, make sure you carry an ashtray beneath it.

With the cat prank, promoting smoking, and my sexist song, what a legacy I left at the Kappa house. Yikes. It's a good thing I'm not running for office.

Finally, together. We were 19 and 20 years old.

Patty Mac and Mike are middle and far right.

Patty Mac and Mike are the two on the right.

Wedding Bells

The first wedding bell rang for my Kappa friend, Miriam Tullah, who married after our sophomore year. She was dating Bill Corning, who had been drafted into the army, and was to be stationed in Seattle. They didn't want to be separated, so they married, and she completed her degree at the University of Washington. What irony that we should become good friends that one year, and then trade locations.

My junior year was full of more science classes and labs, with few electives. If I went to school the summer after that, I would complete making up my lost credits from my freshman year and be able to finish with my class. It was going to be intense, because this meant that beginning my junior year, I would be going to school straight through for the next two years with only a week's break a couple of times a year. The final year of the program was a full twelve months, allowing for clinical rotations at different medical facilities. Graduation would be in August.

Janet Ruth and I saw each other soon after I returned from my summer in Calgary as we began our junior year. She and Vince were still a couple, and as he was a class ahead of us, he would be graduating in the spring, as would Mike. Couples' thoughts often turned to marriage when those situations arose, because in our culture, where we lived, there was no living together. If you wanted to be together, you got married. At least that was the message I got. While things were changing on the coasts, we lived in a conservative world.

A few weeks into the fall, I ran into Elizabeth Marks, Janet Ruth's freshman roommate from Bartlesville who was another artist friend in the same program. She greeted me, but

273

then segued to, "So, what do you think about Janet Ruth and Vince getting married tomorrow?"

I almost couldn't speak. And I couldn't feign that I knew, because I didn't. I'm sure my face told no lies. I felt I had been punched in the stomach. I knew that she and Janet Ruth shared a number of classes and were familiar with each other's schedule, so in the most cavalier manner I could muster, I asked, "So...do you happen to know what class she might be in right now?" Elizabeth was able to direct me.

Maybe I mumbled a thanks. I only recall running, as fast as I could, towards the art building. I had no time to think about what I wanted to say. I just *had* to speak to Janet Ruth.

When I arrived, she was walking down the steps from her class building.

I think she knew by the look on my face that I knew.

"So...I guess you heard Vince and I are getting married. We really don't want to make a big deal out of it. Chuck and Sally are going to stand up for us...how did you find out? Did Marks tell you?"

"Yes...uh...I happened to run into her on campus," I said. "So – she told me. And well...I know you always have your own way of doing things. I just wanted to tell you congratulations." I really did not want her to know my disappointment in finding out this way because I loved this crazy friend. She never did do things the ordinary way. I knew that. That's what I loved about her. She and Vince were close to Chuck and Sally so I understood why they would be there. I needed to be happy for her, but I *was* hurt. I just didn't want her to know that, so I held back my feelings, kissed, and hugged her tightly, and then went home and cried.

College marriages weren't unusual. Miriam had been married since the summer. My friend Terri Constable and her boyfriend, Craig David were talking of marrying, and Mike and I had started the conversation. The Vietnam War was underway and escalating, and once men graduated, if they were single, they were subject to the draft. For those couples seriously contemplating marriage, the prospect of being drafted often accelerated matters.

After Mike completed a summer program at Exxon, he felt sure that he wanted to attend business school after graduation. But I still had another year of college, so he planned to work to allow me to finish school. For both of us, the idea of being separated was unthinkable, as was the idea of me not completing my degree.

In December, we had a date to see *The Sound of Music* and then went back to the little house on Jenkins where Mike lived with Harold. The landlords of these college rentals did little to keep up the houses, but the renters were often neglectful too. The windows and doors were so drafty that Harold wore his hooded sweatshirt to bed. Pulling the hood over his head kept the air off his neck and chin, and when he awoke, he was half-dressed. Mike said he was always so exhausted from track workouts and classes, he just crashed and noticed nothing.

I wasn't crazy about this sieve of a house, but that night it looked special. Mike had decorated a small Christmas tree with lights and ornaments, and with minimal lighting it was romantic. And if the cockroaches were roaming, we couldn't see them.

Our plan was to exchange Christmas presents. I gave him mine first. An electric razor (well – he needed it). And then he gave me a small, wrapped box. I thought I knew what might be coming, but before I unwrapped it, he asked me to marry him. There was no hesitation. Of course, I would. And then I opened the package, an engagement ring – a lovely diamond in a platinum setting. He had picked it out himself, but miscalculated the size, forgetting about my oversized hands. I got the ring on, but I couldn't get it off. We were a little panicked, but we finally found something like Windex to help remove it. Knowing it could be re-sized, we finally laughed. You might think celebratory sex would follow, but no, we would wait until we married.

We made plans to marry June 1 — a Tuesday afternoon. I never had one thought that the choice might be odd. We only had a week between the end of spring term and the summer school we both needed to attend. Mike's engineering program covered four-plus years, and I still needed those summer school credits. Our plan was to travel to Canada on Saturday, be the guest of honor at a shower on Sunday, get our marriage license on Monday, and then marry on Tuesday. We could spend a three-day honeymoon and then fly home the following Saturday, move into our apartment and begin summer school Monday morning. It made perfect sense to us. But I don't believe I ever met anyone else married on a Tuesday.

My mother did most of the planning. We just had to show up, and that was fine with me. I was much too busy with school to worry about wedding plans, and I had no idea of how it should be anyway. I did know that I wanted gardenias in my bouquet, and I picked out my own dress. Beyond that, Mom made the decisions.

Most of my friends wouldn't be able to come because of the travel expense, so my attendants would be my sister and Mike's sister. She and her husband Dwight lived in Massachusetts, and even he didn't attend because of the cost. Janet Ruth was now expecting a baby so she couldn't come, but the expense would have prevented it anyway. It was disappointing, but not unexpected.

Our plan went as scheduled. On Sunday, I was showered with lace and linen table coverings, along with flowered teacups and saucers, not entirely useful for a 21- and 22-year-old, but perhaps we would grow into them. And then on Monday we went to the registry to obtain our license to marry. When we returned to the car and turned on the radio, we couldn't believe it was playing "I'm Getting Married in the Morning" (from *My Fair Lady*).

And then Tuesday came. Tradition demanded we not see each other until we met at the altar. It seemed a long day until four o'clock, June 1, 1965 at Grace Presbyterian Chapel. The Reverend Murdo Nicholson officiated, and Mike's attendants were his childhood friends, Bob Blaker, Bill Dutcher, and Mike Fairley.

As I waited to enter with my dad, a photo shows my dropped head, and I recall a tear or two, registering the significance of the moment. I regained my composure to smile as I walked with Dad down the aisle to meet this man with whom I'd spend the rest of my life.

At the front of the chapel was a contemporary stained-glass window in powerful primary colors depicting children coming to Christ. Whatever chill there was still in the air that early spring, it was obliterated by the sun's strength coming through the glass that afternoon. And at precisely the moment Mike was putting the ring on my finger, we heard a crash from the back of the chapel and saw my fourteen-year-old brother face-planted in the aisle. My dad and Uncle Ed, who was a doctor, pulled him from the church. I thought that my brother had just died at my wedding, but the minister guessed that with the sun's heat and locking his knees, my brother had probably just fainted. The service went on. At its end, we learned that, other than needing a few stitches in his chin, my brother would be fine; Reverend Nicholson had been through this before.

Chip made it to the reception, and though he was a little pale, he stayed until we left. Actually, his drama that day was the most unique thing about our wedding, and the poor guy has had to hear this story repeated for the last 55 years.

I had wanted music, but bands were too expensive. The majority of the guests were my father's business associates, and if I learned one thing that day, I vowed my daughters (if there were any) or their husbands would know every guest at their weddings. But it really didn't matter much. In those days, brides and grooms left the reception early, as did we, to head off on our honeymoon.

We borrowed my mother's car, a little Sunbeam Alpine convertible, for our trip. Mike had little experience with stick shifts; his family's cars were all automatics. Since my family only had a standard shift car, I tried to teach him in high school, but when he tried reverse, he hit the accelerator too hard and flattened our neighbor's mailbox. Though his shifting skills had improved, he wasn't familiar with this car, and he stalled it three times trying to exit the Petroleum Club, with all our guests watching and trying to wave us off. On the fourth try, we were off and on our way to Banff in the Canadian Rockies.

We were booked into the Banff Springs Hotel, where Janet Ruth and my family had gone for a holiday the first summer we arrived. In 1965, the hotel was closed throughout the winter, and had just opened for the season at the end of May. They had barely removed the sheets from the furniture when we arrived, along with the chiropractic and illuminating engineering conventions. Women in moth-balled furs wandered aimlessly about this castle of a hotel, and the only people remotely our age were the help. The bell-hop who took us to our room confirmed our discomfort when he said, "Did you come here straight from the reception?"

Oh my God, I thought. *He knows we're newlyweds!* I was so embarrassed. (He knew we'd be having sex). And to top it off, I was *disguised* in a suit and hat – a dead-giveaway for a "going-away outfit."

When we went to dinner, we found the dining room an empty ballroom, but with a full orchestra in place. Complete with soloist and playing music reminiscent of my parents' time; they could have entertained hundreds. We were definitely fish-out-of-water, and we couldn't wait to find our own pond.

That night we officially became husband and wife. My father, after a few too many drinks at the wedding reception, actually called us to see how we were. I was appalled. Poor Mike. By this time, we also knew we wanted out of this hotel.

We were lucky to have had a few friends at our wedding, and we knew they were staying at cabins over by the Banff dump. This was a popular area because bears came to the dump, and everyone wanted a bear sighting. We had the Lodge's name, and suddenly thought that this honeymoon would be a lot more fun with our friends. When we called the lodge and found out they had an extra cabin, we booked it. We quickly packed up, leaving the gracious old hotel to the gracious old people.

Our friends were speechless when we drove in while they were outside grilling. We joined the party and spent the next few days both with them and by ourselves. It was a perfect honeymoon, and then we all flew home together.

When we returned to our apartment, Janet Ruth surprised us with a visit. I was outside, but I didn't see her get out of the car and only realized it was her when I noticed she was walking towards me with a large bundle in her arms. A bundle of Baby Grant, it turned out, who was born the weekend we'd left. Of course, we knew she was expecting, but we hadn't heard the news; long distance calls were expensive and uncommon. She knew when we were returning, and wanted to surprise us. Mike heard the commotion and came to join us, our trio marveling over this tiny being.

"And now we're moving to New Jersey," she said. "We thought we'd be going the end of the summer, but Vince's mother called us to tell us she'd had a heart attack, so we need to go there now." I knew Vince had found a teaching job, but it didn't begin again until the fall, so I was expecting to spend the summer with Janet Ruth in Norman. I was so disappointed – and stunned.

"I can't go to summer school now," she continued. I knew

by the tone and cadence of her words she was trying to convince herself, as well as me, that this was the right decision. I could only agree. We lived in a time where you followed your husband and put your own goals aside. I knew Mike and I would be moving somewhere after college to a place where he could go to graduate school, but we weren't there yet. In the meantime, he was supporting me as I finished college before he pursued his dream.

Janet Ruth and I knew there was a permanence to this departure. We had made choices and decisions that involved other people, and our futures were no longer our own. As we said goodbye, hugging baby Grant between us, we hated to let go. It would make the parting real. Because this time it was.

Patty Mac and Mike Hewitt. We were 21 and 22 years old.
Photo by Camdale Studio, Calgary, Alberta

Modeling the going-away outfit.

The gracious Banff Springs Hotel.
Photo courtesy: Fairmont Banff Springs, Alberta, Canada

Virginia's dad never forgot his promise.

Lucky in Love

Janet Ruth and Vince packed up their belongings along with Baby Grant and moved to New Jersey. Oklahoma would never again be home to any of them. And Mike and I went to summer school and began a life together.

One thing I never realized about this legalized sex arrangement called marriage was that after having someone make me dinner every night of my life, I was now in charge of putting meals on the table. My mother and every other woman I knew did so, but I'd never given much thought as to how that would relate to me. I knew little more about cooking than Mike did, yet it never occurred to me that we could undertake this project together. Apparently, I was in charge.

I began by choosing familiar meals from home. Spaghetti was a start. My mom made the sauce from Campbell's tomato soup and added fried hamburger, and then the whole thing went over the noodles. I'm not sure I ever saw her drain the spaghetti, but I did know the water and pasta needed to be separated at the end. But I missed the part about a colander.

That first week of marriage, I undertook making spaghetti and put the sauce together like I remembered. Meanwhile I boiled the water for the pasta, added the noodles and when I thought it was done, I took the pot to the sink and started pouring the water from the pot, not considering how to keep the noodles in the pan while getting rid of the water. When I thought I was almost through, the mass of spaghetti noodles gained momentum and shot from the pan straight into the garbage disposal! *Oh, my God. Did I have to start over?*

Mike heard the fracas and came running. When he saw and heard what happened, he just said, "Pull 'em out."

"Pull what out? ...the noodles? ...out of the garbage disposal?" I said.

"Yup. We'll wash 'em off." And so we did, and we ate that mess.

The following week while Mike was at class, I took the car and drove to the Kappa house to pick up some of the last of my things. My house-mother had stored a box for me until we returned from our honeymoon and had moved into our apartment.

At the time, the Kappa house property was elevated a few feet above the neighbor's house to its left. A curved cement driveway led from the front of the house to the back parking lot. Concrete berms bordered both sides of the driveway, and the neighbors erected a chain-link fence which abutted the outside berm. The pronged top of the fencing actually stood a couple of inches higher than the curbing.

After I picked up my things, I left by the front door, loaded the car, and drove out the driveway towards the back. I must have taken the curve a little too fast because all of a sudden, the car jerked to a stop. I tried to go forward, then backwards, but with no luck. When I got out to see what happened, I was astounded to see the car hung up on the chain-link fence.

I felt sick. It was still an hour before Mike was out of class, and I didn't know what to do, except to pace and pace. I imagined how my father would react and felt even sicker. The waiting wasn't helping. I walked to meet Mike.

Once again, I couldn't keep my feelings a secret. Mike took one look and wanted to know what was wrong. I might have cried, but I was just dramatic and told the story in detail. The minute I finished he said, "So what's the problem? We'll just get a tow truck. The guy'll pull it off."

"Really? That's it?" I couldn't believe his reaction. And I kept saying so. Mike was really surprised that I had been so worried and gave me a big hug. We got the help, and the car was lifted up and off that fencing. Other than a few scratches, there were few reminders of my fiasco, and Mike didn't think a thing about it. It seemed we were off to a good start.

His reaction, really, was a foreshadowing of our life together. He never got upset about the things my father would have or those things that unglue most people. Little did I know, but he had his own propensity for humorous kerfuffles. The galvanized water bucket on the barge was one. Over the years he painted himself into a corner when he refinished a floor in the bedroom, got absorbed reading the newspaper and missed a train stop home twice, once wore two different colored shoes to work (same style, though), and installed a screen door upside down, then joked why the lumber yard had sold him a door for kids. I have to say I didn't always express the same understanding he showed me. With the corner painting episode, he told me I had no sense of humor. These stories are now family legends.

By the end of summer, we finished our courses, and Mike graduated with the university's August class. For the next year, he took a job with Phillips Petroleum Company in Oklahoma City while I completed my degree. I had caught up with all my needed credit hours that final summer school session, and was ready to take my place with the other prospective physical therapists in Oklahoma City at the O.U. Medical Center. There I would complete my major.

Those Who Play Must Pay

We finished summer school, Mike graduated, and we left Norman to move to Oklahoma City for my senior year. My friend Terri Constable, married Craig David the same summer, and both of us chose to live in the same small apartment complex directly across the street from where Terri and I would be taking classes at the Medical Center. We lived upstairs, and they lived directly below us. School ran from 8 – 5 PM daily, with classes on some Saturdays, so it was great to be so close and have no need for a car. Craig and Mike needed them to go to work.

The director of the School of Physical Therapy was Miss Gertrude Peterman. She had served as an Army nurse during WW II, and had entered the field of physical therapy when it became a specialized profession. As medicine advanced during that war, wounds often led to long-term disabilities rather than causes of death. The number of patients who survived with amputations rose, and with it, the profession of physical therapy emerged.

Miss Peterman was dedicated, extremely serious, and very traditional. Having two married students in her class was not. She didn't seem pleased that Terri and I were married, but there were no official rules to eliminate us, so she was stuck with us as her students.

Since Terri and I had known each other so long, we were happy to be stuck with each other, studying together and hanging out as couples when we had time. We both worked hard to make our way through this intense final year.

Throughout the fall, I was plagued with headaches, which were new to me. They were painful enough to send me to a doctor, who suggested they might be a side-effect from my birth control pills. The pills were relatively new, and I had begun taking them a month before we married. To a certain extent, the pharmaceutical companies were still figuring out the proper strength and dosages. Once the doctor suggested the pills as a possible cause, I was anxious to quit taking them to see if the headaches would disappear. So I did and they did, and two months later I was pregnant.

Our physical therapy program consisted of strict academics, and many practicums. To learn the different types of treatments, we rotated with our classmates, role-playing as patient or therapist. Some of these treatments, both mechanical and non-mechanical, were contraindicated for certain patients and conditions. And one of the main contraindications was pregnancy.

As soon as I realized I was pregnant, I had to tell the staff of my situation. I certainly couldn't refuse to play patient with no explanation. But, *How was I ever going to tell Miss Peterman? If she wasn't happy with me being married, how would she react to the news of my pregnancy?*

I wasn't a procrastinator, nor a slow remover of Band-aids. But I didn't want to make a public announcement so I made an appointment with Miss Peterman in her office. It was a long, slow walk, because I had no idea what outcome lay ahead. Given that she didn't like married students, a pregnancy situation did not bode well. Also, at this time, if school teachers became pregnant, they immediately lost their jobs when their pregnancy became known. I didn't know if the same rules would apply to me, and be cause for expulsion. None of this made sense to me, but like so many other things, "it was just the way things were."

I arrived on time at her office, and she was ready to see me. I have no idea if she had any idea why I might be there. I knew I wasn't a problem. Yet. But she was all business, as usual. So I guess I was, too.

"I know how important it is for us to fully participate in the role-playing for patient and therapist, but I have a problem. I cannot always be the patient. It seems I am pregnant, and I know that contraindicates certain treatments.

Without missing a beat, she responded,

"Those who play, must pay."

Well, that was a conversation stopper. She started making comments about me dropping out, but it became clear there were no rules forbidding pregnant students, and I had no intention or desire to quit. I had come a long way from my freshman year, and I'd already calculated that the baby would arrive in mid-October. We would graduate the beginning of August. I left the office with my student-status intact.

Though the timing certainly wasn't great, we were excited. I was pregnant. Today couples say, "*We* are pregnant!" I don't really understand that. I get, "*we* are expecting,", but *we* are pregnant? There is only *one animal* that "has a developing offspring in the body." At least that's the way I learned it.

My pregnancy quickly became common knowledge, and my instructors suddenly realized that they had a real-life patient for natural childbirth instructions. The Lamaze method was coming into vogue, and I became the guinea-pig for teaching it. Like it or not, I was on my way to having a drug-free natural childbirth. I bought in.

So, I was not kicked out, didn't quit and never had any medical problems that complicated my continuing in school. I wrote Janet Ruth to tell her our news, but we had little communication. We were both deluged with life, and just kept dog-paddling.

It was a busy winter. Mike applied to business school in Boston and was accepted. His sister's husband had gone to undergraduate college in Boston, and they were now living there. Though neither Mike nor I had ever visited, it was reassuring to know we'd be near family, and his parents were happy.

Once I knew where we'd be moving, I began to think about finding a Boston obstetrician. About that time, we had a guest speaker from Boston who, after his lecture, visited with me and connected me to Dr. Luke Gillespie. He sounded like a character from a popular television show at the time which was good enough for me, so I immediately wrote him and got a favorable response: he would take me on as a patient for the last six weeks. And then I received the biggest shock. As I was reading a *Good Housekeeping* magazine I came across an article on pregnancy and stopped short when I read "according to Dr. Luke Gillespie of Boston Lying-In Hospital." All I could think was, *Wow! I just wanted someone competent, not world renowned.*

August came, and I graduated. Actually, my baby and I both graduated, as I liked to say later. There was plenty of room for both of us under that voluminous gown. Terri and I were both happy to have been trailblazers as married women in the program, and we were both invited to join Phi Beta Kappa. The honor definitely gave us a feeling of satisfaction, especially given the headwinds thrown our way.

Patty Mac and Terri studying and practicing
in our apartment.

My classmate Terri and her husband Craig with Mike and
me at their apartment at Christmastime.

Graduation: I made it!!

Becoming Easterners

At the beginning of September, 1966, Mike and I left for Boston, hauling a 4 x 6 foot U-Haul trailer. To save money, we made our own lunches and had an $8 per night budget for motel accommodations. We did well, until we took a detour to Niagara Falls, where we were blown away by the $25 room, the cheapest we could find. But – the Falls were spectacular, and this was our one big extravagance.

We had pre-arranged a one-night visit with Janet Ruth and Vince in New Jersey on our way to New England. I was so excited to see them. It had been over a year since we had seen one another, and Grant was just a newborn when they left.

It was wonderful to reunite, but at this point, we didn't get much time alone to talk about our lives. Janet Ruth said she was painting – a little, but she hadn't finished school. I felt badly about that, but now we were only a day's drive apart; I hoped we could visit often.

We moved to Boston on Labor Day Weekend. As we drove on the Mass Pike towards the city, I made Mike stop at a rest area, and from a pay phone alongside the highway, I called Dr. Gillespie. He took my call, and we arranged our first appointment. Things were falling into place.

We headed on to Watertown, where we had rented an apartment, sight-unseen. My college roommate Ellen Roberts, had a sister whose husband was a class ahead of Mike at the business school, and had spent time in the Navy. Susan and John Davids had many moves under their belt, and realized how difficult relocating could be, so they took it upon themselves to help us. They found an apartment for us to rent

293

and then found all the house furnishings for $150. Upon our approval, they bought them, stored them, and then moved the furniture in before we arrived. I'm not sure we have ever experienced such generosity from anyone, particularly people we had yet to meet.

Mike began school, and I began looking for things to do. For the first time in my life, I had no obligations. Since we had just arrived, I also had no friends, no money, and no access to a car since Mike needed it to get to school. But I wasn't driving anyway, because I was terrified of the crazy traffic and rotaries in the Boston area. So I made dinner, but short of that, I had endless hours to fill. Fortunately, there were many student-couples in the complex so it didn't take long to meet them; we were all hungry to connect.

My clothes became a bit of a problem. I had plenty of maternity clothes, but they were all summer-wear, sleeveless and totally inappropriate for New England fall weather. I wasn't about to buy new things when we were in a six-week count-down. But, I was desperate, and didn't even want to go out since I truly had nothing to wear. Then we heard about Filene's Basement, an early off-price bargain store located directly below its more elegant sister- store, just called Filene's.

We went on a weekday as school hadn't begun, taking the trolley and following the directions given us. By the time we reached our stop, the crowds were heavy and no one gave way to me and "my condition" as we walked along. It didn't matter as we all seemed to be going in the same direction. The first door to the building led us directly down some stairs which immediately heralded the screech, steam and stench from the subway system. We wondered where we could possibly be headed, when a second short flight of stairs appeared which led to glass double-doors and the magical emporium. A second set of stairs to our right led the commuters to their ride.

Apparently, daily, there was always a *special* in "The Basement." That day it was men's shirts. Most of the merchandise was packaged, but it seemed the female buyers were unsure of their man's size, and so were opening packages to see if they could get a visual feel. That is, until they saw Mike—a living mannequin. In no time, they had him pinned against a wall, arms outstretched like a pat-down. They papered those open shirts on top of him, eye-measuring the sleeves and the rest of him to determine whether they should go up or down in size. Mike didn't know how to refuse their demands, and so cooperated. I looked on as if he'd been called to the stage during a show.

We finally extricated ourselves from this mob, but couldn't resist buying a shirt for Mike before we found the very small maternity department. There, for $8 each, I bought two identical jumpers in corduroy, olive green and brown. *Well, they were cheap.* I could pair them with various blouses and hopefully coast through the next 6 weeks. To this day, my then new friend, Cathy Crawford, vividly recalls those hideous clothes, and how we ceremoniously disposed of them in the dumpster outside our buildings after I gave birth.

October 17, 1966, my due date arrived, but the baby didn't. I was sure it would arrive then, because what's the point of coming up with a date if it has no meaning? Day after day passed, with people calling and asking, "Haven't you gone yet?" (as if it were my choice?!). My only excitement was my weekly trip to see Dr.Gillespie. It took a couple of trolleys and an hour to get to the Boston Lying-In Hospital so that activity filled most of a day. I returned home wondering if it would ever happen. I was reluctant to make plans (was someone going to be miffed if I was a no-show?!) A week went by, and it was time to make that trolley trip again.

Mike was well into his program at school by this time, and was as busy as I was bored. His school used the case-study method where, daily, students were given three real- life written cases of business situations and problems. They were to analyze them and come up with possible solutions. The school encouraged students to form study groups and utilize the skills and backgrounds of its members. Periodically, a single case was handed out to each student on Friday afternoon to be a solo project: a WAC – a Written Analysis of a Case. Students had until Saturday at 6 PM when the typed, written analysis was to be turned in through a mail chute at the school. Often these projects turned out to be all-nighters.

We'd been through one of these projects, and knew another was coming up. I say, "we" because I was the typist and self-appointed editor. I had no business background, but I felt I could tell when something wasn't clear, and I was a built-in spellcheck. Mike wasn't always happy about my suggestions, and we later dubbed these *collaborations* as "WAC-fights."

On October 28, Mike was given his second WAC project of the term and began his analysis. By Saturday afternoon, I was typing ... and typing ... and counting - and counting - contractions. I finally announced that I might be in labor. Mike's response, "Keep typing!"

And I did. It was late afternoon when we finished, and as we lived in Watertown and the school was in Cambridge, it took a while to get there.We dusted off my suitcase (I was now thirteen days overdue), and headed to the school to deposit the paper through the chute and then drove directly to the hospital.

We arrived around 6:30 P.M. and crossed the lobby to check-in. I was careful not to step on the inlaid stork decorating the center of the marble floor. Legend had it, that if you stepped on his foot, you'd be back in a year or so with another baby. I figured one was enough at this point.

Though this hospital was quite old, it was progressive with respect to birthing babies. Fathers were now allowed in the labor rooms here, but not yet in delivery. That would happen by the 1970s.

When we got to the floor, I was directed to change into a hospital gown, and once I was situated in the labor room, Mike was invited to come in. It wasn't long before I was mentally thanking my instructors for all the Lamaze training I received in school. I was especially happy to have Mike by my side for this first part, coaching me through the breathing and panting.

"Take deep pants and then breathe," He told me.

I listened, but amended, I think I need to breathe first, and pant later. But you're doing great!"

After all this waiting, I was so ready to have this baby. I was lucky because labor moved quickly as I focused on a wall photo of an elephant until it finally lost its trunk somewhere close to my giving birth. After an examination when the pushes were almost uncontrollable, I was whisked away to delivery and Mike was sent to the father's waiting room to receive word of our baby's birth. He didn't wait long. Three pushes and at 1:10 AM on Sunday October 30, 1966 our daughter Patricia Christian Hewitt was born. We called her Chris.

It had been 10 years since Janet Ruth and I first met as 12-year-old girls playing softball against one another. We grew up together, and in that short time we had entered the world of our parents, married with children. But we were never grown-ups, alone. We would become grown-ups *with* our kids, not *ahead* of them. And by now I realized our friendship would forever be a long distance one, but one I would work very hard to keep. And what were some of the hopes I had for this beautiful little girl who came into Mike's and my life? I hoped that she could do the things boys did, like play sports, have a paper route, and swim naked at the Y. If she wanted to. But my biggest wish was that I hoped she'd find a friend like Janet Ruth along the way.

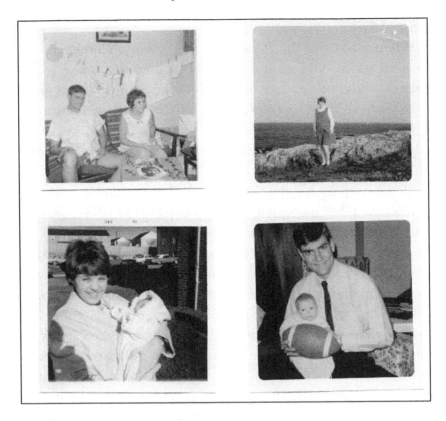

Waiting for our baby...
and Patricia Christian Hewitt arrived!

Where Did S.H.E. Go?

Janet Ruth and I never lived near each other again. And neither did many of our other friends. Despite our affection for Bartlesville and our life there, after college graduation, nearly all our band of merry little women scattered. We headed to Massachusetts, Maine, New Jersey, Minnesota, Montana, Colorado, California, New Mexico, Arizona, Texas, Florida, the Washington, D.C. area and sometimes overseas. A few remained in Oklahoma.

We'd return for family and class reunions, and sometimes we made our own reunions elsewhere. Through phone calls, cards, letters, and later, email, we stayed connected, but not with the regularity of today's social media. We were growing up, privately, and sometimes painfully. There were some divorces, unplanned pregnancies, spousal abuse, and abortions, all whose existence only filtered out as the years went by, not as the events transpired. We weren't able to avoid the turmoil the rest of the country experienced.

As unmarried women, Janet Ruth and I missed participating in some of the landmark movements that were percolating ahead. But many of this group did not. After graduating in international relations, and as a single woman, Marie was stymied from going overseas with the government unless she was a secretary. Since she had no interest in that, she went back to graduate school. After completing her degree, she was intrigued with the newly created Peace Corps program and became the first woman to go with a group to Western Samoa to work in a world health program. When she returned, she went on to study nursing and practice in that field. She has a son who is a talented musician leading a bluegrass/rap band out of Brooklyn.

Virginia and her high school boyfriend, Larry Winston, married after their junior year of college, ten days before Mike and I did. After all those years of her dad teasing us about the ramshackle cabin being our honeymoon cottage, he sent Mike and me a telegram on our wedding day which read, "Yours and Virginia cottage awaiting. Congratulations and best wishes. Mr. and Mrs. Isaac Smith."

After Virginia and Larry graduated, she found herself stateside while Larry completed three tours of duty in Vietnam, including two as a helicopter pilot. Meanwhile, she joined the Head Start program as a teacher. Larry made a career as a pilot in the military while Virginia built a career in education while raising a son and a daughter. She is a breast cancer survivor and volunteers wherever she is needed. She's never changed.

Nancy Lord ended up in California after a couple of early detours. Nancy began working for small high-tech start-ups as she loved computers, but when her husband gave her a Mac, she was unsure how to use it. When she learned that the company was hiring temps, she decided it would be a good "free" way to learn the ins-and-outs of this new device. That led to a full-time job with Apple until she retired. Nancy was widowed soon after she and her husband moved to a retirement community in the California desert, but she has remained there and is happy as she gathers friends and animals "as quickly as cockle burrs stick to your jeans while walking through a pasture." We see each other annually.

Jan Everett was an artist who went into education. Early on, however, she ran into an interesting stumbling block when she was student-teaching: her youthful looks and sweet voice made it difficult to distinguish her from some of her students. She said it was hard to maintain her confidence as a teacher. During college she had become involved with Campus Crusade for Christ, a Christian group focused on campus ministry, so she joined their staff at Southern Methodist University for two years before beginning to teach art in the Dallas school system. She has two sons, and today is a talented portraitist of people and pets and continues to paint and be involved in her church.

And what of Ada Lee Bean? After high school graduation I never saw or heard anything about her, nor any of the other Black students. When the Civil Rights Movement occurred, I often wondered how those changes might have affected them. Fifty-five years later, I got the idea to try and find her via the internet. We have now shared many conversations and emails about her life and friends, many of whom were in my classes. Like me, she has stayed connected with her friends through Douglass School reunions held every three years for decades. These were totally unknown to me and many of my friends. Sadly, I have learned that several of her group have died of cancer or respiratory diseases. Because the number is so disproportionate, Ada Lee and her friends question the cloud of waste from the zinc smelter that hovered over their neighborhood every afternoon. I have to wonder about that, too. No one wanted to be near it.

Ada Lee has her own fascinating career story. After she graduated from high school, she took a job, (in her own words) as a "maid" at Edwards, a fashionable women's clothing store in Bartlesville. There were few job options in town for Blacks, so she felt lucky to get one, though it was far from anything she might have wanted. The first summer, two white girls from the class behind us, were hired as salesgirls. They both knew Ada Lee through classes they had shared, and they knew how smart she was. After a few weeks, one girl went to the manager and told him that Ada Lee "was a straight-A student." He was surprised, but apparently intrigued enough to question Ada Lee. When she confirmed their information, he said, "How come you never told me?"

She replied, "You never asked."

He then asked if she would like to learn about the business side of retailing. Ada Lee told me she couldn't accept fast enough; she couldn't wait to quit cleaning. And so, she learned, and continued to work there.

When an opportunity arose to join two of her sisters in California, she left Oklahoma. Once in California, she went directly to department stores to apply for jobs. After she described her skills to the first interviewer, the woman replied, "Oh, you were in 'unit control,'" to which Ada Lee agreed, having no idea that was the name of what she'd done in Oklahoma. By the next interview, she presented herself as skilled in "unit control." She was hired at Livingston's in San Francisco, and built a lifetime career at major retail stores. Her jobs took her to Joseph Magnin, Gumps, and Mervyn's, and covered every aspect of running a department store: from unit control, to buyer, department manager, store manager, systems control manager, bringing and updating computer services and capabilities, to retail stores. When she and I have talked about our lives, and I recall the effect she had on me, she recalls the two girls who spoke on her behalf who opened a door, which she exploded through, when given the chance. Today Ada Lee is retired and lives with her son and his family in California. Because of her great-grandmother's lineage to a slave of the Cherokees, Ada Lee and her offspring are members of the Cherokee nation.

Susie Reinfeld was always our Google. We could ask her anything, and if she didn't know the answer, she could come up with something that convinced us she did. After college, she headed to a California beach town, and never left. There, she married, had two boys and spent her business career with an insurance company. Along the way, she became the town volunteer organizer. In 2004, she was awarded the Chamber of Commerce Woman of the Year. My guess is that she could have taken that honor any number of years.

Our last visit was a mini-reunion in the California desert

where she and I were looking towards our 70th birthdays. She turned 70 on January 28, then had a stroke and died on January 31, 2014. There's a bench on the town pier which the S.H.E.'s gave in Susie's honor, and her ashes were strewn from the end of the pier. Totally illegal. So, what's new? I think the police were out with the "blue-flu" that day.

Our group of friends was similar to an early tribe without a written history. We kept our stories alive by the telling and re-telling, an oral tradition. Even as we were creating new tales, we enjoyed reliving the past ones; I think that's why they remain so clear in our minds.

One spring, after an unexpected back surgery, I realized I would not be able to be very physically active that summer. I decided that I would begin to write down some of these stories I had been telling to my children and grandchildren. The youngest two, who were getting their fill at this time, called them "Janet Ruth Stories."

Once I began, I couldn't stop. I joined a writing group, and found writing guidance from long-distance teachers, editors, and friends who were good readers. A book grew from these writing adventures.

As for Janet Ruth and me, we work hard to visit one another. We call to update each other when things happen – or we don't. Neither is annoyed; we have never been high maintenance friends.

Artwork by Janed Ruth. After a castration. First called, "I Don't Need No Damn Balls." Cleaned up to "Sassy." I prefer the first name.

"Let's Do Lunch!"

Artwork by Janet Ruth. When made into a notecard, the inside read, "And will there be carrion?"

Artwork by Janet Ruth.

Janet Ruth became the artist she always was. Her medium varied along the way, but she always found a way to keep painting. When her marriage to Vince ended during Grant, Chuck, and Vicki's teenage years, she moved to Odessa, Texas (or "O-desolate as she liked to call it") to be near her parents, and took a job with Phillips Petroleum Company to start anew. Her entry level job led to working on the *Permian Basin News*, an in-house publication which she was running within six months, doing the photography, layouts and writing articles. And on the side, she painted.

Within a couple of years, she met Tom Johnson, a young engineer at Phillips, and fell in love. When she called to tell me she was getting married again, she began, "Guess where he's from?"

"Bartlesville!" I said. She laughed, told me his name, and I continued, "But I don't remember him."

"Yeah…well, he's five years younger than we are. I'm robbin' the cradle." No one knew anyone that much younger unless you babysat them. My brother was seven years younger than I, so I asked him if he knew Tom.

"Oh sure, I knew him. I dated his younger sister in high school," Chip said.

After marrying, Janet Ruth and Tom continued to work for Phillips until a downturn in the oil industry prompted Phillips to offer early retirement packages to some employees. Tom and Janet Ruth jumped at the opportunity, ready for something new, though not yet sure what it might be. After investigating several possible business opportunities, they bought a foundry in New Mexico which created molds and produced jewelry and sculptures from artists all over the area. At one level it was a world they knew nothing about and a formidable undertaking. But with Tom's engineering skills to keep the machinery running, and Janet Ruth's artistic talents and ability to keep the employees laughing, they became successful.

During these years, Janet Ruth created her own jewelry line. She once made me a woman's warrior pin, a sterling-silver shield accompanied by a spear and a stemmed rose. If you were in a good mood, you slid the rose aside the shield. If not, you replaced the rose with the spear. Fair warning, I guess. Meanwhile, she kept painting.

When she and Tom sold their business, they retired to an old former gold-and-silver-mining town in Colorado and opened a gallery for Janet Ruth's paintings, jewelry, and objects d'art. The dead-end resort-canyon town became home. First, they bought a house, and then an 1880s building to house the gallery. As you step inside the old building you immediately realize you are standing on a sloping floor. Then a sign catches your eye, "We're on the level, but you're not!"

She sees the world and what's in it, with a sense of humor that draws people to her and to her paintings, capturing moments in time with paint and words that bring a smile: the front porch of an old strip-motel with its three empty metal chairs reflecting the day's end light and shadows is called "Waiting for Happy Hour." And one of my favorite paintings is of a baby vulture, painted with the detail of Audubon, its beady scarlet eyes boring into the viewer and is captioned, "Let's Do Lunch." She often makes notecards from original paintings. When she wrote me on the one with the vulture, the inside read, "And will there be carrion?"

I took a job as a physical therapist three and a half months after our daughter Chris was born, and it took the two of us to manage her along with Mike's school and my work. He pitched in because he didn't know anything different, and I expected the help because I couldn't figure out how I could work full-time, take care of a child, cook, and clean otherwise. The three of us grew up together, and Mike and Chris became soul mates.

The loyalty ties to Phillips Petroleum Company were still strong when Mike graduated from business school, so he felt a pull to work for a subsidiary company in South Carolina. But soon after our arrival it became clear that this was not the direction he wanted. Our daughter, Katherine, arrived during this year, but she and the rest of us soon left her birthplace and headed back to Boston where Mike was offered a job at an investment company. For the next forty years, he built a career in that world, and I oversaw the other parts of our lives. Our son, Michael was born five years after Katherine and completed our family. Today Mike and I live in New Hampshire, and our three children live in Minneapolis, New York City, and Amsterdam.

My McKinley Grade School dreams of "doing things that boys did, like play sports, have a paper route, and swim naked at the Y" took a while to be realized. I got my naked swim one September night in the waters off Bermuda. I was married with three kids, but it was worth the wait. When my son Michael was in middle school, he had a job delivering the local evening paper. It was going well until he got a role in a school play which conflicted with his paper route. So, off I went through the neighborhood, on foot, taking over the route for the duration of the play. One afternoon, when I found myself annoyed with this chore, I laughed when I realized that this was exactly what I wished for when I was growing up!

My biggest dream was participating in sports, and though there was little fanfare when it happened, it brought many years of joy. Mike's college track teammate, Harold Close, came to stay with us in Boston one spring when he ran the Boston Marathon. Our family found a spot on Heartbreak Hill to cheer Hal on, and I became enamored with running. My first foray led me back and forth a few blocks, but within three years I had run two marathons and numerous other races of varying lengths. I finally found my sport. Often, I placed in my age groups so I wondered if I could make some real improvement with a coach and team to train with. Tufts University was nearby, so a call there led me to the Waltham Track

Club and Coach Joe. I was hooked. My daughter Katherine once told her Nana Hewitt, "Don't be buried on a Tuesday 'cause that's my mom's track night, and she might not come." I loved the training process even more than the competition, but a highlight of those years was when I raced in the 800 meters at the Dartmouth Relays. I certainly didn't place, but I wasn't last. I was in my 40s racing against 18-22-year-olds. I was finally an athlete.

My physical therapy career was short-lived. When I entered the field, most jobs were full-time, and I found raising three children to be that. After a serious automobile accident in 2000, with multiple surgeries and rehabs, I decided that I'd spent more time as a patient than I ever did as a clinician. But what really bothered me about not having a career in those early years, was filling out the "occupation" question on forms — medical, legal, and credit. I hated writing "housewife." So, I started making things up. Once, at a party, some fellow asked me what I did, and I answered, "I sling dirt."

"Oh, you write pornographic novels?" he said. When I laughed and confessed I was a housewife, he immediately turned to speak to someone else. Finally, I began to answer the question with "concubine." I said it in person, and I wrote it on forms. No one seemed to read those forms anyway, but the verbal response usually drew a few laughs.

When we made our retirement move, we found a lawyer to update our will. Days later when we arrived to sign the documents, we were told not to proceed until the lawyer called in his female assistants. Apparently, they wanted to meet the woman who gave her occupation as "concubine." Those forms were going to follow me all the way to my grave.

And now Janet Ruth and I are growing old. We have had wonderful, but not perfect lives, and not without dark times, but with great husbands, three children each, and multiple grandchildren, we have been fortunate. As they say in Oklahoma, though our "lives are going by like a Cadillac speeding to Tulsa," we're still trying to make memories. Janet Ruth once wrote me, "When we open our old ladies' home, we shall have aerobics, golf, and brain games to tease our forgetty heads and maybe some softball. I sincerely hope we get do-overs. I'd like to be your best friend all over again."

And so would I.

Celebrating birthdays...

Faces change...the message doesn't...

HAPPY BIRTHDAY, OLD FRIEND!!

Janet Ruth and Patty Mac

Acknowledgements

This feels like the academy awards where you have one public chance to thank all the people who helped you along the way. I better apologize right now because there will undoubtedly be someone who listened or read one of the many versions of my five year hobby that I neglect to mention. I didn't begin this project to be a book, but as a record of oral story telling. As I kept writing and enjoying the memories and connections, it occurred to me that this could work itself into a wordy scrapbook. I began sending the first stories to my mother who loved to read, had plenty of time, and was a definite positive audience. Her amazing memory helped me document facts and her comments ranged from, "I didn't know you did this!" to some sadness in reading my memories about my relationship at times with my dad. She read all the chapters minus the very ending, and missed the book publication by two years, but I have to feel she is enjoying it somewhere. My husband Mike was my in-house listener and reader, and though he'd never make a copy editor, he was very good in every other way, keeping me on track and filling in some blanks, as he was somewhere in the picture for many of the stories. I thank my sister Pam Clinton and my brother Chip Sloan for their part in making my family and letting me tell parts of their stories, but mostly for being siblings that I love and work hard to be around.

To recount the many stories, I relied on my memory and then the confirmation, refutation, or documentation of Janet Ruth and my early tribe of friends. I had numerous conversations with them to hear their accounts of our adventures, individually, and then assembled the tales. Several of them offered pictures and other memorabilia as they related. I particularly thank them for their part in creating the book and to all the other classmates who appeared throughout. As their names have been altered, I cannot be the spoiler here.

There have been many other readers and listeners, most certainly the Janet Ruth of the tales as well as her husband, and her daughter and husband. My children, Chris Whitford, Katherine Cherian and Michael Hewitt, and my granddaughters Sophia, Zoe and Eloise have all weighed in on the stories as they unfolded. My grandsons Zach, Toby, Sebastian, Ellis and Willem have been waiting for the book to be published.

I would like to thank the late Allison Fennell Grossman, Carrie Rowley Baker, and Robin Rogers MacNeil, friends of my daughter Katherine who read some early tales and introduced to me to the LOL acronym which they marked alongside some of the stories they read, giving me confidence that younger women might also relate to these dated times.

I would like to thank my friends and readers, Gerry De-George, Emily Kaplan, Michaele Benn, Sally White, Alexis Wallace, Jan Smith, Christine Smalley, Carolyn Sundquist, the late Marilyn Schmidt and Judy Crystal who weighed in at various early and late writings. My Tuftonboro Library Writer's Group with Phil Soletsky, Ron Sundquist, Alexis Wallace, James Cross, Dan Lake, Carole Shea, Joan Magrauth, Lynne Horton, Andrew Bridgeman, Steve Morse, Rosalie Triolo and Alexander Dunford have heard various stories over various years but all have served as solid inspiration to keep writing and moving forward, not to mention just helping make the act of writing something I want to do daily. Thanks also to Julia Attaway with her help in putting together a CV for book usage.

Photo credits have been noted in the book, but I would like to mention special thanks to Debbie Neece at The Bartlesville Area History Museum who went out of her way on several occasions to help me find particular photos. I also made several contacts with Craig's Photography speaking to Heather or Melissa regarding using photos from Winston's collection which Craig's now own. Linda Stone at the Frank Phillips

Acknowledgements

Foundation at Woolaroc provided access to several old photos I wished to use and was most helpful in the search. The Reverend Stephen Carl at First Presbyterian Church gave me permission to use an old bulletin cover for a particular story, and I spent a wonderful few hours at the Bartlesville downtown Public Library pouring over old phone books for old addresses and names. I am appreciative to Kim Reis at USA today for permission to use Examiner-Enterprise photos and to The Fairmont Banff Springs for use of its photo.

This first foray into book writing required many writes, rewrites and guidance which I received from Judah Le Blang, Peter Havholm, and Terri Trespecio, all writers and editors themselves. I finally decided that age needed to dictate the finish line; if it wasn't soon, I might lose my audience. Finally, I thank Piscataqua Press at the RiverRun Bookstore in Portsmouth, New Hampshire, the independent press with Tom Holbrook and Kellsey Metzger who produced this wordy scrapbook, my magnum opus.

Bibliography

Oil Man by Michael Wallis, published by Doubleday, a division of Bantam Doubleday Dell Publishing Group, Inc., 666 Fifth Avenue, New York, 10103, 1945

Woolaroc, published by the Trustees of Frank Phillips Foundation, Inc., copyright 1965

Killers of the Flower Moon by David Grann and published by Doubleday, a division of Penguin Random House LLC, New York, 2017

The Dismissal of Miss Ruth Brown by Louise S. Robbins, copyright c 2000 by the University Oklahoma Press, Publishing Division of the University

O Ye Jigs and Juleps by Virginia Cary Hudson and published by The MacMillan Company, a division of The Crowell-Collier Publishing Company, 1962

Centennial, Foundations for the Future, Special Edition, the first 100 years, published by the Bartlesville Examiner Enterprise, 1997

Frank's Fancy by Gale Morgan Kane, published by Oklahoma Heritage Association, 201 Northwest Fourteenth Street, Oklahoma City, Oklahoma 73103, 2001

Made in the USA
Monee, IL
29 June 2021